D1587669

Mark of the Lion

The Story of Capt. Charles Upham, V.C. and Bar

By the same author:

DEAD SECRET

DEAD RECKONING

KENNETH SANDFORD

Mark of the Lion

The Story of Capt. Charles Upham, V.C. and Bar

 CENTURY HUTCHINSON

CENTURY HUTCHINSON NEW ZEALAND LTD.
An imprint of the Century Hutchinson Group.
32-34 View Road, P.O. Box 40-086, Glenfield, Auckland 10.

Century Hutchinson Ltd.
62-65 Chandos Place, Covent Garden, London WC2N 4NW.

Century Hutchinson Australia Pty. Ltd.
16-22 Church Street, Hawthorne, Melbourne, Victoria 3122.
89-91 Albion Street, Surry Hills, Sydney, N.S.W. 2010.

Century Hutchinson South Africa Pty. Ltd.
P.O. Box 337, Bergvlei 2012, South Africa.

First published 1962
© Kenneth Sandford 1962

This edition © 1987

Printed in Hong Kong

ISBN 0 09 172731 6

Contents

Illustrations

Unless otherwise stated, all the above photographs are from the collection in the New Zealand Government Department of Internal Affairs (War Histories Branch), to whom acknowledgment is gratefully made.

Mark of the Lion

FOR centuries the Lion has held a double place in British tradition:

* As a hall-mark of quality, an emblem that sets a standard, against which all else may be measured. So, an Act of Parliament in 1739 provided:

> '*The Standards* (for gold and silver) *are both for the Honour and Riches of the Realm; and such shall be marked* . . . *with the MARK OF THE LION.*'

* As a symbol of nobility and strength, as in the words of the Royal Warrant of 29th January 1856 instituting the Victoria Cross:

> '. . . *The Cross shall only be awarded to those officers or men who served us in the presence of the enemy, and shall have performed some signal act of valour or devotion to their country.* . . . *A bronze cross* . . . *in its centre a Royal Crown, surmounted by a LION.*'

or in the simple design of the War Medal 1939–45, awarded to all who served in the Armed Forces for twenty-eight days, the official description reading '. . . *a LION standing triumphant.* . . .'

Introduction

CHARLES HAZLITT UPHAM, the New Zealand infantry officer who during World War II won the V.C. twice, is a man noted for his extreme modesty. It was only the intervention of his former Commanding Officer, the late Major-General Sir Howard Kippenberger, K.B.E., C.B., D.S.O. and bar, E.D., that finally extracted from Upham a reluctant consent to this biography being written.

But Charles Upham is not given to talking of his own experiences, so most of the events in this book have come from the eye-witness accounts and reminiscences of a host of independent observers, friends, and war-time comrades. They range from generals to batmen, scattered as far afield as South Africa, England, Australia, New Zealand, even Trinidad. To them, who in scores of interviews and hundreds of letters have supplied the bulk of the biographical material, I express my gratitude, and particularly to those who have critically reviewed chapters within their own intimate knowledge.

Many an incident in this story has had to be checked and re-checked a dozen times. So if some of my informants now find that the printed version differs from the way they related it, may they be consoled in the knowledge that the weight of evidence and the facts of history have had to prevail. But often truth itself has clearly emerged in a stranger and more dramatic form than many first believed.

To Charles himself and his wife Molly, my thanks for their kindness and hospitality. In many pleasant hours I have spent around his fireside Charles has revealed (perhaps unconsciously at times) some of the thoughts and feelings that accompanied the deeds of which he is so disinclined to speak. But in the end he has been kind enough to read the manuscript and to point out some errors of fact that escaped an otherwise exhaustive checking. And after much prompting, and with his characteristic reticence, he has supplied the true version of what had been little more than legend concerning several episodes in his war-time career: notably the grisly death-cellar at Mersa Matruh; his escape attempts from Weinsberg prison camp, and his twelve hours of hard-won freedom en route to Colditz Castle.

I acknowledge very gratefully the help of the editors-in-chief of the official New Zealand War Histories; first the late Sir Howard Kippenberger, and then his successor Brigadier M. C. Fairbrother, C.B.E., D.S.O., E.D. They have kindly given me permission to quote some passages from the Official Histories and to reprint certain photos.

Any war biography inevitably creates the impression that every battle was fought by only one man or by only one unit. But there is simply not room to tell of the others. Charles Upham hopes, however, that this book can be read, not as a tribute to him, but to all those others—the men with whom he served.

I would be more than pleased if the story can be read that way, if there can emerge an appreciation of the qualities of the ordinary New Zealand soldier, to be read alongside the exploits of this remarkable man.

K.S.

I

Advance Copy

HE FLINGS himself over . . . gropes to his feet, staggers to the bank at the side of the road, climbs up it . . . then seems to pause a moment on the summit of the ridge.

He has chosen the very spot, the very instant.

And now he throws himself forward, loses his footing, goes sprawling, rolling over and over down the slope. His withered arm gives him an awful twinge.

Near the foot of the embankment he scrambles to his feet, sets off running towards the trees. . . .

He seems to have gone only a few yards before the bullets come. The S.S. men, well-trained marksmen, are into action in seconds. Leaping from their truck, they line the top of the bank, have a clear view of him as he races across the fields below.

With sub-machine-guns and rifles the fusillade starts, fire pouring towards the hapless man as he sprints desperately for cover.

And the word spreads from truck to truck, like a silent, sympathetic flame: '*It's Charlie Upham.* . . .'

*   *   *   *

He had a rifle again. But with his arm in a sling it was a heavy, almost useless, weapon for a one-armed man. In the fork of the tree, though . . .

Two of them to get.

Only one hand to hold the rifle, to pull the trigger, then work the bolt after the first shot and bring the second round into the chamber.

Would he have time for the second shot?

They came closer . . . carefully . . . for they could see the clearing ahead, and they were looking for his body in the grass.

He lay dead still, hardly breathing, the barrel of his rifle resting snugly in the fork of the branches.

Close enough . . .

13

He squeezed the trigger. The crack of the gun seemed to shout back from the trees. He saw his man pitch forward.

Like lightning he shifted his one good hand to the bolt . . . a moment's fumbling would be fatal . . . seized it, drew it back, pushed it home again . . . with the other man looming over him.

When he fired the second shot the man's body fell against the muzzle of his rifle.

. . . close enough.

*   *   *   *

And now he is at the main wire. He seizes the strands, begins climbing steadily. It is easy. In no time he is at the top.

All around there are dozens now watching. Others are catching sight of him for the first time and are staring in amazement. A wire-break in broad daylight! What maniac is trying that!

Some who recognize his small wiry figure call out softly to those near: '*It's Charlie Upham*,' and there are some who remember those same words, passed from mouth to mouth, when he ran from the trucks alongside the river. There is a sudden aching sympathy for a man who will dare such fearful odds.

They wait for the volley of fire any moment, wait to see his body crumple up and fall from the wire to the ground, like a sack of old clothes.

But those who wait for that haven't counted the guards today.

*   *   *   *

It is a long dash down the hillside. There can be no reconnaissance, no flanking movement. It has to be an assault into the very muzzle of the guns, straight down the lines of tracer, straight towards the German armour.

And as Upham runs, and he sees his boys all running with him, unhesitating and unflinching, a deep, savage pride possesses him. What men they are!

But they are not thinking of themselves. They are looking at the fury ahead, and they are watching Upham as he races out in front of them, and they are saying . . .

*   *   *   *

'. . . Australia? Well, if you're going all that way, you'd better take your own cutlery . . . and take a bath-tub, too.' Johnny Upham did so.

It was about the beginning of the century when the vastness of Australia summoned him. After studying medicine at Edinburgh, then serving as a book-keeper to a tea firm in London, young Johnny Upham told his parents that he was off 'down under'.

He turned up on a sugar plantation in Queensland at a time when the Boer War was the talk of the Empire. He met a friend on the plantations, and in no time found himself in the swing of the independent, rugged life of the pioneers. Quickly, and despite his formal education in France and England, he acquired a power of picturesque language that seemed to rest incongruously on his slight, rather pedantic figure.

But his greatest surprise was to find that his friend was deep in a political intrigue with quite amazing objectives. The principal scheme was for the northern half of Queensland to sever itself from the rest of the state, secede from the Commonwealth, and declare itself an independent, sovereign nation under a newly constituted monarchy.

Upham's good friend was to be no other than the King of this new domain; and lo! in tribute to his advanced education, Johnny Upham was named as the proposed Prime Minister!

Startled by these crackpot ideas, Upham extricated himself from his friend's ambitious clutches and made his way back to London. It was learning life the hard way when he found all his luggage stolen by the rogue who offered to paint his name on the leather for a modest fee. Some of the picturesque phrases from the plantation came in handy at that moment. But he was a cultured philosopher by now, and promptly decided that this blow to his self-esteem would best be solved by making another sea voyage, this time to New Zealand, where he would visit his brother in Lyttelton, near Christchurch.

From Christchurch Johnny Upham never returned to his homeland. There he studied law, married, and lived his days as a prominent barrister and solicitor.

His wife was the daughter of a widely respected clergyman in the district, descended from a family who had landed with 'the first four' in the mid-century days of Canterbury colonization. She was a woman of especial grace and charm, by nature gentle and shy, but possessed of a determination that was implacable.

Mr. Upham was a deceptive lawyer. Rather short of stature, mild of voice, his air of erudite respectability gave one a feeling that this was a lawyer of the old school, precise, unbending, but not a very dangerous adversary. Woe betide any who felt that way, for behind his kindly blue eyes was a courageous and fighting brain. In court the harder the going, the more resolute he became. He feared no one.

The Uphams had four children—three daughters and a son. They

were all born and bred in a comfortable two-storeyed home in Gloucester Street, Christchurch; reared in the English manner, with a nurse, a
housemaid, and a gardener making up a satisfactory domestic establish-
ment.

For such a family, the future might well have appeared safe, assured,
and comfortable.

Their son, Charles Hazlitt Upham, was born on 21st September
1908. He grew up a quiet, rather shy little boy, very gentlemanly and
courteous, and 'no trouble at all' to 'A'—the nickname of his nanny,
Ethel Turtill. She was with him until he was five years old. They would
walk daily in the park, the lad punctilious about walking on the outside,
even if that meant stumping along in the gutter before 'A' noticed the
lengths to which his courtesy extended.

But from the very start there was something about him. As a child
it was obstinacy; as he grew older it was called perseverance. In the light
of history it was at all times nothing else than rigid single-mindedness.

He didn't like fish as a boy. Requiring him to eat it one day, Miss
Turtill took him for his daily walk in the park some two hours after the
fish luncheon, wondering why he remained so silent. She questioned
him about it, receiving only grunted replies. At last he suddenly smiled
and said: 'It's gone,' and triumphantly explained to her that he couldn't
be bothered holding the fish in his mouth any longer. Nanny had once or
twice held a fish-bone in her mouth for a few minutes, so as to observe
common decencies, but it startled her to think of a mouthful of fish
being obstinately held for over two hours.

He was not a strong child physically, and his parents' concern over
his health was accentuated when he developed a pronounced limp,
which lasted several months. The doctor's report that one leg was shorter
than the other caused them to wonder if some feverish attack had really
cloaked a mild bout of polio—known as 'infantile paralysis' in those
days.

When Charles was nine he was sent to Waihi, a boys' preparatory
boarding school near Timaru. There five years, he left no impression of
scholastic or athletic eminence, but developed a spirit of independence
that his masters specially noticed.

'Puggie' was the nickname he earned at Waihi, sometimes shortened
to 'Pug'. There was no suggestion of his being a bully—that was the
very opposite of his character—but his face was cast in an aggressive line
for a boy of his age, and he was already displaying a spirit of mild
belligerence towards things he did not believe in.

He accepted authority only if he could be shown that it was right.
At prep time this characteristic often appeared. Advancing to the master

in charge, Charles would stand alongside the table and ask a question. The answer would be given. Charles would shake his head (either in genuine or simulated ignorance) and say: 'But I don't understand why it should be, sir.' Another explanation, a very clear one, would follow, and then: 'Now go back to your seat, Upham.'

Shaking his head, Upham would retreat a yard, declaring that he still did not understand. Shorter, more pithy, explanations would be flung at him. He would retreat further; and then a step-by-step argument would finally see him driven back to his seat, still muttering vaguely about the injustice of it and how the book must be wrong.

Peace would reign for five minutes, then out of the silence the voice of Upham would be raised: 'But, sir, you told us yesterday . . .'

The rest of prep would see the master becoming shorter and shorter of temper, and young Upham becoming more and more deliberately obtuse.

The trouble was that he would have developed a theory of his own from which he was not prepared to depart, no matter what the master or the books said.

To the delight of his form-mates, this kind of running war occupied many an evening's prep.

Charles Upham was more liberally whacked than many of the others at Waihi. He could be quite exasperating, with his constant inquests into the rightness of the conclusions reached by the writers of the school-books.

'A Boy-Proof watch, is it?' he said enquiringly, as a relative generously presented him with a pocket watch for his eleventh birthday. He offered the appropriate thanks, being well trained in the drill of acknowledging presents from relatives.

But immediately they were gone he stole upstairs. 'Boy-Proof', eh? That's what it said on the face of the watch. But he would have to see to that for himself, make his own tests.

Leaning out over the balcony, he cast the watch out into the air, watched it crash on the gravel drive beneath.

As he picked up the shattered remains, he nodded wisely, saying to his friends: 'That shows it wasn't boy-proof.'

*   *   *   *

From 1923 to 1927 Charles Upham was a boarder at Christ's College, Christchurch. One of the oldest and most beautiful of New Zealand's colleges, Christ's follows the English public school tradition of stern scholarship hand in hand with religion and sport.

B

No mark was carved by him at college. Although he won prizes in English, Science, History, and (surprisingly) Divinity, he was not regarded as a scholar of any note. His successes were those of the determined plodder and his intellectual attainments suggested that his place in life would not likely be found amongst the professions, but in the more practical sciences. That was just as well, for he had already set his heart on being a farmer. Even at Waihi, holidays on farms with his school friends had fired him with love of the land, especially the great spaces of the broad sheep stations of Canterbury, where men live amidst the grandeur of country that knows few barriers save the wide sprawling rivers and the snow-capped ranges in the west.

Mr. H. E. Solomon, Upham's housemaster at Christ's, said of him: 'He was quiet and unassuming, despite his nickname of "Puggie". Rather shy, not a very good mixer, he would walk over to school with a group of boys, not talking and chaffing with them, but head down and brow furrowed, completely wrapped up in his own thoughts. He took things more seriously than others. He was a lone ranger. Though normally placid, now and then he showed he was capable of a deep fierce temper if he were aroused. But you could rely on him implicitly. I would risk anything on his word—and once having given his word, nothing would budge him.'

To steal out of Flower's House at night, out through the window, then stroll grandly down to the pie-cart near Cathedral Square, was an adventure that Charles shared with others. The deadly thrill of it appealed to him, especially as the road to town took him right past his own front gate.

But his deeper feelings seemed to be reserved for occasions when he saw injustice being done, when the weak were oppressed by the strong. Schoolboys rarely show their emotions, but it was kindness that Charles showed more than anything else. He inherited that from both his mother and father. His resolution came from them, too.

When, as a mere new boy at Christ's, he intervened between three louts who were teasing a little fat boy, shouting at them: 'Leave him alone, you pigs!' he drove them back, not with the threat of his fists—for they would have availed him nothing—but with a passion that flowed from his icy-blue eyes. It was something that indicated a force of personality lying deep within him. They desisted, worried and frightened by the look that blazed from him.

That characteristic—the hatred of wrong—appeared only briefly during his early years. But as he grew to manhood the intensity of that quality set him out from his fellow-men.

*   *   *   *

Mr. Upham was a disappointed man when his only son elected not to study law and join his father's practice. But Charles said: 'I'd always be jealous of my friends on farms.' So Mr. Upham did the next best thing. He enrolled Charles at Canterbury Agricultural College ('Lincoln College'), where the practical and theoretical sciences of farming are taught at university level.

Going from Christ's to Lincoln in 1928, Charles rapidly found himself enthralled with the work. He plunged into the farm and study courses with an enthusiasm that convinced his parents that, after all, it was the right choice.

For two years he was first in agriculture, and gained firsts also in veterinary science and economics. Here indeed was a field of study in which he left behind the rather prosaic results that had been his in the classical subjects at college.

They were happy and stimulating days at Lincoln. Agricultural research and experiment are both highly active in New Zealand, and the young men graduating from the agricultural universities form the brains trust of each new generation of farmers. Upham has always acknowledged his debt to Lincoln College, for the life of practical scholarship, in close association with other ambitious and rugged young men, materially helped shape his own character.

Life at Lincoln brought out more of the lightness of his character, and when some years later he returned there for a further course, he was famous as a raconteur. The atmosphere of the land, and the men who worked it, appealed to him more than the stricter channels of civilian life. He was more gregarious, less the serious lone ranger.

But he was already displaying a kind of ruggedness, both of speech and mind, that seemed at variance with his educated and respectable upbringing. He was already a critic of sham. Flash clothes were sham.

The College Principal met him on the path to the dining-hall one morning and stopped, looking mildly surprised.

'Good morning, sir,' Upham said politely.

'Good morning, Upham. By the way, got a match?'

'Yes, sir . . . here.'

'Then put a match to those clothes you're wearing!'

And in language he was developing a free vocabulary suitable to most occasions, like the day he and John Sandall were returning to Lincoln on a motor-bike.

As they passed a stationary bus an old man suddenly stepped out into the road, right in their path. They crashed into him violently, all three went flying over the road, the bike careering to a stop on the far side.

Upham and Sandall picked themselves up, found they were intact, and shook the gravel from their clothes.

'Now where's that silly old bastard?' Upham asked.

They found him lying hunched up on the roadway, dead still, his eyes closed.

'The bloody old fool's dead,' Upham announced unsympathetically.

Sandall bent over more closely. 'No, not yet. But the bloody old fool's drunk.'

Then the 'corpse' stirred, and a bleary eye opened and surveyed them painfully. And then the old man spoke. 'You're both wrong. I'm neither dead nor drunk. But you've bloody well broken every bloody bone in my bloody body.'

Charles looked down in mute admiration.

*　　　*　　　*　　　*

The college was heated with coal. Students trundled the sacks from the railway station to the college bunkers, and nothing was said when they occasionally dropped off a sack or two for use in the studies. But one shipment was so heavily raided that barely one sack finally reached the bunkers.

The Principal addressed the students. 'About this coal, gentlemen,' he said. 'Although it is forbidden for students to use coal in their studies, I have known for some time that you have occasionally helped yourselves to a sack or two. I've turned a blind eye to that—but this has gone *too* far.' He continued for a while in that vein.

When he had finished, Charles got to his feet, eyed the Principal seriously, and said: 'Sir, on behalf of the students, I wish to lodge a protest. The quality of the coal in this last shipment is much below standard and . . .'

The delighted hoots and laughter of his fellow-students drowned the rest of his words.

The Principal joined in.

*　　　*　　　*　　　*

With the Diploma of Agriculture, Charles Upham left Lincoln in 1930 to begin life on the land.

For the next six years he learnt his craft in the hills, gullies, and plains of Canterbury. He acted as shepherd, musterer, farm manager—in fact in every capacity; four years of this time being in the high country where men have to match the ruggedness of nature with their own ruggedness of physique and temperament.

Island Hills, Glen Wye, Rafa Downs, St. Helens—sheep stations whose names were known to all the graziers of Canterbury—Charles lived through their hot dry summers with the parching north-westerlies; and the snows of winter came down from the Alps, and the rivers rose, and the men on the stations rode the tracks and waded through the floods, living often alone in remote musterers' huts.

It was a life for men of only the tough variety. It built Upham into a man of wiry strength, of great physical endurance. He gained an eye for country, a complete indifference to personal comfort, and he came to judge men by what they did and not by the clothes they wore or the titles they carried.

Now and then he appeared back home. His hair unkempt, clothes scruffy, accompanied by a pair of dogs, he cared not for the comparison with the well-dressed young bloods walking out from Christ's College just a few yards down the road from home. He revelled in the rugged life, distrusted ease, scorned social graces, and appalled his mother with the unconscious array of oaths that he learnt from his years in the out-back.

Perseverance marked this stage of his career. If a dog were slow to learn he would spend weary hours coaching and cajoling it, even though other musterers might be kept waiting. Breaking in a horse would never beat him—he would persevere to the end. Rivers, mountain slopes, outrageous weather—he never surrendered to the elements. He accepted difficulties as part of normal life, as things one had to surmount. He surmounted them with a total disregard of considerations that deterred other men, such as wet clothes, lack of sleep, tiredness, or shortage of food. They were secondary considerations. The objective came first.

Charles attended the local dances that were held in his neighbourhood, but he was one of those who preferred standing in the corner. Nevertheless, he never wasted an evening, for he soon found someone with whom he could argue solidly and intently. As an arguer, he was the same as when breasting a mountainside. The more difficult the argument, the more determined he became not to give in to the other man's point of view. The weaker the case he had, the more hotly did he contest it.

The girls made little progress with this rather shy, but rugged, product of the out-back. He seemed so little interested in small talk, so contemptuous of the fripperies, so intent on more serious subjects.

'But, Charles,' they cooed at him, 'what do you do for washing when you are living all alone? Who washes your socks?' And they tittered at the thought of the solemn young man bending over a washtub.

'My socks?' he queried. 'Well, it isn't really necessary. When they're dirty you throw 'em in a corner. They freshen up again in three weeks!'

There were week-ends at home, performing the evolutions of polite society. But he did enjoy the nice blend of society with nature when he could attend the races. He loved horses, the striving, the will to win, the ruggedness that was close to the silks and satins.

It was at the races one Saturday in 1935 when he first met Molly McTamney. She was a dietitian on the staff of the Christchurch Hospital, after a period of four years hospital nursing. Molly was brunette, pretty, and gay. They danced together that evening; and next day Charles was waiting as she came off duty. He had an armful of red roses for her.

It was Molly from then on.

In from the hills he came whenever he could. She liked red roses, so there he would be waiting outside the nurses' home, bouquet in hand, perhaps some attempt made to control the unruliness of his ragged hair.

They went for drives in his ancient car. It was a car with a canvas hood which flapped backwards in any sort of wind. They wore oilskins in bad weather, because when the hood flapped back there was nothing between the passengers and the rainy skies above. Charles never thought it needed repairing. Molly withstood it, for she began to understand that in Charles's mind rain coming through the roof of the car was a trifling thing.

*   *   *   *

Charles began to think that life ahead required something more secure. Perhaps Molly helped him towards that conclusion, for she had a more practical approach to some problems that Charles never recognized.

So in March 1937 he joined the Valuation Department. First under supervision, then alone, Upham quickly assimilated the techniques of land valuation. He was aided by the scientific knowledge gained at Lincoln College, but much more by his extensive experience of Canterbury land during his six years' work in the province. Very soon his superior officer reported on him: 'He is very conscientious, very obliging, and anxious to get on. I find that he is inclined to be easy in his values, but every month seems to be increasing his efficiency.'

Then around came the Valuer-General in person, visiting his branches and meeting the staff. Charles stood in the ante-room, waiting his turn for interview.

The man acting as usher drew him aside, pointed disapprovingly to a rent in Upham's coat, mildly suggested that it would be politic to change.

'But it's only a hole,' said Charles. 'What's wrong with that?'

The usher had no chance to say any more because it was now Upham's turn, but he listened outside the door.

Upham was being asked his opinions. He gave them freely, embellished with some of his more ebullient phrases gleaned from the high country. It went on vividly for some time.

At the end the Valuer-General shook hands cordially, a little surprised at his new recruit. And as Upham turned to leave, he said rather sadly: 'Upham—you'll never make a civil servant.'

And Charles couldn't understand why.

*   *   *   *

To his fellow-valuers, Charles's physical toughness was a byword. If they returned late from the country their thoughts turned to a hot meal, a bath, and a warm bed. But as often as not, they found that Upham was interested only in going to sleep, and he did precisely that, curling up on the large table in the Timaru Valuation Office.

Once Cliff Muir and Charles went out on location, Charles going on ahead to try to engage accommodation. He did so successfully, proudly showing Cliff through the little cottage he had rented for the duration of their stay.

'That's your bed, Cliff,' he said.

'Thanks, Charlie, that's fine. But it's the only bed in the house. Where's yours?'

Charles pointed unconcernedly to an old tent-fly, folded up in a corner on the floor of the living-room. 'That's mine,' he said.

In 1938 Charles and Molly became engaged. They had only a few happy months before she left New Zealand to visit her sister in Singapore.

From there, early in 1939, Molly went on to England. By that time the situation in Europe was darkening, Charles was beseeching her to return home, and he himself was planning seriously for his future career.

*   *   *   *

Granted leave from the Valuation Department, Charles returned to Lincoln College in February 1939 to take a course in valuation and farm management. Now somewhat of an elder statesman, by virtue of

his earlier days at the college and his wide farming experience, he
became a popular favourite of his fellow-students. He helped them
liberally with their own studies, he played football with just as much
vigour as before, and he was always in demand for the fund of humorous
anecdotes he had accumulated during his years on the stations.

The course he took was restricted to men of wide practical background and was designed primarily to train men for managerial posts in
Government departments. At the end of the year Charles had no
trouble with the necessary exams, obtaining his Diploma in Valuation
and Farm Management, and it was only his entering camp before the
end of the year that probably lost him the chance of becoming gold
medallist for 1939.

'An experienced, educated, well-bred rough diamond,' was how one
man described him at this time.

But the darkening months of 1939 saw Upham thinking more and
more deeply about events on the other side of the world. Slowly he
evolved his own ideas of where lay the rights and the wrongs. Once he
had convinced himself, his mind was made up for a lifetime.

With the call for volunteers in September 1939, he lost no time in
putting his name on the lists. His career, his own future, his life ahead
with Molly—none of these could be assured, he reasoned, unless the
menace in Europe was quickly halted.

He enlisted out of conviction that the Nazis had to be stopped. Not
for him the quite popular feeling that Hitler was a somewhat comic
figure with enough ability to bring order out of Germany's chaos, that
Mussolini was a good business man to drain the swamps and run the
railways on time. No.

He marched into Burnham Camp, near Christchurch, with the first
draft of New Zealand's First Echelon. He stood in the queues, found his
slat bed in the hut, chafed impatiently at the slow gearing of the Army
system that took so long, he thought, to get down to the business of
learning to fight. He found he was in A Company of an infantry
battalion.

He was Private Upham now, a soldier with no special qualifications,
no influence, nothing that appeared to differentiate him from the
hundreds of others.

He was not to know, and does not recognize to this day, that already
there lurked within him some qualities which seemed to be waiting for
warfare to nourish. The needle-sharp courageous brain of his father,
intent on fighting legal points; the gentle, but unyielding determination
of his mother; the traditions of his schools; the toughening experiences
of his years on the stations; the eye for country—either scanning it for

the best track or assessing its value; the hatred of oppression; all these influences had made their mark on him.

The Principal of Lincoln College in 1939 was Professor Eric Hudson, a man of notable appearance and reputation, who had served overseas in 1914-18. He believed that the way men behave under fire is almost always unpredictable. The timid counter-salesman who dislikes killing a chicken might well be the coolest man under a barrage. The tough champion boxer, abrim with self-confidence, could be the one man of an infantry platoon who won't go over the top. You need to know a man a long time before boldly asserting that he will be a good man in action. You can guess, but experience shows that your guesses are too frequently wrong.

Professor Hudson saw the men march out from Lincoln College during the war, men who were studying farming and the land, men who were more likely to be solid than flash. Perhaps they were better equipped for soldiering than their city brothers, because of their knowledge of country and their physical adaptability. Hundreds of them went from Lincoln into the training camps during the six years of war. Hudson was tempted to write commendations for many of them, knowing that his position and name would command respect.

But conscious of the fallibility of his own judgment and the judgment of other men as to whether a man would make good in uniform, he refrained throughout the whole war from writing to the military authorities about his students. Before him there at Lincoln he had the finest possible material. Yet he paused. Only *one* exception did he make in all those years, the only student he ever wrote about. And even with that one student Hudson decided to be as brief as possible and avoid anything fulsome.

Early in October 1939 he wrote his only letter. It was:

> 'Canterbury Agricultural College,
> Lincoln.

The Commanding Officer,
    Burnham Military Camp,
        Burnham.
Dear Sir,
        A young man by the name of Upham has left the College to join your unit. I commend him to your notice, as, unless I am greatly mistaken, he should be an outstanding soldier.

> Yours faithfully,
> E. Hudson'

2

Men Marching

IN THE three mobilization camps at Hopuhopu, Trentham, and Burnham there were skeleton staffs of former Territorial officers and N.C.O.s and a smattering of Permanent Staff instructors. But from the miscellaneous ranks of those who had just arrived a number had to be chosen to act as temporary N.C.O.s. Choosing men in those circumstances depended on very undependable factors—a man's apparent enthusiasm, his appearance, his 'air' of leadership, his tone of voice. If these were false indications of a man's real worth his true measure would soon become apparent. There were other criteria, too.

Captain Frank Davis, Adjutant of the infantry battalion at Burnham, went through the list of names with the C.O., Colonel H. Kippenberger. 'Let's sort out a few who went to boarding school,' he suggested. 'Most of them have cadet training and annual camps. We could look that lot over.'

'Good idea,' Kippenberger agreed. 'The other lads will make just as good N.C.O.s in time, but it takes longer to pick them out. Here—you take this lot, I'll go through these others.'

The cards were flicked through in silence, every now and then one being put aside.

Kippenberger paused, card in hand. 'Upham,' he mused. 'Christ's College boy. Farm valuer. Lincoln College.' He turned to Davis. 'Here's one we could try. Have a look at him anyway. I know his father—Johnny Upham, a lawyer in Christchurch. Well-known good family. And I've had a note about this chap from Eric Hudson at Lincoln College.'

They put that card aside, went on working through the others.

Just as they finished there was a knock at the door. Steele, the R.S.M., put his head inside.

'Come in, Sergeant-Major,' Kippenberger nodded. 'And before you leave we've got a list of men here we'd like to have a look at for temporary stripes. Now what's the matter?'

Steele said: 'The men know there's no leave this first week-end. But

26

there's a chap here wants to make a special application for leave. Personal grounds, he says. I told him no show, but he has asked to see you. Determined sort of beggar.'

'All right,' the Colonel said. 'The sooner I get to know them the better. Send him in. Who is he, anyway?'

'His name's Upham. In A Company. I'll get him.'

Charles Upham was brought in, uneasy at the formality of his intrusion.

'All right, stand at ease, Upham,' Kippenberger said. 'The R.S.M. tells me you are asking for leave. There's no leave being granted, you know, except in special circumstances. What's your trouble?'

'Well,' Upham replied hesitantly, 'it's not exactly trouble. I just want to get leave for personal reasons.' And he looked straight ahead at the wall behind Kippenberger's head.

Adjutant Davis studied the man as he stood there. Rather an unkempt individual, he thought. Hardly the usual product of Christ's College. A rugged-looking face. He noticed the eyes too—intense, rather chilling eyes.

The C.O. said: 'Well, I'm sorry, Upham, but you'll have to tell me the personal reasons before I can consider it. What's the matter?'

Upham hesitated again; then spoke suddenly: 'I want to give a chap a hiding; that's all.'

There was a short, rather surprised pause.

Kippenberger found it necessary to adopt a more than usually solemn tone to control his startled amusement. 'I think that's the first time I've heard that one,' he said. 'But go on, Upham. Tell me more about it.'

Upham turned his eyes on the Colonel. 'I sold a man a car,' he said. 'He owes me £12 10s. on it and he says he's not going to pay it. If I don't get my money I'm going to take it out of his hide.'

The Colonel looked interested. 'Do you know where he is?'

'Yes, at the Grosvenor Hotel in Timaru.'

Kippenberger looked hard at Upham. Then he decided. 'Yes, Upham,' he said, 'you can have your leave. There'll be only one tag to it—when you get back I want you to report personally to me. Understand?'

Upham nodded shortly. 'Yes, sir. And thank you, sir.'

R.S.M. Steele marched him out.

Kippenberger chuckled, then thumbed through the cards again till he found Upham's. He re-read the details on it.

'You know,' he said to Davis, 'that chap's got something. But he's not a bit like his father. Old Johnny Upham is a very respectable sort of family lawyer. This chap looks as if he'd be happier in the mountains than a lawyer's office.'

The week-end came. Upham walked out of camp in company with a very favoured few.

Monday morning he reported again at Battalion Headquarters.

'You told me to report to you, sir, after I came back from leave.'

'Oh yes, Upham,' the Colonel said. 'Tell me—did you find your man?'

'Yes, sir.'

'Did you get your money?'

'I did not,' Upham replied tersely.

'M-m, bad luck.' A pause. 'Well, then—did you give him his hiding?'

'Yes, sir, I did,' came the answer, and a look of satisfaction showed momentarily on Upham's face.

He had barely returned to his hut when the Orderly Sergeant came after him, telling him he was wanted again at Battalion H.Q., this time by Captain Davis, the Adjutant.

He walked back obediently.

'You're a graduate of Lincoln College, aren't you?' the Adjutant enquired. 'Diplomas and all that? . . .'

Upham nodded.

'That means you've studied soils, laying out of crops, grassland cultivation, and all that sort of thing, doesn't it?'

'Yes, that's right, sir.'

'Well, just come back inside. There's someone here you know.'

Inside the Adjutant's room Upham came face to face with R. H. Bevin, who had been his tutor at Lincoln College a few days before.

Davis said: 'You know Mr. Bevin, don't you, Upham? He's cver here to help us. You see, they've decided to lay down a lawn around Camp Headquarters. We asked Lincoln College if they would send someone to advise us. Mr. Bevin came over. But he's a pretty busy man, and he says if anybody ought to know how to lay down the lawn it's you. So you've been detailed for the job.'

Upham stared blankly at him.

Then Bevin came over and said briskly: 'I've brought all the stuff over, Charlie. . . .'

And Upham stood there silently while Bevin handed over the goods and then made his departure.

When he had gone Upham looked at Captain Davis stonily. He said: 'Is that right—you're going to get me to lay down a bloody lawn?'

'That's right,' Davis said. 'You're just the man. And mind your language when you're in here.'

Upham gulped. 'What happens to my training while I'm doing that? We're on Lewis gun and bayonet today and I don't want to miss it.'

'Plenty of time,' Davis said soothingly.

'Well, I don't know that there is,' Upham blurted out. 'The war's not going to be won by laying down ruddy lawns. Is it an order?'

'Yes, it is. And, you know, Upham, you can't win the war today.'

Upham looked at him without speaking. No, he couldn't win the war today, he knew, but he'd have a mighty good crack at it if he had the chance.

So that afternoon he laid the lawn.

And that night a torrential downpour washed out all his seed and he had to sow it all afresh the following morning.

And there is great doubt if any lawn in the world has been laid to the accompaniment of such profanity and discontent.

Because lawns don't win battles.

*   *   *   *

Towards the end of October the training camps were told that men would have to be chosen from the ranks to train for commissions. Nominations were called for.

In Burnham, where the infantry now bore the title of 20th Battalion, Colonel Kippenberger went through the lists again with his Adjutant, Davis.

Upham's name came up once more. He was getting himself noticed now by the almost ferocious intensity he was bringing to bear on his training. He gave the impression that he regarded his competence as a soldier as of tremendous importance. And to the little section of men, over whom his new one stripe gave him command, he conveyed an air of dedication and urgency.

Kippenberger said: 'What about him?'

'He's got a good background,' Davis agreed. 'Doing a good job as a lance-jack, too; he's older and got more savvy than most of them. But I wonder if he knows enough about it yet?'

'Hear about him at Tai Tapu?' Kippenberger queried, referring to manœuvres from which the battalion had just returned. 'Held up the whole advance half an hour. I was chewing him up, but then I found out the reason. He'd been out scouting on his own. He came upon an 'enemy' section, rushed in on them, and demanded they surrender.

Trouble was, they *wouldn't* surrender. Reckoned the battle hadn't started. Upham was late getting back because he stayed to argue with them.'

Davis nodded. 'And I heard more about that today. The stream was running four or five feet deep, and the 'enemy' reckoned it would be all right to post men only on the bridges. But I'm told Upham took it more seriously. He didn't have a go at the bridges; said that was crazy. He made his men wade the stream—up to their armpits. Won his little battle, all right, but it didn't make him too popular. A bit too realistic, they said.'

Kippenberger listened with interest. 'Yes . . . and Archie MacDuff told me he did a camouflage job that was pretty good.' He sat silently for a little while.

Then he continued: 'A determined man. Probably get himself shot the first day we're in action. Yes . . . I'll have him. Put his name on the list. Then we'll parade these lads and have a talk to them.'

The fifty men were lined up on the parade ground. Twenty of them had to be chosen for the Trentham Officer Cadet Training Unit. Frank Davis looked them over before the Colonel arrived.

He said to them bluntly: 'You blokes have been sorted out for the chance of going for commissions. The C.O.'s going to pick out twenty of you. They'll go up to Trentham this Friday night. But if any of you aren't interested, better fall out now.'

One or two shuffled their feet uncomfortably.

Ross Westenra, standing alongside Upham, said: 'I've got a race-horse I want to see run at Ashburton this week-end. Suppose I'd better drop out.'

Davis said: 'Please yourself. . . . Any others?'

Charles Upham looked hesitant. Then he said to the Adjutant: 'I don't want to be mucking about in New Zealand. What happens if I go to this school? Do I get away?'

'Don't ask me,' Davis replied. 'Try the C.O. He's coming now.'

Kippenberger walked over from the orderly room.

He spoke to them in his quiet, sincere voice. 'This is an opportunity for you men. We are badly in need of good officers. Every one of you could earn a commission if you worked reasonably hard. But don't be under any illusions about it. You'd go overseas as second lieutenants, and I think I can fairly warn you that the prospects of a one-pipper at the beginning of a war aren't particularly bright. Now, are there any questions?'

He looked along the ranks. . . . Silence.

Then he noticed an arm held up, rather like a boy in school.

'Well, Upham, what do you want to say?'

'If I went up to Trentham, sir, would I still get overseas with this battalion?'

Kippenberger looked at him straight. 'I couldn't give you any guarantee about that.'

'In that case, sir,' Upham replied, 'I'd like my name taken off the list.'

Kippenberger was all the more certain then that Charles Upham was the kind of man who would put his head in the road of a bullet in a comparatively short time. But he didn't realize then, as he did later, that behind Lance-Corporal Upham's anxiety to close with the enemy lay a brain that was very quickly mopping up the fundamentals of military skill.

The men who survived battles were often found to be those who could calculate the risks a soldier could fairly take; who could distinguish, in the heat of conflict, between futile risks on the one hand and, on the other, risks which were reasonably worth taking for the objective in view.

In his later military career Upham was sometimes branded as a foolhardy, reckless, and lucky soldier. That was not a fair appraisal. He took fearful risks, agreed. But examination of them shows that they were all 'on'. And every one, if successful, stood to gain some worthwhile advantage.

To be brave and foolish can be heroic. But heroism takes on a higher quality if bravery and judgment go hand in hand.

*   *   *   *

It was as the battalion returned from a long route-march after midday on 4th December that the word passed rapidly around the lines: a small advance party was about to leave for overseas, the men had been chosen, and any minute the lucky names were to be announced. Final leave for them right away. Here was the hour for those who were most anxious to be away to the wars.

They were lined up in the mess queue when the R.S.M. bustled along, sheet of paper in one hand.

'Where's Corporal Upham? Ah . . . there you are, Charlie. You're in the advance party, Charlie. Get your gear together straight after mess, and report to Battalion Headquarters 1400 hours. You're going on final leave right away—lucky beggar.'

For a moment Upham looked incredulous. Then an excited grin spread over his features. 'Where're we going, Sar'-Major?' he shouted.

'You'll know before I do. . . . Better get on with your lunch.'

But this was too wonderful to absorb right on mess time. Face alight, he went around his friends, telling them of his good fortune, leaving his lunch plates untouched.

There were ten others chosen from the battalion to form part of the advance party. The others seemed to enjoy their lunch. Charles was too excited to care.

From all the training camps in the country fifty-two men were selected for the advance party. It may have been significant that Upham was singled out for special duties. Perhaps his commanders already suspected that, despite a civilian career that had been promising but unspectacular, Charles Upham had certain qualities which fitted him well for the exceptional demands of war.

He was promoted to sergeant six days before they sailed.

3

The Impatient Sergeant

EARLY 1940 was the time of the shadow war. Some called it the 'phoney' war, though it wasn't phoney for the comparative few who saw the bullets and bombs. There were the troopships churning overseas, the factories almost reluctantly switching to war materials, the psychological change that was necessary to make a nation ready to meet fancied threats ahead. And some wondered if the threats were real.

Then suddenly, with a violence that shook the world, there came the panther springs of Hitler's Germany, swallowing up the little countries of Europe, startling the old soldiers with a kind of warfare that most had refused to recognize and only a few had warned against, like voices in the wilderness.

The success of it was awe-inspiring. As April turned to May, France, totally bewildered, began to crumble. Then Mussolini of Italy decided that he too would like to share in the glory.

During that time, while the New Zealand Division trained in Egypt, Charles Upham worked as a sergeant. He did not become renowned as a particularly smart sergeant. Intent on learning the essentials of fighting, and nothing else, he showed no affection for parade-ground niceties, little respect for the conventions of Army life and rank.

Indeed, it is a wonder he escaped arraignment for plain insubordination. He would speak bluntly to everyone, whatever their rank. He became quickly intolerant of the many artificialities of the Army system, outspoken against anything that did not immediately appear to help the business of fighting and winning a war. All else was sham, unwanted. If he thought an officer was wrong he would tell him so to his face—not out of insolence, but from sheer honesty, from the burning sense that men had to be trained right, the war fought right, the right orders given, and the right men appointed to give them.

Late in February he was demonstrating the Bren gun to a squad of men. He told them clearly what had to be done and he gave his own practical demonstration of it.

C   33

An infantry captain came up behind him as the lesson progressed, watched for a few moments with a disapproving eye.

'Just a minute, Sergeant,' he interrupted. 'That's not the right way to clear that stoppage.' And he proceeded to expound to the squad what he claimed was the proper method to follow.

Upham looked on silently, his brow darkening, a rather ominous glint in his eye.

'There, Sergeant,' the Captain concluded. 'Teach it the way I've just shown you.'

Upham held his heels at attention. But all the stripes in the world were not worth being told he was wrong when he *knew* he was right. He had just passed out of a weapons course at Tel Aviv, and he knew his Bren completely. He snapped out: 'I'm sorry, sir, but you're wrong. I was showing them the *right* way.'

The Captain eyed him. 'You'll teach it the way I've just shown you,' he repeated steadily.

Upham's eyes flared. There was a moment of silence, then he could not contain himself. He blurted out: 'Who's supposed to be giving this lecture? Me or you? If you reckon I'm wrong, well go ahead—there's the gun, there's the squad; teach 'em yourself!' And he looked his defiance as he saw his three stripes melting into thin air.

The Captain turned and walked away.

Upham glared after him, then turned and eyed the squad stonily. It was a few moments before he spoke. Then he said: 'Forget what he told you. He doesn't know what he's talking about. Right . . . we'll have a smoke.'

And his men grinned at one another; and they rather thought their sergeant was the sort of bloke they wouldn't mind going into action with; that is, if he didn't end up in the ranks himself for talking to officers like that.

But Upham kept his three stripes, for the Captain was a well-liked officer who was wise enough to recognize his own mistake and to count his blessings for an N.C.O. who had the spirit to stand up for himself.

It was the right and duty of every soldier, Charles thought, to speak his own mind if it would help win the battle. As a sergeant and later an officer, he was on familiar terms with all his men, calling them by their first names, or merely swearing at them affectionately. They called him 'boss' to his face, 'Charlie' behind his back. He asked for their opinions, considered them soberly; dismissed them brusquely if he thought fit; adopted them with enthusiasm if they were good. He expected to be allowed to express his own views in the same way to those above him in rank. To him it was natural to do so.

Likewise, it was natural for him to disagree flatly with a superior officer and to tell him so bluntly, with no embarrassment on either side. Of course the officer needed to know his Upham, to know that no disrespect was intended, that it was just the mental honesty and straightforwardness of the man that accounted for it.

The 20th Battalion went out into the desert on training manoeuvres. One company would establish a defensive position, another would reconnoitre and attack it. Colonel Kippenberger himself would watch and later give comments.

It was on such an occasion that Upham's forthrightness went almost as far as it safely could. Out into the desert went A Company to establish a defensive position and hold it against attack. They also had to employ the newly issued anti-tank rifle, and this required a little more thought than the usual dispositions for a company in defence.

Sergeant Upham was given command of his platoon, and soon had his sections well disposed. Probably it was his training in the hills, or some inborn ability, but he had a natural eye for ground, which others took months and years of active service to acquire. He seemed able to assess immediately the tactical potentialities of any area.

A supervising officer arrived, looked searchingly over the sergeant's plan, and roundly condemned it. This section should be further this way, that section closer to the ridge, etc. He told Upham to move his men accordingly.

This was learning warfare, Upham reasoned. Rank did not enter into the discussion. His men's lives would depend on his own decisions in months to come.

So he said: 'No, sir. I'm not moving them.'

'Why not? I've told you you're wrong.'

Upham gave his reasons, carefully thought-out reasons. To others within earshot they sounded convincing. 'It would be bloody stupid to move those sections up there,' he concluded brassily. 'Just plumb crazy.'

The officer had had enough. 'All right, Sergeant,' he said, 'I make it an order.'

Upham shook his head stubbornly. 'Those positions are right,' he maintained. 'I take my orders as to where the whole platoon goes. But it's my job to place my sections. That's my responsibility. I'm sorry, I'm not shifting them.'

'Then if you don't do what you're told, Upham, I could have you placed under arrest and removed.'

There was a rather long silence. Upham let his eye range over his section posts again. He knew he was right. The officer was wrong. Orders might be orders, but men's lives were more important than that.

Arrest, eh? But his mind was inflexible. He always was inflexible, once he had carefully mapped out a course of action and embarked upon it. No deviation. No side issues.

But there was a hint of a smile in his eyes as he replied. 'Have me arrested? I don't think you could do it, sir. We're out in the desert here, and I'd have a right to insist on two N.C.O.s of equal rank to escort me —and there aren't two other sergeants within three miles.'

The two men looked at each other. Then the officer said: 'I'd escort you myself, Upham, if I felt about it seriously enough. Lucky for you I don't. Say we get on with the war, then—and we'll see how your positions stand up to it. You'll find out you are wrong. Then perhaps you'll learn your lesson.'

So the exercise continued, but history does not record whether Charles's positions were proved right or wrong. All the story shows is that this rather brash sergeant was determined to lead his men according to his own ideas, and he wasn't mealy-mouthed over telling other people what he thought of theirs.

It was just a few days after this incident that the Battalion Adjutant, looking over his lists of N.C.O.s with a critical eye, said to Colonel Kippenberger: 'This Upham ought to go to O.C.T.U. some time. His O.C. says he knows platoon tactics backwards, and he's a tiger with the bayonet and the Bren. Though I doubt if he'd make a good officer. Rough as guts. And on the parade ground he's about the world's worst. He's the scruffiest we've got, but he's a hell of a good soldier.'

Kippenberger didn't need to be told. He already had Upham on his list.

'Pity he couldn't smarten up his drill,' the Colonel said. 'He's pretty rough, isn't he?'

'Could be smart if he tried, I think,' the Adjutant replied. 'But he's got no sense of time, no rhythm; and I think he reckons it's all a waste of time. He wants to be killing Germans. He's out there now taking his platoon on drill. Like to look?'

They strolled out of the orderly room and walked over towards the platoon. It had just faced round in a rather straggly left-form, and now was marching off towards the edge of the training area. Sergeant Upham strode along at the side, concentrating deeply, his stride a shade out of step with the leaders of the front rank.

They came closer to the edge of the square.

One or two of the front rank glanced sideways at the sergeant to make sure he hadn't forgotten them, and that he would soon give the required order to face them round and march them back towards the centre again.

But the order didn't come. Further and further they went. Upham had an intense, furious expression on his face as he strove vainly to remember the right command. It was something absurdly simple, he knew full well; but his mind had been preoccupied with a thought he had had about firing a Bren gun from the hip.

Kippenberger gazed in perplexity.

The Adjutant said: 'There's an example of it. He's forgotten what foot to give the about-turn on.'

'He won't have any platoon left if he doesn't do something,' the C.O. murmured. 'If he doesn't call "Halt" pretty soon I'll call it myself.'

But Upham also knew it was now too late to turn the platoon about. He had to stop them somehow. What was the command to stop? What foot?

In final desperation he filled his lungs, lifted his head and yelled: 'Whoa!' Like well-trained horses from the hill country of Canterbury, the platoon came to a sudden halt, and permitted themselves a friendly grin at the sergeant.

Upham swallowed hard, pushed down his web belt, and addressed his men: 'You beauts. I suppose if I hadn't said anything you'd have walked right into the bloody wadi. That was one of the roughest halts you fellows have ever done. Remember, it's—halt, one, one-two. Now we'll turn round and do a proper job of it in front of Kip. Right—turn round. . . . I mean—about . . . turn!'

So they swung back across the sand determined to put on a good show while the Colonel and the Adjutant were watching.

Upham judged his time, ordered: 'Platoon . . . *halt!*'

They came to a staggering stop, one after another, and looked with mild reproof at the sergeant who had failed them.

But the sergeant was too busy with the officers.

The C.O. said: 'Your men can do better than that, Sergeant. You gave them the "Halt" on the wrong foot.'

Upham nodded, cursing himself silently. He never seemed to be able to pick the right foot.

Then he said hopefully: 'Well, sir, even if I did, *they knew what I bloody well meant.*'

Kippenberger found that unanswerable.

He said to the Adjutant as they retreated to Battalion Headquarters: 'Does he often swear like that?'

'Most of the time, I'm told. Just a habit. Educated fellow of course, good family, Christ's College. Must have picked up all his profanity when he was mustering. Now it just pours out of him naturally. Funny thing, though, it's not offensive. He's even sworn at me. Anyone else I'd have on the mat, but with Upham you know he doesn't mean anything by it.'

'What about his men? Does he swear at them too?'

'They tell me he'll swear at anybody, no matter who. I expect his men swear back at him. But they're all *for* him. He looks after them so well. A real fighter for his own platoon.'

Kippenberger paused, stood outside in the sun for a few minutes. Then he said: 'I'll send him to O.C.T.U. later on. But those English instructors will give him hell. What I'm thinking about is this, though—when he's commissioned would we want him back in the battalion? What do you think?'

The Adjutant considered. 'Depends what we are going to do. If the div is going to stooge around in Egypt much longer, doing routine stuff, Upham wouldn't be any special gain to us. He's a very thoughtful, intelligent chap, but he's too impatient.'

'But what if we go into action?'

'Here in Africa? Can't see that happening.'

'Well, I can tell you this—Italy will be in the war in the next few weeks.'

'The Ities! My word, that's great. . . . And Charlie Upham? I can picture him now—walking in with a hundred prisoners, holding 'em up at the point of his pipe. Capture by will-power!'

Kippenberger said: 'That's it exactly. And that's why I'll try to get him posted back here after he's commissioned. We want to win our battles!'

Capture by will-power! Charles Upham's personality and strength of will were already manifest to those whom he commanded and those who were in command over him. Without speaking a word, men possessing these qualities often radiate their power to those around them, so that men say in a puzzled way: 'There's something about him. . . .'

It is demonstrated in a hundred little ways. There was the day back in New Zealand when Upham stood in the queue buying tickets for the cinema. For himself and his mate they would cost about 5s. He handed over a £1 note. The cashier, quick as light, handed him the tickets and pushed over only 5s. change, as if believing that only a 10s. note had been tendered.

Upham said nothing at all. He did not pick up his change, just stood there watching.

The cashier finally looked up, aware of the silence. She saw the man's strange blue eyes steadily fixed on her.

Not a word was said. But, as the silence lengthened, finally the cashier slowly moved her hand, groped for a 10s. note, then added it to the rest of the change. She smiled hesitantly. She felt relieved when those unusual eyes at last turned away from her. There was something frightening about them. . . . Capture by will-power!

*   *   *   *

On 10th June 1940 Italy declared war on Britain. It seemed to Mussolini that the pickings of Europe were there for the taking.

All it did to Charles Upham was to make him the more impatient to get down to business. But it was not a mere blind lust for fighting—he never had been a belligerent man. But fighting the war, fighting it physically, was the only way he could see of ending it the sooner. He begrudged the weeks and months of training, though he hurled himself into it with something like passion. It was the inexorable passage of time that worried him.

He already comprehended that the man who could do the enemy most damage, and at the same time have the best chance of survival, was the man who made himself expert with his own weapons. So he became an expert with the Bren. He tried to train his men to be experts also.

At an early stage in training, when there was only one Bren gun for the whole company, Upham utilized every second of the time the Bren was allotted to his platoon. Every man had to know the Bren better than his own hand. He drilled them on gun stoppages without respite.

Next time the Bren came round he found that one of his men, Alex Meldrum, did not know his 'immediate action' on a Bren stoppage. Upham gave him the lash of his tongue, and Meldrum had difficulty in finally getting in a word to explain that he had been on fatigues when the lesson had been taught.

Quick to blame, quick to retract if wrong—that was how they always found him. Instantly he arranged with Meldrum that they would meet that evening. And after evening mess Upham arrived at Meldrum's tent, the Bren under his arm, and spent an hour giving his one-man squad an intensive and individual course in Bren-gun stoppages. He couldn't afford to let such a vital thing wait another day.

So likewise he became an expert with the grenade—not merely proficient, but expert; in distance; in direction; judging how long it could be held before throwing, to make sure the enemy could not throw it back; what damage it could do both to men and morale; how many he could possibly drape around his body before going into action.

Later, when his exploits made legends throughout the British forces, the stories were always garnished with details of how many grenades

Upham carried about with him. Some said he carried a sugar-sack of them as he waded through the circle of fire during the amazing break-out at Minqar Qaim; others claimed that he wore a special bandolier of them as he earned his first V.C. on Crete; that on Ruweisat Ridge there was a grave shortage of grenades in his company because Upham had coralled them all.

Whatever the truth, it was common ground that Upham cherished the grenade as his favourite attacking weapon, and he went into every action carrying as great a load of them as he could bear.

But in some of the formal aspects of military life he was lost. With little musical sense, and knowing himself that he had a poor sense of rhythm, parade-ground drill continued to be an unpleasant effort.

On several occasions he had to act as Battalion Orderly Sergeant, whose job at Battalion Parade was to dress the companies in proper line. This is accomplished by the sergeant looking down the line of each rank, moving men up or back; then, when satisfied, repeating the process with the next rank. Upham was well known for making a bungle of it more often than not. The other N.C.O.s laughed at him and the men squirmed silently. Upham hated the whole thing and realized he was hopeless at it.

Then there was the occasion when he was Guard Sergeant. . . .

Changing the guard is one of those formal things that higher officers love, R.S.M.s regard as setting the standard of the battalion, and men patiently endure. But the crisp exactness of a well-drilled guard gives some satisfaction to all who take part.

It is the Orderly Officer of the day who inspects the incoming guard and sends it on its way to take over from the old guard. The new guard is first paraded by its sergeant. Then formal salutes are given to the Orderly Officer. He returns the salute, inspects the guard, then sees it march away to its duties.

In the fussy exactness of guard-mounting Upham saw nothing that would win the war. He believed in guards, of course, but had little time for the attached ceremonial.

On this day he was the Guard Sergeant. Impatient with the routine, he waited for the Orderly Officer to arrive. He checked his men again, thought they looked reasonably well turned out, and shifted his weight from one foot to the other as the minutes ticked by. It was hot. Damn the ceremonial!

Word came that the Orderly Officer was delayed, would not be long.

Patience exhausted, Sergeant Upham took up his station in front of the guard, brought it to attention, inspected it meticulously, and forthwith proceeded to change the guard himself. The Orderly Officer arrived, boots shining, Sam Browne belt immaculate, to find that he was too late, his functions usurped, the parade ground deserted, the new guard safely installed.

*   *   *   *

The men of his platoon were the salt of the earth. Their welfare became his first thought. He would fight for their interests tooth and nail, doing it with a smile if that seemed the best approach, but more often winning his way by a persistence that finally wore down the opposition.

Swear at them as he did, drive them mercilessly to become expert soldiers, show them a poor example of military precision, yet they came to regard him as a man who would risk a lot for their sakes.

They marched back from a long desert manœuvre that gave them a good taste of sand in their mouths. The march back was dry, hot, and gruelling. The administrators had trucks to commute to and fro, with no special difficulties attached to the bringing up of rations.

But as the men staggered to a halt for lunch on the long way home, the word came down the line: 'No tea—just hard rations.'

That wasn't good enough, Upham argued. He went straight to his Company Headquarters. On the way he seized the handle of a pick-axe, took it with him.

'My men are just about all in,' he complained. 'If the ration blokes can't turn on tea pretty smartly, then I'll take this bloody pick-axe to them!' And he shook it angrily under their noses.

'Calm down, Sergeant,' the officer told him. 'And put that thing down! Don't behave like a savage. I'll see that your men get some tea.'

He did see to it.

But some thought that it would have been only hard rations 'if Charlie hadn't lost his temper'.

*   *   *   *

Often intolerant of the Army system, impatient with its slow gearing, he was also quick to criticize any apparent abuse of the powers of rank. By nature he always sided with the under-dog, risking his own rank to uphold what he thought was justice.

One day in Cairo three Military Police were sauntering along the footpath. They were big, powerful men, capable of handling trouble. Trouble came.

First it was three drunk soldiers, badly, abusively drunk. They swaggered past the M.P.s, swayed across the footpath, threatening and obscene.

Upham was standing nearby with a group of fellow Kiwis. They watched in amazement as the hefty M.P.s looked casually over the lurching soldiers, then let them go past unmolested.

One of the watching men muttered: 'Scared of them. Frightened it would be too tough.'

Upham had almost a pathological dislike of M.P.s as a class. No logic about it—just one of his prejudices. Nor did he pause to consider that these M.P.s might not be authorized to arrest soldiers of *all* Allied nationalities.

In less than a minute another drunk appeared, this time an enormous, belligerent man. Everyone visibly quailed as he set sail down the street, bent on trouble. The M.P.s pretended not to notice.

Until five minutes later, when a half-pickled little Tommy came waltzing timidly along, cheerful, peaceful, happily tipsy.

The three M.P.s pounced on him, roughing him up as they hurried him to the kerb.

'Are we going to stand for that?' one of the New Zealanders asked his mates.

They muttered darkly, began edging slowly towards the M.P.s, circling around them, doing nothing wrong, but helping the other pedestrians crowd in on the little group. Jostling began.

Upham had seen it all, was seething with resentment.

A taxi was stopped. Into it the M.P.s bustled their diminutive prisoner.

Then the men acted. Ostensibly to beat the M.P.s for the taxi, they rushed forward, elbowing and shoving. Into the taxi hustled the Kiwis. Out sprawled the M.P.s, shouting and threatening.

With a roar the taxi started up. But one M.P. hung on desperately, grasping the handle of the door, feet on the running-board.

Then from amongst the bystanders there appeared a soldier's boot, firmly and swiftly kicking the hand away, sending the M.P. back on to the road. Off went the victorious Kiwis with their rescued Tommy. Into the crowd disappeared the owner of the boot, losing himself rapidly in the throng that had gathered.

Just as well he disappeared fast. A man like that would never have been sent up for a commission if that exploit had come to light. It is still a secret, hard to prise out from those who were there.

4

Leggy Meets His Lieutenant

THE handful of New Zealanders who entered the officers' training unit in August 1940 contained Sergeant Upham. He was a reluctant candidate. He dreaded lest the war should come to the New Zealand Division while he was detached in some backwater at Base. But he was persuaded that the Italians planned no sudden inrush on Egypt, that it was a matter of duty to accept appointment to the school if that was what the Army thought best for him.

Like most officer-cadet courses, it was a solid test of all-round ability. Men worked hard night and day. The instructors knew their subjects, according to the standard of military knowledge believed adequate up to that time. Tactical training was based on the lessons of the Great War of 1914-18. The German lesson of Poland and France, just a few months old, had not yet filtered down.

But somehow Upham thought the tactics were wrong. He was born with an enquiring mind, and he was tremendously worried by what they taught him. Bert Steele, the 20th's R.S.M., was in the course with him. Steele readily absorbed the tactical lessons, knowing they were the product of experience and had stood the test of time.

But after one such lesson Charles spoke to him as they came out into the sun. 'Bert, I dunno—but I just can't understand these tactics.'

'Don't worry, Charlie. It's just common sense.'

'Common sense, Bert?' Upham queried, looking at him in a puzzled way. 'Well, if it is, I just can't get it. . . . I can't get it.' And he walked away with his head down.

That night in the mess, over a pot of beer, he raised the subject again. One or two of the other New Zealanders were around him, and the talk turned to the tactical lessons of the day.

'They don't say anything about surprise,' Upham complained. 'The element of surprise—surely that's the most important thing. These fellows don't mention it. But that's how the Huns wiped up the Frogs.'

'You might be right, Charlie,' one of them said. 'But these Tommy officers know their stuff. You can't expect to get anywhere with them if you just stand up and say "I think that's a lot of rot". You'll get fired from the school if you say that again.'

'But it *is* a lot of rot,' Upham argued. 'Look—these instructors are set-piece men. They read it straight from the book. That was all right for the last war. But things are different now. We're going to have lots of tanks, aerial co-operation; you know—modern ideas. Set-piece tactics won't be any good against these German panzers. Look at France.'

'Yes, all right, Charlie. But why not wait till we get our pip before being too dogmatic about it? Arguing with the instructors won't help. And what did you go and tell the Commandant, Charlie? Come on . . . what did you say to him? He looked a bit surprised.'

'The Commandant? Oh, nothing much. I just told him I thought his ideas were *obsolete*. What's wrong with that?'

And Upham looked round at them with his eyebrows raised innocently.

He couldn't understand why they laughed so loudly.

But Upham learnt the tactics they taught him, studying every word with a grim intensity, as if his life would depend on being word-perfect. Perhaps it would. And on top of the 'set-piece' stuff they gave him he was quietly and earnestly fashioning some ideas of his own.

The course went on. Charles mastered his map-reading, desert navigation, military law, Army administration, intelligence, drill, tactics, weapon firing, hints on command, vehicles, street fighting, aircraft recognition, gas, and the rest.

And at the end the Commandant said to the New Zealand Military Secretary:

'Upham's got through all right. But you'll never make an officer out of him. They pass out tomorrow. Here's the grading list of the men from your division.'

Sure enough, the Commandant's opinion of Upham was reflected in the results. It never pays to argue with the boss, does it?

Down the list of successful cadets the Military Secretary ran his eye. He already had in mind where he would be posting each new subaltern. Those near the top of the list would be welcomed by this unit and that. Those near the bottom would not be so heartily welcomed. But they would have to be placed somewhere.

He nodded as his eye picked out the names he knew—the A grade passes, the B grade, the C grade—until he came to the end.

His eye dwelt as he came to the very last name. The name at the *very bottom* of the list read—'*Charles Hazlitt Upham*'.[1]

The same Charles Hazlitt Upham who later won two V.C.s, whose leadership was an inspiration, whose skill and whose exploits made his name a legend; of whom the London *Times* said: 'Mr. Upham's courage was superhuman. . . .'

*   *   *   *

On passing out of the school the new subalterns were posted temporarily to a Base depot, waiting there for appointments to the battalions and regiments. On the first night in the new mess Upham found himself in a corner alongside a New Zealand artilleryman named Atchley.

'You sound English,' Upham said to him. 'Been in New Zealand long?'

Atchley told him.

'Listen,' Upham said. 'I've just come from O.C.T.U. They had instructors teaching us infantry tactics. Now you're a gunner—just listen to this stuff they taught us and you tell me if it makes sense to you. I don't know—it's still got me beat. . . .'

'Don't ask me about infantry tactics,' Atchley protested. 'I just fire the guns.'

'Never mind—just listen. You're English—perhaps you'll understand it better than I do. Now take the case of a company making a night attack. . . .'

Atchley resigned himself to listening. He listened to infantry tactics that evening—all phases of company and platoon tactics, by day and night, in attack and in defence, with and without tanks, machine-guns, and artillery. And he listened to Upham's exposition of his own views, contrasted with the official view taught at the school. They coincided most of the time, but where they clashed Upham was anxious and disturbed.

'They must be wrong,' he claimed. 'Hell—I don't know anything about it—but I just know they *must* be wrong.'

The second night in the mess, Upham opened up the subject again. Atchley tried to head him off, but he was too late.

And again a night later.

It can be said that Trevor Atchley, after three nights of listening,

[1] To this day Upham still manfully protests that he did not pass out bottom of his O.C.T.U. class. He admits that he was amongst the C grade passes but that, as the names in that grade were published alphabetically, it thus happened that his name appeared at the bottom. However, the late Major-General Kippenberger, whose knowledge of Upham was complete, did not support Upham's contention.

knew a lot more about infantry tactics than he ever expected to. He
knew, too, that the character who cornered him every evening had a
curious mind—a determination to grasp the whole of a subject, to thrash
out any problem to its conclusion, to match his own reasoning against
the reasoning of others, and to adhere like a limpet to the final decision
he came to.

*   *   *   *

When N.C.O.s from a unit were sent to O.C.T.U. for commissions
it was not the practice to post them back to their old unit.

Colonel Kippenberger of the 20th had sent in some of his best
N.C.O.s. He knew they would make cracking officers. He wanted them
back to the 20th. He went to see the Military Secretary about it.

But there was no change of policy. The Military Secretary went
through the names of Kippenberger's men, all of whom had passed
successfully out of the school and were waiting at Base for their
appointments. No. The rule had to be followed—no posting back to
their former units.

Kippenberger pressed hard for all his men, including his former
Sergeant Upham.

The Military Secretary said: 'Oh well, he's at the bottom of the list.
I don't suppose it'll matter much with him. All right, you take him back
if you like; but I can't do it with any of the others.'

Kippenberger closed the deal quickly and eagerly. He knew his man.
He knew that Upham's place on the gradation list would mean little
when the bullets started flying.

Without further ado, he left instructions for Second Lieutenant
Upham to report to the battalion in the Western Desert. Number 15
Platoon of C Company would have him.

The New Zealand Division was at Baggush at the time Upham was
required to report back to the 20th, so, to make use of his services en
route, he was put in charge of a draft of reinforcements travelling out to
Baggush by train.

The reinforcements had known more comfortable train travelling in
their day. Some of them were from the 3rd Echelon not long arrived
from New Zealand. Others were seasoned men of the desert, returning
to the division after spells in hospital, at courses of instruction, or at
Base.

Packed in the train amongst his larger fellows was a rather
small man whose topic of conversation centred around race-horses and
their mysteries. He was voluble in his condemnation of the present

travelling arrangements. He was listened to with respect by those around him, for he was not a newcomer. He had been with the division some time, had served as a batman to a Lieutenant Fountaine of the 20th Battalion. But he and Fountaine had parted.

The officer-in-charge wedged his way into the carriage. The little man noticed that the officer was a brand-new one-pipper, albeit with a rugged-looking face. He stuck his small chin upwards and launched into a general complaint.

The new officer listened sympathetically. 'What's your name?' he asked.

'Le Gros,' the ex-batman answered. 'What's yours?'

'Upham,' the officer replied mildly, while those around grinned at the little man's cheek.

'Well, look here, Second Lootenant Upham, these carriages aren't good enough for pigs. I bet old Kip wouldn't allow it if he knew. What are you going to do about it?'

Upham was amused by the perky confidence of the small man. He said: 'I suppose if you think she's too crowded you could jump off and walk. Take longer, though.'

Le Gros shrugged his shoulders. 'O.K., boss. She'll do. Typical Army. I expect you officers have got an air-conditioned carriage, with a case of grog, nurses, red tabs everywhere, eh?'

Upham smiled at him. 'I haven't found a seat for myself yet. You're the lucky one.'

The train ground on. The officer went on his way. Le Gros resumed his discussion of the 1939 Grand National.

When finally the train halted and everyone gratefully clambered out, Upham saw Le Gros again. The small man had little to carry. Upham had more than his own gear. He walked over.

'How about helping me with my pack, Le Gros? I've got a job to do here and I've got other stuff to carry. What about it?'

Le Gros stared at him incredulously. 'Christ!' he said. 'We're all soldiers, aren't we? What's wrong with you?'

'Never mind, never mind,' Upham quickly replied. 'Forget it. . . .'

The look of shocked surprise on Le Gros' face suddenly changed and was replaced with an air of benevolent tolerance.

'Aw relax, boss, relax. I'll take it. Here—give it to me. . . . Feels like a bottle of whisky in here. You'd better not be too long getting after me.'

And, with a cheery, but slightly evil grin, Le Gros heaved Upham's pack on to his shoulders and marched off.

It was two hours later when Le Gros received a summons to attend before the new officer of Number 15 Platoon. . . .

'How would you like to be my batman, Le Gros?'

'Well . . . I dunno. But I suppose—seeing as I carried your pack about ten ruddy miles—all right, I'll take it on if you like. *But on one condition, though.*'

'What's that?' Upham enquired dubiously.

'I don't do any guards, eh?'

Upham nodded humbly.

*   *   *   *

Major Wilson of C Company warned Charles about 15 Platoon. They were mainly from the West Coast of the South Island, he said —the isolated, law-unto-itself part of New Zealand where the scent is still strong of the hundreds of saloons that catered for the gold-rush days of last century.

Men from the West Coast were rugged. They presented some problem in military discipline. They needed an officer who could talk their language, who could be more rugged than they.

They were lined up for Upham's first inspection. They muttered between themselves, wondering if they could 'have this fellow on'. They had known of him as a sergeant in A Company, a rather short, wiry man, hopeless at drill, a bit grim as an instructor. They waited for his arrival.

He turned up smoking his pipe, a knobbly stick, like a musterer's, in his hand. He stood silently in front of the platoon, letting them look at him. He knew they were summing him up, trying to judge how far they could go with him.

He looked from one man's face to the next. What he saw pleased him. They were tough, they were individualistic, they were a little scruffy, but they looked completely dependable; they looked the sort of men one would like to have around when the going was difficult.

What should he say? Say that he was pleased to be put in command of them, that he hoped they would work well together, that there were dangerous days ahead and they would have to pull their weight, there was a lot to learn, etc.? No, that wouldn't go down with these hardy birds.

Finally he slowly took his pipe from his mouth and lowered his head. They saw the curious cold glint of his eyes. He said: 'I'm your new officer. My name's Upham. You look a pretty tough mob to me. But you don't look fit. In fact you look like a lot of boozers. . . .'

*   *   *   *

Charles Upham was a forceful platoon commander in those days late in 1940. But that was no greater a quality than others possessed. His tactical ideas were thoughtful and sound, his training of his men painstaking, based on a determination that they must know their job thoroughly. His personal attitude to his men was more casual than military tradition preferred. 'This having to salute you chaps is a damned nuisance,' he complained.

He held independent views on the value of different kinds of training. 'This won't help,' he would frequently complain, when he found he was expected to take his platoon on some exercise or scheme that did not seem to him to increase their efficiency for real fighting. 'War is fighting,' he argued. 'Why bother with anything that doesn't help you to fight? Let's concentrate on things we'll *have* to do when we're in action.'

As his knowledge of his men grew, so grew his concern for their well-being. To the Company Quartermaster he became a constant thorn —enquiring, demanding, making sure his men got the best of food and supplies.

But in those early days, as 1940 turned into 1941, no one claimed that Upham shone above his fellow-officers in any way other than in his violent and unremitting attention to the comfort and safety of his platoon. Men of discernment like Kippenberger guessed it would only be the demands of action that would really plumb the depths of Upham's character.

The King's Commission did not stop the picturesque side of Charles's speech. A deep-thinking and quiet man by nature, it yet never seemed incongruous to hear him swearing. Nor was it due to the commonest reason for swearing—the inability of the speaker to choose suitable vocabulary. Upham was not a ready conversationalist, but if he became interested in a subject or a conversation he took his part with more than average humour and enthusiasm. His vocabulary was normal for a man of his education and age. The choicest oaths seemed to drop from him as an inoffensive and natural accompaniment to the discussion.

Kippenberger watched him develop. A curious mixture, this young man, he thought. A rugged exterior, a rough bluntness that would be downright rudeness in another man, superimposed on a modest, shy fellow whose bellicose intensity contrasted strangely with his intelligence and retiring nature. Kippenberger knew now how stubborn he was— he heard the stories—and yet the man was soft-hearted and easily led.

'That's a hard-working platoon you've got there, Upham,' he remarked to Charles one day. 'They were a pretty tough lot—how do you think they'll do in action—enough discipline?'

D

'Discipline?' Upham queried, looking puzzled. 'I don't really know, sir. I get on all right with them, I think. They know their stuff really well. They'll loaf if I let them; but they'll spring to it if I tell them to. No serious crime amongst them. . . . I suppose you could say their discipline was all right, sir.'

'Yes, I expect so. One thing, Charlie—do you think it's a good thing to swear at your men? You do it a lot, you know. I don't believe in it. I'd like you to cut it out.'

'Swear at them, sir? I never thought . . . I mean . . . I didn't think I swore at them much.' He looked concerned.

'You probably don't know you're doing it,' Kippenberger observed drily.

'I'll do my best, sir. I'll certainly cut it out if you think I've overdone it. . . .'

The C.O. moved on, while Upham turned thoughtfully back to his men working a few yards away. Yes, he'd have to cut out swearing if it was bad enough for Kip to notice. He watched what his platoon were doing, noticed the mess they were making of a camouflaged dug-out they were trying to construct. His gorge suddenly rose at the shoddy display.

'You lazy bloody loafers!' he shouted at them. 'With Kip standing right in front of you you put up a ruddy shambles of a thing like that. You . . .!'

They grinned shamefacedly. They knew they'd done a poor job.

A chain away Kip paused as he heard his subaltern's tirade. He thought of turning back, of giving Upham a real dressing-down this time; but he thought better of it and walked quickly away out of earshot.

He muttered to himself: 'It *was* a ruddy shambles, too.'

*   *   *   *

Corporal McKegney was a 'kidder'. He could almost always get a bite out of the boss. To rush up to Upham and say breathlessly: 'I heard the Major was wanting you,' turned out to be really worth while, for Upham responded with reckless haste, only to find that the Major was absent from the battalion that day. Keg managed to cover up by explaining that he 'heard it the day before yesterday'. The boss patiently pointed out that it might be good fun for Keg to do that behind the lines, but it would never do in action. McKegney knew that too.

One day two generals watched the slick 15 Platoon at work. Upham's N.C.O.s put on a demonstration of quick range-finding.

Upham rapped out the command to range on to a white rock protruding from the sand about 600 yards in front of the squad. The generals watched McKegney fling himself down behind the rangefinder, apply his eye to the viewer, turn the knobs with brisk efficiency.

Then Keg lifted his head and, with tongue in cheek, loudly announced: 'Two thousand yards!'

The astonishment of the visiting generals at such a blooper was rapidly increased by the words of the platoon commander as he roared at the 'kidder' corporal: 'You *bloody bastard*, McKegney!'

The generals blanched and walked away.

5

Knight Without Armour

MUSSOLINI'S entry into World War II was unimpressive, to say the least. There was Graziani's rout in North Africa in December 1940-then, when the Italians invaded Greece, they found themselves counter; attacked to such effect that 7000 Italians were prisoners within a few weeks. To protect his Balkan flank Hitler had to take over.

In February 1941 the United Kingdom Cabinet cabled the New Zealand Prime Minister:

'. . . We have taken full cognizance of the risks involved in the despatch to Greece . . . of so large a proportion of the troops available in the Middle East . . . [But] our failure to help this small nation putting up a gallant fight against one aggressor, and willing to defy another, would have a grave effect on public opinion throughout the world.'

'Public opinion' certainly; but military opinion should have convinced the Allies that an expedition to Greece could only be an honourable, possibly disastrous, gesture. For it was no more than a gesture. The German attack had been in progress only *six days* before the Greek Commander-in-Chief suggested that the Allied forces evacuate.

Nevertheless, the New Zealand Government promised support, though not without forebodings. Prime Minister Fraser said to Whitehall that the operation was 'a formidable and hazardous one'.

Before it even started the situation deteriorated. The Greeks were unable to conform to the defence plan that had been jointly arranged. 'We found a changed and disturbing situation on our arrival here, and an atmosphere quite different from our last visit'—cabled the British Mission.

And in New Zealand anxiety increased. Fraser cabled London:

'The operation, which had always been regarded as highly dangerous and speculative, is now obviously much more hazardous.

... Pressure by the Germans might perhaps lead to a rapid collapse of the Greeks, which would leave the British force in the air. . . .'

Fraser's prophecy was proved exactly true.

Churchill himself sensed the inevitable. He said to Eden, who was leading the British delegation in talks with the Greeks: 'Do not consider yourself obligated to a Greek enterprise if in your hearts you feel it will only be another Norwegian fiasco. . . .'

That is what it turned out to be.

Yet, somehow, in the face of all this advice, the politicians were swayed by the moral appeal, leading them to discount the military realities. From the very beginning the end was obvious.

During March 1941 the New Zealand Division was shipped across the Mediterranean, moved up through the Greek mainland, and took up defensive positions near Katerini, 300 miles north of Athens.

Charles Upham's platoon found itself in a little Greek hamlet called Riakia. There they stayed for seventeen days, digging in, erecting wire, settling their defensive lay-out in anticipation of the German attack that would assuredly come down the road straight into their village.

The ability to lay out and construct a good defensive position depends so much on the type of ground one is offered; but there were many opinions expressed that Upham's positions were outstandingly well done. Here at last he was able to mesh his own downright opinions with those of the text-book writers; and he drove his men on to accomplish a lot of work in a short time. Den Fountaine, then second-in-command of the company, and later to become a full colonel, has since described Upham's work at Riakia as 'a marvellous job'.

Upham, too, respected the importance of camouflage. He studied it eagerly, made his men work at it hour after hour. It was one of those things he became very intense about.

One day he gave a lecture on camouflage to a large audience, expounding his theories with fervour and sincerity. When it was over he stood alongside Frank Hill, a quartermaster-sergeant whom he had known since 1939.

'How did I do?' he asked Hill, his voice shaking.

Hill was surprised to notice that Upham was still trembling with nervousness.

To a man who is normally intense and highly strung, illness can be a greater burden than to others. The battalion had not been long in Greece before Upham developed dysentery. At first it was not disabling but it saw him becoming irritable and quick-tempered. He became loudly impatient too often and too quickly, and was unduly bitter against the alleged inadequacies of higher commanders. But it was only the approach of real war beginning to expose the depths of his belligerence and hatred for the enemy. Illness merely put an unpleasant sharpness on that side of his character.

On 6th April 1941 Germany attacked Greece and Yugoslavia. They had already been in Bulgaria, on the north-eastern border of Greece. Now they attacked across the border, soon ravaging Salonika and advancing south towards the New Zealand positions near Katerini.

In addition, they swept into Yugoslavia and made short work of opposition there. That gave them a clear run through Yugoslavia into Greece by the central route. If they pressed on down there through the Monastir Gap they would isolate the Katerini defences on the east coast.

If anything favourable can be said about the Greek campaign it was the speed with which decisions were taken, and implemented, to protect our forces from being cut off. Barely forty-eight hours passed after Germany's declaration of war before the New Zealanders were moving back from the Katerini positions, in realization that the collapse of the Yugoslavs opened up Monastir and made Katerini untenable.

Two brigades dropped back to the Mount Olympus area, leaving the Divisional Cavalry to nibble at the enemy and slow down the advance. The 4th Brigade (including the 20th Battalion) was sent over to the central front, on the road running south from the Monastir Gap, to an area near the town of Servia.

There, Upham's platoon was posted at an important local crossroads to check the streams of refugees beginning to pour down from the north. There were civilians with their pathetic burdens, Yugoslav troops, Greek soldiers with nothing left to fight with but courage, and an expected proportion of fifth columnists.

It seemed quite a friendly war at first. Overhead came German reconnaissance planes, confident in the skies in the absence of British aircraft, flying casually low over the hill-tops.

Upham waited for the real war. He disregarded the observation planes. It was futile trying concealment in these positions.

Kippenberger had other thoughts.

'Why aren't your men under cover?' he demanded sharply.

Upham said it was waste of time.

'Then when the real thing comes,' Kip continued, 'you'll find your men will be too slow. They'll think it's another snooper. You'll have casualties.'

Upham learnt quickly.

During 11th April bombing and machine-gunning from the air could be seen ahead. Refugees thickened. More enemy planes appeared above. One German pilot flew brazenly low over the defenders, waving from his cockpit. The Kiwis admired his cheek and waved back. The plane flew on, banked, and swung back along the same route. Another wave?

War came to the 20th Battalion as the pilot, his little game over, abruptly dived and strafed them savagely.

Then they turned as they heard the sound of more engines, coming up from a new direction. Our planes this time?

Upham watched them too, straining his eyes to identify their shape and markings.

Suddenly he yelled: 'Duck quick . . . they're Heinkels!' And as his platoon went to earth, clinging to the mud in their shallow trenches, the bombs came raining down.

Upham's cross-roads became a favourite target. More and more planes came over, dropping their bombs along the roads, into the villages, seeking out the artillery positions. They had it all their own way. British planes had done their best but there had been pitifully few of them from the start.

Upham stood by a large rock as German fighters swept overhead. John McIlwraith, a sergeant of C Company and an old friend, squatted beside him and wondered why Charles wasn't wearing a tin hat. Upham's men often wondered at that later. On Greece, on Crete, into the inferno of Minqar Qaim, through the disaster on Ruweisat Ridge—Upham often wore no helmet, but came on to the battlefield wearing an officer's soft cap, making him look like a casual observer who had wandered into the wrong territory.

It was not till after the war that he offered the only known explanation. Pressed by a friend for his reasons, finally, rather gruffly, he said: 'Because I could hardly ever find a tin hat to fit me.'

He certainly had a large head—a 'leonine head', one writer described it. If he found a suitable hat he would wear it. But if he couldn't get the right size in the first three or four he tried it is likely he gave up the search. The subject of tin hats would be dismissed from his mind from then on.

McIlwraith checked the Bren gun in his hands. The next plane that came in low enough he would have a good go at. At least it would make them fly a bit higher—might even get a lucky hit.

Over they came, confident, almost contemptuous.

McIlwraith cocked the gun, swung the barrel up, and emptied a whole magazine at the nearest plane as it zoomed past at tree-top level. He clamped another mag into the Bren, watched silently as the plane banked round at the end of the valley. It was going to make another run at them.

Then there was a voice beside him. 'Let's have a go, Mac!' and Upham was eyeing the Bren gun eagerly.

But now the plane was shrieking down at them again, and suddenly Upham was shouting 'Get down, Mac!' and snatching the Bren from him.

McIlwraith felt himself thrust behind a great boulder, and saw Upham standing upright in the open, lining up the attacking plane as it roared in to strafe them; and then a long sustained burst from the Bren, and then the plane was above, gone, and Upham was cursing furiously because he had missed it.

Then he was moving away, running quickly from one section to another. 'You chaps all right?' he was calling.

* * * *

By 13th April 1941 New Zealanders sat astride three of the main lines of advance into southern Greece. Greek armies were on the western side of the peninsula. New Zealand 4th Brigade was around Servia, in the centre; the 5th Brigade on the slopes of Mount Olympus, with the 6th a little to the rear; while a solitary battalion squatted on the extreme east coast watching the Platamon rail tunnel. All these routes converged and joined together as they continued south—so that a successful German attack down any of the four routes would cut off the defenders holding the other three.

That turned out to be the story of Greece. The Germans attacked down every line, suffering heavy casualties at every place where they ran on to the New Zealand defences. But down the western side the Greeks had no weapons to match the German panzers, and it was only a matter of time before the invaders would sweep through to the south, regardless of how long the defences in the centre and the east held out.

Next day, the 14th, the air blitz continued. But already it was obvious that even the new defences could not be held. It was all very well to hold the German attacks at Servia, and on the defiles over Mount Olympus, but further to the west the Germans were moving down through the shattered Greek forces, whose sturdy fighting against the Italians was now no match for the resolute, well-equipped Germans.

Enemy pressure increased on the 15th. On the Servia front German infantry moved towards the New Zealanders, but were heavily manhandled.

But successes like these had no sweet taste. There was no advance and counter-attack to emphasize the enemy's discomfiture. Minor victories had to be won merely to gain time for retreat. Good soldiers hate that kind of fighting.

A new defence line was formed at Thermopylae, far to the south across the narrow waist of Greece. Towards Thermopylae the withdrawal began, first under cover of darkness, and then of necessity in daylight. And while daylight lasted the bombs rained down on the convoys and the planes ranged up and down the roads at will, their machine-guns spraying the jam-packed trucks.

Even at Thermopylae the line could not be maintained. Hardly had the New Zealanders arrived there before word came that the Greeks on the western side had broken up and capitulated. The Germans would be in behind Thermopylae before many hours passed. No more could be done for Greece. Evacuation was ordered.

The 6th Brigade held Thermopylae while the other two brigades fell back towards the beaches. Time for evacuation had to be gained. Artillery attached to the 6th fired 30,000 rounds in fifteen hours, then destroyed their guns after they had fired their last shell. Then the 6th turned and made for the coast.

Now the 4th Brigade, the men who had stood at Servia, had to act as the delaying force. While the 5th and 6th went to the beaches, the 4th took its stand near Kriekouki, not far from Athens. They thought they could hold on there for two days, but orders came that they would have to stay an additional twenty-four hours. Kriekouki was christened 'Twenty-four Hour Pass'.

* * * *

C Company of the 20th was alongside the road at Kriekouki Pass. During the three days the battalion was there, many a question was asked why messengers from C Company—from 15 Platoon in particular—kept foraging around for tins of condensed milk.

'They're for Charlie Upham—the boss,' came the reply. 'He can't eat anything else. Got dysentery. Can hardly walk. Be lucky if he gets away.'

And for three days his faithful platoon fed Upham with condensed milk while his weight went down and down.

If he couldn't walk around his section posts then he would ride. So Kriekouki became used to the spectacle of Charles astride a donkey, painfully moving along the hillsides, up to Company Headquarters and around his section posts. He rode in to Battalion H.Q. on the final day to thank them for his tins of milk. He looked very sick.

It was difficult to move around. While he did what he could on his donkey, Upham found he had to use Eric Le Gros for more message work than usual.

Leggy and Charles bandied abuse at each other. There was probably never a more disrespectful batman. Indeed, the platoon sometimes wondered who was batman to whom.

Leggy returned from a long walk to Battalion H.Q. Charles was sitting on the ground, face drawn, but his voice cheerful as he said: 'Thanks, Leggy-boy. Get there all right?'

'Yeah. I found the bludgers. I bet they'll clear out and leave us here . . . you see.'

'You reckon, Leggy-boy? I don't. But, here . . . I've made a mug of tea. Have some. You make such a lousy cup of tea I reckon I might do it myself in future.'

Leggy took the mug, tasted it carefully, then pulled a face. 'Christ, that's awful,' he said. 'Can't you make better tea than that?'

Upham laughed. 'Grateful, aren't you? You know, you're a damned awful batman, Leggy. I should have taken Spout Fountaine's advice and given you the chop months ago. . . . Now, where are my boots?'

Leggy looked uncomfortable. 'You mean—the spare pair?'

'Yes.'

'Well . . . actually they're gone. I gave 'em to an old Greek geezer when we were passing through Larissa.'

'Gave 'em away? What the hell for?'

It took Leggy-boy quite a time to admit that he was one of a number of bright lads who found a bombed-out bank in Larissa. There were banknotes everywhere. Leggy helped himself to a good collection and was still having great trouble finding enough room for them in his pack.

'Well, what's that got to do with my boots?'

'Don't you see, boss, someone had to keep a look-out for the M.P.s. Couldn't expect the old boy to do it for nothing—so I gave him your boots. Do you want a share of the notes? Reckon they're worth a good lot.'

Upham looked at him more in sorrow than in anger. 'If you weren't on active service, Leggy-boy, you'd deserve to get court-martialled for that. But I suppose the Jerries would have got them if you hadn't. So shut up about the whole thing. Now get me that donkey. I want to go down to the 18th . . . eh, what's that?'

Leggy hastily retrieved the donkey from a quartermaster-sergeant in the 19th, to whom Leggy was hiring the donkey at so much per hour.

*   *   *   *

Finally, in the nights, the ships came and lay off the beaches, while 40,000 troops were taken off to safety and to fight again elsewhere.

'That's a heavy load, soldier,' the Navy type would say, as the exhausted soldier clambered aboard. 'Here, I'll look after it.' So the soldier gratefully surrendered the pack of extra food, his bedroll, looted money, and precious comforts that he had been jealously harbouring all the way from Monastir. And the Navy man's method of looking after it was to pitch it into the sea. 'No room for it, chum—got to get eight hundred men on here tonight. Go on, get down below. You'll find plenty of cocoa and bread-and-butter.'

Below decks it was all warmth, kindliness, and generosity.

While down at the southern tip of Greece, at a little port called Kalamata, the New Zealanders took part in the last organized resistance. One by one the beaches had been closed by the advancing Germans until, at the end, the last few thousand defenders gathered uncomfortably in Kalamata. But no miracle of rescue could be done for them, though many could have been saved but for inescapable confusion in a time of great difficulty.

But here in Kalamata, with rescue gone, the New Zealanders still fought. For a few hours lightly armed Aussies and Kiwis disputed the town against the might of a German panzer unit. Jack Hinton, a forthright sergeant of the 20th, won his V.C. as he moved around the streets, destroying enemy nests that were gradually pressing the last Allied troops closer into the sea. Others fought with him, courageous but hopeless little battles, with the inevitable end only a matter of time.

*   *   *   *

Looking back on the futile Greek campaign, it gives a little comfort to believe that it served some good moral cause, and that it delayed the eastward advance of Hitler's armies. The truth of history is not so comforting. It is now apparent that the political decision to enter Greece was taken without the fullest military appreciation that was necessary; all the facts were not disclosed to the New Zealand and Australian Governments who were to supply the bulk of the fighting troops; and, from the moral viewpoint, it is an open question whether the helter-skelter withdrawal, so soon after the fighting began, did Britain's prestige more harm than the good created by the noble effort to help a threatened little country.

With adequate air support the original plan might possibly have checked the Germans. But when the Greeks reduced the measure of their own contribution, and Middle East Command had to retain in the desert some of the forces previously earmarked for Greece, the project became more than merely hazardous. It became quite hopeless.

Hopeless causes sometimes have to be fought. It is at least doubtful if there were sufficient reasons for such a hopeless cause as this one when it is weighed against the sadness in 2500 New Zealand homes (or 6600 British homes for that matter) whose sons died, suffered, or went into captivity.

It was only the courage and resourcefulness of lesser men that atoned in some measure for the ill-judged decisions of the greater ones.

6

Invasion of Crete

FORTY THOUSAND MEN could not have been rescued from Greece if the Navy had delivered each ship-load to Egypt before returning for more. So the majority of the Allied troops were dropped off at Crete, the Greek island lying sixty miles south of the mainland.

By chance, some well-equipped troops were taken straight to Egypt. By equal, but unhappy, chance, a great many more arrived in Crete with few arms and fewer supplies. There were drivers without trucks, artillerymen without guns, signallers without wire. These men, of reduced military value when parted from their specialist equipment, had to be fed and clothed like the rest. The 400,000 Cretan civilians also now expected the British forces to maintain them.

Crete possessed some strategic value, and Allied Intelligence did not have to work hard to discover that the Germans intended to invade it very soon. Appreciations were made that correctly judged the weight and manner of the expected attack and where the invasion forces would strike. It would be an attack from the air with paratroops and troop-carrying aircraft, designed to drop the invaders into several obvious target areas under cover of powerful bombing and strafing attacks.

A seaborne landing would also be attempted, but that could safely be left to the Navy to deal with. But the air invasion could not be stopped half-way, and the commanders knew that the day would come when the air would be black with German men and machines, dropping out of the sky, testing our men in a new form of modern warfare.

The New Zealanders had nearly a month on Crete before the blow fell. They were given an area to defend that stretched from Canea, a town on the northern coast, westward along the shoreline to the Maleme airfield—a strip about ten miles long. It was laced with ridges and streams running from the central mountains to the sea, clothed with olive trees and vines, with only one substantial road that ran parallel with the northern coastline.

It was certain that the air assault would be directed at the airfield and on other flat ground within the New Zealanders' defences.

The Kiwis camped and dug under the olive trees, swam on the beaches and in the streams, and waited—and waited—for the equipment to come that would give them a reasonable chance of fighting the battle on equal terms.

But when the battle came, and was fought, and lost, it was not the courage of men that failed. It was the failure to give them the tools of war that rendered their defeat inevitable.

There were few picks and shovels, so men dug trenches with bayonets. Any unit that had a truck was envied. Mortars without base-plates, Vickers guns without tripods, artillery without sights—from the beginning, right through to the end, it was a pauper's campaign. Even the combatant units were often makeshift affairs—great lines of country were held by Greek battalions totally untrained; infantry tasks had to be given to patchwork units formed from artillery-men, truck drivers, and even concert entertainers. Food was only just adequate.

Major-General Freyberg, the New Zealand G.O.C., was put in command of all Allied Forces. He accepted appointment as a duty, but regarded the chance of successfully defending the island as precarious. He signalled his Government in New Zealand:

> 'The decision has been taken in London that Crete must be held . . . it can be held only with the full support of the Navy and Air Force. The air force on the island consists of six Hurricanes and seventeen obsolete aircraft. Troops can and will fight but, as the result of the campaign in Greece, are devoid of any artillery and have insufficient tools for digging, little transport, and inadequate war reserves of equipment and ammunition. I recommend that you bring pressure on the highest plane in London either to supply us with sufficient means to defend the island or to review the decision that Crete must be held.'

That was on 1st May 1941. The New Zealand Government supported him. Fraser cabled Churchill stating that the situation was regarded as one of the utmost gravity.

But Wellington received no reply to the request that the decision to hold Crete be reviewed. The days and the weeks conveniently passed, until finally it was too late to do anything but fight the invaders with such means as Freyberg had available to him. Middle East Command, under Wavell, did its best to feed in supplies, but it was a profitless enterprise, with ships able to unload for only three hours in the middle of each night. Freyberg realized his peril and sensed that others did not. He signalled Wavell to 'introduce a little reality into the calculations for the defence of Crete'.

The Germans bombed the island incessantly. Suda Bay, the main harbour near Canea, became a graveyard of ships, with a huge pall of smoke overhanging it night and day. The bombers and fighters paraded overhead, looking for targets, softening up the vital areas where the defenders knew the attacks would come.

The nights were bitterly cold. It was merely in conformity with the general shortage of supplies that there were no groundsheets and bedding, and one blanket had to be shared between three men. This involved neat mathematical problems, made only a little easier when more supplies later came to hand and enabled only two men to share a single blanket. Putting on every stitch of clothing they possessed, even hats and boots, they settled down for the night in a spirit of generosity, each man believing that he was giving his mate just a shade more of the blanket than he himself retained. But as men turned in their sleep, and clawed at the meagre covering during the freezing small hours, they unconsciously dragged the blanket from each other. Bosom friends would awake in the night and argue so bitterly over the disputed blanket that many a friendship was irretrievably broken.

Charles Upham and Eric le Gros shared their blanket, and night after night woke in mutual accusation, hotly blaming the other for taking more than his fair share.

One night their disagreement reached its climax. Each vilified the other in language they would never use in the warm light of day. But in the icy night more instinctive passions were aroused.

Upham suddenly stopped their verbal war. 'All right, Leggy,' he said calmly. 'There's only one way to settle this. . . .'

He told Leggy his idea. The batman nodded agreement.

Officer and man clambered to their feet, stood there stamping for a few moments to try to get warm.

Then Upham said: 'Right-oh. You take that end, I'll take this. . . . Now fold 'er over . . . right? Now get your bayonet. . . .'

And with elaborate care, each making dead sure that the cut did not deviate a hair's-breadth from the centre, they used Leggy's bayonet to split the blanket down the middle, solemnly dividing it into two equal, satisfying, but utterly useless halves.

*   *   *   *

'We'll go in to town today, Leggy-boy,' said Upham. C Company of the 20th was in a reserve position, a mile or two west of Canea, close by Divisional Headquarters.

Canea was rather desolate. There was little food, the shops were low and dirty, drinks of various colours could be purchased with ease, the Cretan population still inclined to regard the war as something remote. They were on cheerful terms with the Kiwis.

Eric Le Gros strolled knowledgeably beside his officer. He already knew which dives served the best and the worst liquor, he knew the inside reason why Hess had just flown to England, he knew the essential words of Greek that generally caused squeals of delighted laughter from the local lasses, and seemed able to open doors when other means failed.

'Look at that now,' he said admiringly. 'You wouldn't see a prettier bit of goods in New Zealand. My oath, I wouldn't mind taking her out. Hey, cutie!'

'Shut up, Leggy! You're out of your class. She'd go out only with officers.'

'Why don't you ask her yourself, then?' Leggy grumbled. 'You reckon you're an officer, don't you?'

'Come on, we'll have a drink instead,' Upham replied firmly. 'Get these thoughts out of your head, Leggy-boy. . . . Mind you, I agree she's not bad. Not half bad. Actually, she's pretty good. In fact, I'd say . . .'

Leggy looked alarmed. 'Heh, cut it out, boss. I saw her first.'

They reluctantly dragged each other away and went and drank something coloured green. Then they tried the purple stuff, which tasted awful. After that the blue liquid with orange peel in it. And they talked, as officer and batman often do, of folks back home. And the more they drank of the many colours, the more sentimentally they talked.

They walked slowly down the road towards the 20th as the evening drew in. The invasion seemed far, far away, and not at all likely.

*   *   *   *

Invasion came on the morning of 20th May 1941. The battle lasted nine days, but the Germans had won Crete by the evening of the first day.

It began like most other days. At six in the morning the planes were overhead, bombing and strafing, but this morning there seemed a greater intensity about it. Yet when this bombardment fell away, and allowed the troops to begin their breakfast, there was little to suggest that this day would be different from the others.

But about a quarter to eight a new attack developed. Overhead the bombers swept in again, fighter planes swooping amongst them, and against vital targets an air blitz of great ferocity was mounted, rising to a continuous roar.

Maleme airfield came in for special attention and around the perimeter the intensity of the bombing was so severe that men who had gone through the artillery barrages at the Somme stated later that this was more terrible. Further afield, from out over the sea, the roar of an approaching air armada beat upon the ears.

Then through the bedlam and the fiery skies planes of strange shape were seen manœuvring, coming in over the island little more than 400–500 feet up.

All at once the fury seemed to abate, as if to leave the skies clear for something new. And to the men clinging deep in their slit trenches a spectacle as bizarre and unreal as anything in the history of warfare was unfolded.

Black dots suddenly fell from the bellies of the low-flying planes. In an instant the dots were blossoming into parachutes, hundreds upon hundreds of them, swaying swiftly earthwards, filling the sky with their different colours.

There seemed then a moveless pause, as if the defenders were transfixed by this amazing sight. But only for a few seconds. There was no long delay as the parachutes wafted down. On the contrary, they seemed to descend with quick and dangerous suddenness. There was hardly time to aim and fire, but then the crackle of rifle-fire began, swelled into a chorus, Bren guns added their chatter, and the bodies of paratroopers began to twist and squirm as they came near the earth.

Many fell out of range of our guns, organized themselves quickly, picked up their supplies and heavy weapons that had floated down with other 'chutes, and moved swiftly into attacking formations.

But those who fell close by the New Zealanders learnt a lesson that Hitler never repeated during World War II. Of 136 who landed near 18th Battalion only two survived. The rest were destroyed in the air or within minutes of their landing. A hundred more dropping near the village of Galatas fared no better.

A wave of paratroopers swung to earth by the lines of an engineers' unit. Their descent was watched by an infantry headquarters not far away.

'Ring up those engineers,' the infantry C.O. ordered sharply. 'Can't

E

expect sappers to deal with paratroops. Tell them we'll send over
help.'

Back came the reply. 'Thanks, but don't bother. They'll all be dead
before you can get a man over here.'

The engineers were almost true to their word. On one German body
was found the unit nominal roll, showing that 126 men jumped that day
into the teeth of the belligerent sappers. A mere fourteen escaped the
fate of the 112 others.

These were minor examples of the torrid reception that the defenders
of Crete gave Hitler's prize troops on the first day of the battle. The
enemy landed 10,000 men that day. By nightfall only 6000 remained
active.

But the parachutists were not all. As the skies fluttered into life,
and death, and brave young Germans felt their first fear as the bullets
came racing up to meet them in the air, the defenders saw another sight
that was new to soldiers' eyes.

Long-winged, stubby aircraft came sidling in over the defences,
completely silent, planing steadily downwards, or circling cumbrously
like great useless birds. Gliders. Towed six at a time by heavy Junkers
planes and released when they crossed the coast, the gliders swept in low
over the defences, inexpressibly menacing and sinister.

Warned as they had been to expect this kind of attack, nevertheless
the New Zealanders who looked into the skies that sunny morning can
still recall the feeling of unreality and disbelief, of being part of a dream
too fanciful to be true. But the novelty of the spectacle did not awe
them. Like the paratroops who dropped into the lion's many mouths,
the glider troops were hotly engaged the moment they came within
range. But many gliders chose the safe undefended ground west of the
Maleme airfield, bumping and crashing their way to earth, disgorging
their crews into sheltered valleys where they could re-form and prepare
for battle.

Back in its reserve area near Canea, the 20th Battalion watched the
landings and listened to the growing noise of fighting.

Charles Upham said to his batman: 'They told us it would be this
morning, Leggy. Good Intelligence work somewhere.'

'I suppose they knew what time it would be, too,' said Le Gros dis-
believingly, looking at his watch.

'That's right,' said Charles. 'We were told to expect it between eight
and nine o'clock.'

'Jeezes,' Leggy said wonderingly, looking over the ridges towards
the smoke and fire in the direction of Maleme. 'Didn't think these
Jerries could be *that* accurate. . . . Heh—had your milk this morning?'

Upham nodded rather heavily. His dysentery had become worse. He could take only condensed milk. He was feeling pretty weak.

Le Gros went on cooking some rice.

Then Den Fountaine came running over. He was in command of C Company now that Major Wilson had gone over to organize a crowd of Greek recruits somewhere up in the battle-line.

Fountaine said: 'Charlie, some paratroops have come down over there between us and the 19th. Get a few men there smartly and clean 'em out, will you?'

Upham called on a handful of men from his platoon and moved quickly away, down through the trees, along a gully, then up to a ridge. Over the ridge they saw the 'chutes lying on the ground, tangled in the trees.

'Cover me!' he said shortly. They knew what to do. They had practised it often enough. The men went to ground, picking their cover, and began firing steadily into the area where the 'chutes lay. Upham went round the flank, moving quickly forward and out of sight.

Five minutes later they heard a flurry of shots. Then silence.

He was soon back, appearing suddenly out of the olive trees, swinging a German helmet in one hand. 'She's right now,' he said, his voice sharp with excitement. He didn't tell them any more.

The main German landings were made in three areas. One large group dropped into the Prison Valley, a few miles inland, and quickly scattered some Greek forces; but by the end of the day had made little progress against the New Zealand defence line in that area. Another group landed west of the Maleme airfield and continued to be reinforced throughout the day. There were no troops available to keep them engaged.

The most serious lodgment was made around the Maleme 'drome, held by the 22nd Battalion of 5th Brigade. The fight there went on all day. However, all communications broke down, pockets of paratroops caused casualties if the defenders attempted movement, and the Germans diverted more and more men to the attack on the airfield, the capture of which would open all western Crete to the invaders.

By late afternoon the Kiwis around the 'drome were out of touch with their own headquarters and with one another. Battalion and Brigade Headquarters further back gained only a confused and pessimistic view of the situation.

With the Germans gradually gaining a foothold on the vital airfield, counter-attack was imperative. If 5th Brigade could not lay on the counter-attack with their own men, then someone else would have to do it—4th Brigade, no doubt. In command of 4th Brigade was Brigadier

L. M. Inglis, later to command the division and to become an Occupation Force judge in Germany. With his brigade not heavily handled, Inglis knew that his should be the counter-attacking role, his the task to move inland south of the busy 5th Brigade, then turn northwards up the Tavronitis River straight on to Maleme 'drome. He thought he could do it successfully with two battalions. So he asked for orders to counter-attack, conscious that delay would be fatal. All day long he could see the signs of a big enemy build-up proceeding unmolested in the safe areas west of the airfield. That build-up had to be interfered with. Time was of the essence.

But back in the places where greater decisions had to be made there was the knowledge that the enemy were also landing at Retimo and Heraklion, two other airstrips on the island, and reserves might be urgently wanted there; that more waves of airborne troops might any moment descend on the same hills and valleys that would be left only lightly defended if much of 4th Brigade moved away westwards to the counter-attack. A seaborne landing, too, was known to be in the German plans. Troops had to be kept back to meet that threat.

When finally the word came through to Inglis—'Counter-attack not permitted'—his Brigade Major leapt up and shouted: 'Then we've lost Crete! We've lost Crete!'

Inglis snorted: 'You don't need to tell me that.'

Night came. There was no communication with the men on the airfield. German airborne troops seemed to be in nests and patrols everywhere. We had had some sharp losses. There was to be no counter-attack on the 'drome. So the vital decision was taken—withdraw from the airfield.

It is idle to speculate what would have happened to the battle for Crete if that withdrawal had not taken place. But undoubtedly, if the men of the 22nd had been allowed to stay, and a counter-attack had been quickly and strongly laid on, the battle would have run differently.

After the war Inglis spent an afternoon with General Student, the German commander of the invasion.

'What would have happened,' Inglis asked, 'if I had been permitted to counter-attack you that afternoon?'

Student said: 'If you had done so, I could not have held Crete. You had knocked me about so much that day, particularly my paratroops, that I could not have resisted a counter-attack. After the way you smashed up my units on landing, all day long we waited for your counter-attack. We feared it, we thought it must come, and were amazed that it didn't.'

And so, with the wisdom of hindsight, and the detachment and knowledge that only history can give, we know now that Crete was lost on the first day. Had Student been successfully counter-attacked, would Hitler have persisted, flung more and more troops at the obstinate New Zealanders? Probably yes, and probably with ultimate success. For the Germans had uninterrupted command of the air, and control of the air would finally have been decisive.

7

Crisis at Maleme

THE next day, 21st May 1941, saw the Germans massing reinforcements into Maleme. Some of our guns still played on the airfield and on
the nearby beaches, where troop-carriers attempted landings; but by
afternoon planes were landing on the 'drome at the rate of one every
three minutes. With Maleme secured, the German plan would be to
advance east to Canea, rolling up the New Zealanders on the way.

There was sharp fighting with our advanced battalions, but the
enemy made little progress against the defences. Smarting under his
heavy casualties of the opening day, he was content to concentrate on
building up men and supplies, probing forward where he could.

During the day it was belatedly realized at Force H.Q. that all
would be lost unless Maleme were recaptured. A counter-attack had to
be made. But by day the air strafing was insuperable and prohibited
practically all movement. So the counter-attack on the airfield would
have to be a night show. It would have to go in that same night—
another day's delay would make success impossible. Even now it might
prove to be already too late.

It was decided that the attack would be given to the 20th and the
28th Battalions. They would first be moved up to a start line during the
early hours of the night; then, when all was ready, they would advance
westward, side by side, a distance of about four miles, until they reached
the 'drome. They would have to swarm on to the field and capture it
before dawn, or daylight would make them open targets for the German
guns.

The four-mile strip of ground the attackers had to cross before
reaching the 'drome was known to be occupied by the enemy. How thick
the enemy were, and how many guns they had defending that ground,
could be found out only in the face-to-face experience of the night
attack. For such an enterprise against unknown dangers, few better
troops could have been allotted than the keenly trained men of Kippenberger's 20th and the fiery Maoris of the 28th.

No forward move could be made, however, until an Australian unit arrived by truck from further east, took over the 20th's defence positions, and handed over its vehicles to the 20th to take the men forward to the start line. With the Australians scheduled to arrive about 8 p.m. all would be well; the 20th would embus and move west. By 1 a.m. the four-mile advance against the aerodrome would begin.

Dusk came; drifted into night. Restless and impatient, the 20th waited in their slit trenches amidst the olive groves, listening for the sound of the Australian convoy. They were keyed up for the occasion, ready and eager to fight, all ranks knowing that the counter-attack on Maleme that night was crucial.

The hours passed. Eight o'clock . . . then nine . . . ten . . . and Lieutenant-Colonel J. T. Burrows, now commanding the 20th while Kippenberger had a brigade, felt his anxiety growing, as there was still no sign of the Australians. Every hour of the night was precious. It would be madness if his men were still in the open when the next dawn rose up over the vales of Crete. But he was helpless and immobile. The arrival of the trucks was out of his hands.

Eleven o'clock . . . then twelve . . . and still they waited.

It was not till 1 a.m.—the very hour when the attack should have been going in—that the first party of the unfortunate Aussies arrived. They had been bombed and strafed when they started, delayed for hours by casualties and wreckage suffered at the very beginning of their move. Even now they brought only enough trucks to lift two companies of the 20th—less than half the battalion.

'Get started with what you can,' Burrows was told. 'Start the advance with only two companies. The rest will follow.'

Burrows had no choice. C and D Companies hurriedly embussed and went churning forward towards the start line near Platanias. Burrows reported there to Brigade Headquarters for his orders. It was 2 a.m. By now he was desperately anxious, horrified at the short notice available to him and his men, with no time for reconnaissance, no information, and with only a portion of his battalion ready. 'We knew then that we would never reach the 'drome before dawn,' he said. 'We knew there were mine-fields laid by our own troops which we would have to get through, but there was no time to get information about them. But we knew the attack *had* to go in. The fate of Crete depended on it. There would not be another opportunity.'

It was half past three before the advance started. Burrows had waited a final agonizing half-hour in the hope that his other two companies would arrive in time, but the delays to the Australians made that impossible. Because there was no alternative, the vital attack had to begin with only two companies of the 20th. The other two companies would follow in when they arrived.

The battalion was to move westward, in a line extending from the beach on the right, inland to the main road, a front of about 700 yards. D Company took the right-hand side, C Company the left. Upham's platoon of C Company was on the extreme left end of the line, his flank man Hill-Rennie having to walk up the ditch bordering the road.

The other attacking battalion, the 28th, was already waiting in position, its line of advance being on a front further inland from the road. It began its move forward when the 20th came abreast.

The attack on Maleme began.

They moved off in the darkness, sections spread out, just a few muttered words setting the whole line in motion.

Down into a shallow gully, up the other side, all trying to keep quiet, through a hedge at the top, and across the first field of vines. Then there were trees, looming dimly through the night like broken buildings.

Each man strained his eyes ahead, peering into the darkness, watching the shadowy outlines of the country gradually unfolding. Four miles of this before they reached the 'drome. . . . Each man glancing to his right and left, keeping spaced out from his mates, hoping against hope that it wouldn't happen, knowing for sure that the time would come, sooner or later, when flame and death would suddenly, without warning, shriek at him.

They were advancing against the line of the country—all the gullies ran across their path, all the vines and hedges had to be climbed through, one after another.

They made the first mile in that fashion. Close at hand the night was eerie and silent, though in the distance a tank could be heard clanking along the main road, a machine-gun fired an isolated burst which seemed to come from miles away, and out over the ocean mysterious flares told the only story of the German sea invasion that the Royal Navy utterly destroyed that night.

Out on the right somewhere was D Company, its flank advancing along the beach. Then came C Company, and across the road, somewhere in the darkness, the Maoris were picking their way forward. But over them all the dark bowl of the night was already beginning to fade—a new day was not far away, and not a shot had yet been fired.

Then sharply through the night came the first rifle-shot, not a hundred yards away, then another, and another, and suddenly the air was filled with the sound of it. Machine-guns broke into their chatter, and through the darkness lines of tracer came weaving in fiery patterns.

The New Zealanders surged ahead. But they found now, and as the attack continued on and on, that the Germans had spread themselves right through this country, with posts established behind trees, in houses, in ditches, wherever there was cover. Pockets of enemy riflemen and machine-gunners were scattered in depth along the whole route of the advance. As our men pressed forward the fire came at them in front, from the sides, even from behind.

Upham's platoon had moved steadily forward across the fields, waiting for the first sound, wondering how far they would go before it came. They climbed up a rise, through a small hedge; shook themselves out again into line, then moved cautiously across the open field. There was a large tree square in front of them. They had passed many trees like that one, warily and with every muscle tense. Nothing had happened so far. Would this one be any different?

They plodded on, each man's feelings and fears like a huge private world inside him.

It came suddenly, with an awful violence that made every man feel he was the one target. With a dinning gabble, a machine-gun burst into action from behind the tree, only sixty yards ahead.

They were in the open. The tracer swept amongst them before they realized their danger.

'Down! Down!' Upham was shouting, and they hurled themselves to the ground. But it was already too late for some. Four of the platoon were hit.

Now came the test of training. Each section-leader had to make his own instant decision. Could his men survive where they were or must they find better cover?

Some stayed where they dropped to earth, relatively safe in the undulations of the ground. Others wormed their way on their stomachs to better cover, lay there panting while the tracer bit through the air inches above their heads.

Now it was up to the platoon commander. One machine-gun can't stop an advance. His was the next responsibility.

Upham crawled from one section to the next, giving them their orders, showing them the route they had to follow. They all had to get nearer—closer in on the gun. So one by one they moved again, squirming from cover to cover, with Upham in front of them, till finally he had them barely forty yards from the tree. Then they waited for him to make the next move. He told them what he planned to do.

They began firing at the tree, at the gun-flashes, at the patches of deep darkness that lay in its shadow.

Hill-Rennie, the man on the extreme left of the platoon, watched Upham moving like a hunter round to the side, drifting silently from one shadow to the next. The comparison to a stalking animal was too vivid to be comfortable. Here was no task for the upright guardsman, brave and straightforward; nor for the belligerent tough who might shine in a brawl. Here was something almost primitive—but far more skilful and deadly.

Hill-Rennie wrote a report later. He said:

'As we kept up the fire the platoon officer, Lieutenant Upham, cautiously crawled round to the side and slightly to the rear of the tree. Although it was still dark, we could tell by the way the Jerries were shouting to each other that they didn't like the look of the situation. . . .'

Faintly through the gloom he could see Upham lying full-length, head towards the tree. The Germans were firing wildly now, conscious that some out-flanking movement was under way, but pinned down by the steady covering fire from the grounded men of the platoon.

Upham was drawing grenades out of his pouches, loosening the pins. He drew one pin right out, held the grenade in his hand, fingers pressed down on the lever.

It was curious the way he was feeling. There was excitement and tremendous tension; but above all he was aware of an icy fury possessing him—not a feeling of hot reckless rage, but a deliberate deep savagery—and it had started the moment he saw four of his boys roll agonizingly to the ground. The first moment they had really seen action —and now they were dead or wounded. The hatred of it took hold of him, the hatred of war, the hatred of the enemy—the enemy crouching behind that tree, just a few yards away in the semi-darkness.

Hill-Rennie was watching his every movement, every stealthy step, every silent rustle of the grass as Upham squirmed closer.

And now Upham was almost behind the tree, his figure a mere shadowy outline as Hill-Rennie peered at the spot. He saw Upham gathering himself up on to his knees, crouching forward, poised as if to spring.

This was the moment—the almost unbelievable tension of it—when one man had to risk everything in a burst of tremendous action.

Hill-Rennie saw it all happen—and recorded it in his mind, just as he wrote his written report on the incident a few days later.

Upham suddenly moved. In one rushing moment he was up on his feet . . . his arm swung over . . . the grenade arced towards the machine-gunners . . . there was the splitting crash of its explosion. . . .

And he was rushing in . . . hurling another grenade . . . and another straight after it. The succession of bomb-bursts hit against their ear-drums like a repeating hammer.

Straight at the German nest Upham was running, and he was firing his pistol ahead of him . . . there seemed to be a burst from a sub-machine-gun, firing straight at him. . . .

The others watched the sudden fury of noise and action. Then he was calling to them in a high-pitched, penetrating voice, and waving to them to come forward. They leapt to their feet and ran to the tree. He was standing there beside the gun, breathing heavily.

There had been eight paratroopers there—seven with sub-machine-guns; another behind the bigger gun that had first torn into the platoon. They were all dead.

'There'll be plenty more like that,' he said sharply. 'Come on, let's get cracking again. Don't bunch . . . spread out. We don't want to get copped standing here.'

They attended to the wounded, re-formed their lines, then began pushing on slowly again. By this time it was much lighter, and they could see the shape of a house standing on the edge of the road just ahead. Behind it was a shed.

And again it suddenly came—the fiery stream of tracer leaping towards them, and the staccato of the enemy machine-guns, one from a window of the house, another from the shed.

They literally flung themselves to the ground this time, rolling like seasoned veterans into the nearest cover. They were learning the basic facts of life and death in battle in as many minutes as it would take months in base-camp training.

They got the Brens into action, firing short sharp bursts at the windows, watching for any sign of movement.

Then in the half-light they saw Upham running again, dashing ahead with head bent low, racing past the house and up to the walls of the shed. For a few moments he was protected there, while he edged his way along the wall towards the door.

They kept up a rain of bullets to cover him while he crouched there in the open.

It was light enough now to see him reaching for his grenades. They were beginning to realize that he was carrying grenades all over him. One dead German lay with arm outstretched through the outhouse door. They watched Upham pull the pin of a grenade, jump forward and place the bomb fairly in the dead man's hand, then crouch back.

With the explosion, Upham was shouting to them, his voice ringing through the night so loudly that it was heard by men of another company moving up behind.

'Come on!' he roared back to them. 'Come in quick!' And the platoon sprang forward as one man and dashed towards the buildings.

It was enough. Half a dozen Germans came tumbling out of the house, hands held high. Inside the shed eight more were found wounded.

On again . . . on . . . on. The men of 15 Platoon found Charles amongst them one moment, the next he was out in front, scouting the way ahead. He was talking excitedly, shouting encouragement, drawing them on by his personal example. And all the time the light was growing stronger.

More vines . . . more hedges and trees . . . the houses were becoming thicker. There was fire everywhere now, out towards D Company on the right, over the road where the Maoris were, straight ahead where their path lay, and the tracer seemed to draw curved lines across their path, as if to say 'this far and no further'.

They couldn't burst through this line of tracer. It was coming in from the right, in long fiery bursts, flashing across their front from a gun way out on the flank. There was no dodging this one. They hesitated, crouching low in the grass.

But now Upham was beside them. He was saying: 'It's high, chest high. That won't hurt anyone. Come on . . . we're going to crawl through underneath.'

And on hands and knees he led them towards the path of the tracer, closer and closer, and they watched him go right underneath it, rise to his feet on the other side. They followed, resisting the temptation to go flat on their stomachs as they crawled past the deadliest spot.

Now there were more houses. The Germans were on the roofs, in the lofts and upper storeys, firing from them all. The desire to lie in a fold of the ground, or behind a tree, was almost overwhelming, but the leadership of the officers and N.C.O.s drew them onward, right through, right down, the lanes of fire.

Upham was in sight of his men the whole time, calling and shouting, rushing here, stalking there like a hunter of big game. He was possessed by the fighting—tremendously stimulated, swearing violently, driven on and on by a hatred that now seemed to be welling up out of him.

There were few men not afraid. As in all fighting, there were moments of cold terror. But Upham's men found themselves watching the boss, wondering at his apparent indifference to fear, prepared to rush in and follow so long as he led.

There were brave and resolute men in that platoon, as indeed there were right along that advancing line of New Zealanders. They needed resolution, pushing forward over unknown ground, treading on mines, tangling with barbed wire, moving steadily straight towards the guns, every minute of approaching dawn making them better targets for the defenders to see. Men of less resolution could have faltered, decided with some justification that the pace was too hot, and allowed themselves to fade into the safety of the ground.

Another machine-gun barked suddenly at them. There it was—in that window in the corner. One of our men was hit—in the stomach—and he let out a cry and rolled on the ground in agony. His mate dashed to him, tried to hold him still.

Upham's face contorted. He looked towards the gun and the words came out of him like a vow. 'Leave that bastard to me! I'll fix him!' He made this his personal war.

So while the others covered him with fire, he moved quickly round to the flank, Le Gros close behind him. Then when there was no more cover he broke out, rushed straight for the window, grenade in hand. Away went the pin, he threw it like a baseball player, and the crash came as it exploded inside the window.

Le Gros had a Tommy-gun. He kept firing at the window while Upham raced round to find the back door.

Something stuck into Le Gros' back—something like the barrel of a gun. He shouted, stood dead still. In a moment Upham was back, sprinting round the corner of the building, saw the hefty German towering over Le Gros. Upham flung himself at the man, hitting him with his fist, beating him to the ground.

But another German, confused or unheeding, came stumbling in from the fields, making for the house. He carried no weapons.

Upham shouted at him, but the German was not blessed with a knowledge of English. 'Up! Up!' Upham yelled.

The man didn't comply, bore in towards them. Upham drew back, clenched his fist, and clouted the German on the side of the head.

He fought back savagely. Upham seized him round the neck, started hitting him over the head with the butt of his revolver.

Gradually he broke the German's resistance, sent him sprawling on the ground. 'Get him out! Take him away!' he ordered loudly as his platoon swarmed around.

At this moment Peter Maxwell, one of D Company's officers, appeared in the morning light. He had not had a hard time so far—his real fight was yet to come—and he had come over to see if Upham needed any help.

Maxwell said: 'Why didn't you just shoot him, Charlie? You don't want to get so savage.'

But that was futile advice. Upham had a vendetta now. He would show the Huns they couldn't kill his boys without answering for it.

Forward again. Now into a little village called Pirgos the platoon moved determinedly. It was almost full daylight now. It seemed that every house held a German, firing, sniping . . . They moved from house to house, clearing one after another.

He had lost his rifle—or some say he threw it away—and had taken possession of a German sub-machine-gun. Company Commander Den Fountaine came up alongside and Upham urged him to get one for himself.

'What about ammo?' Fountaine asked. 'Got any?'

'No, but I'll soon get some,' Upham replied.

'Throw it away,' Fountaine advised.

Upham shook his head and produced a German Luger pistol he had also just acquired. He'd get ammo, he claimed, from the next German nest they winkled out.

Fountaine ran to find his other two platoons.

Fire started coming at them from yet another house in front.

Eric Le Gros kept close beside Upham, followed apprehensively as he began walking straight up the garden path towards the house.

They arrived at the door. Upham listened. There were bullets flying around, close enough to Leggy to make the locality undesirable, but apparently unnoticed by Upham. His objective for the moment was this house. Bullets from other directions were of no more than nuisance value when he had an objective in mind.

To make a smaller target Le Gros pressed himself against the wall. Then he watched as Upham began circling around to the back.

Charles turned, appearing to notice Le Gros for the first time. He scowled. 'You stay there, Leggy-boy,' he ordered.

Le Gros shook his head, swallowed hard, and pressed on after his officer. 'No . . . I'm coming too. What's good enough for you, boss . . .'

Upham turned full round to face him. 'I said stay back there!' he shouted. 'You get out of this. You'll get killed. . . .'

'What about you?' the batman replied.

'I'll put you under arrest,' Upham snapped back. 'This is too dangerous,' and he turned again to the building.

The platoon moved up cautiously, then demonstrated the art of house clearing. While the rest of the building was kept under fire, one of the N.C.O.s kicked the door in suddenly, threw in a grenade, and they rushed in before the dust cleared.

But now there were casualties coming faster and faster, and the thump of a captured Bofors gun was reverberating through the village. Hill-Rennie and two others crept up the ditch towards the Bofors. It was behind a stone wall. They began firing at the gunner, forcing him to keep down.

Upham waited till his men were all firing. Then, dropping to his stomach, he squirmed his way forward, yard by yard. . . . thirty . . . twenty . . . fifteen . . . ten yards, unslinging his beloved grenades as he inched closer.

Then sharply, surely, over swept his arm, a grenade curled through the air, and with a roar Bofors and German gunner were destroyed as the boys raced in to support their leader.

House after house they edged onwards. Daylight now; what hope was there now of capturing the 'drome? How had D Company on the right got on? A lot of fighting over there by the sound of it, and they seemed to be further forward. They must be close to the airfield.

Now there was a culvert, with Germans holed up beneath it, firing along the road. Colonel Burrows with his Battalion Headquarters was right up now with the assaulting troops, watching 15 Platoon go to work on the culvert. The same tactics, the same covering fire, with Upham rushing forward alone, grenade in hand, the throw, the pause, then another grenade after the first, the explosions, and Upham dashing in with his pistol, shouting and firing.

Corporal McKegney had started off with eleven grenades hung around him. They were nearly all gone, but the boss seemed to have an inexhaustible supply. 'He had a haversack full of 'em,' someone said.

Next they came to a line of bamboos. Upham broke through them first, McKegney close behind, with Puck Wesley alongside.

The two Germans were standing not five yards ahead, waiting for the New Zealanders to come into the open. They looked startled, but the one with a sub-machine-gun was quick to react. He lifted it sharply to his hip.

Upham moved like lightning. His pistol flashed up and he pulled the trigger before the German could steady his gun. The man pitched to one side and the gun dropped to earth. One gone.

But from out on the flank Fountaine saw the incident and caught his breath in sudden alarm. For the second German was raising his rifle quickly, while Upham seemed to be still watching the man who had just fallen.

Fountaine could see it all happening, but he was too far away to intervene.

But Upham was awake to it. Up came his pistol again. He pressed the trigger.

The pin clicked on an empty chamber. With the vision of the German already about to fire, he seized his other pistol, the Luger, fumbled desperately with it, not sure that he knew exactly how it worked.

He would have been dead an instant later. But Wesley, quick to size up a moment when life hung in the balance, threw up his rifle, fired quickly, and killed the German. The muzzle of his rifle was within inches of Upham's ear as the shot blasted out, left Upham dizzy and half deaf.

Charles turned quickly to him. 'Thank you, Puck,' he said gratefully. 'I was a goner.'

But Wesley didn't hear. He was busy searching the two dead Germans. Nice chocolate many of these Jerry paratroopers carried with them.

But as the fighting progressed through Pirgos, this morning of 22nd May, the opposition became more inflexible. It was 7 a.m. by now, and casualties were mounting gravely. With Germans established in buildings and behind walls, any movement in the open became more and more hazardous. Obviously the attack was grinding to a halt. Burrows knew that he could get no further. The Maoris, too, had struck immovable opposition on their inland route.

What of D Company, though, hard by the beach? Striking light opposition in the early stages, they had pushed ahead fast, outstripping C Company on its left. Forward they pressed, till finally, in full daylight, their forward sections reached the edge of the 'drome. There they came under tremendous fire, making it utterly impossible to attempt a crossing of the 'drome, and forcing them to fall back a few chains to a position of cover. B Company, one of those who had made a very late start, followed in behind, and it, too, reached a point not far short of the 'drome. Then it was pinned down by the violence of the enemy fire.

Lieutenant Jack Bain, a platoon officer from Headquarters Company who had followed behind C Company, came up to Upham in Pirgos. Men were lying wounded in the open, casualties were piling up, and progress now was irretrievably halted.

Upham said to Bain: 'What do we do, Jack?'

'We'll have to get out,' Bain said. 'Everything's bogged down.'

Upham swore. 'If we'd had another hour,' he said, 'we'd have been through to the 'drome. Had no show, starting so late. Another Army gafu.'

'Someone's got close,' Bain said. 'Listen to that shooting over near the 'drome. Sounds as if D Company's getting stuck in.'

Upham said: 'We'd better get Fitz here out. He's wounded. Wait till I get a door.'

So Charles broke a door off its hinges from a nearby house. Bain, Upham, and two others lifted Fitzgerald on to the door. Then they

Green & Hahn, Christchurch

Charles Upham's birthplace in Gloucester Street, Christchurch, New Zealand

Schooldays at Christ's College, Christchurch, New Zealand

Green & Hahn, Christchurch

Too ill to walk, Upham rides a donkey at Kriekouki, Greece

'The Victoria Cross has been awarded . . .' Surrounded by his platoon, Upham is congratulated by Sgt Bob May. Eric Le Gros is second from right

started back, straight down the street in full view of the enemy. The others watched, waiting for the machine-gun to mow them down. But the few decencies of warfare were still being observed by the Germans. Fitzgerald was carried safely out of danger.

Around the airfield further progress had stopped. Maxwell of D Company was believed to be holding his ground, rather precariously, a short distance from the edge of the field. It was thought that B Company were near him. The air was full of planes and it would not be long before troops in the open would be strafed and bombed.

They had done their best, but Burrows had feared it was hopeless from the start. Now he knew that nothing more could be done. Any movement from cover was drawing murderous fire. If he attempted to press the attack any further he would gain nothing and probably sacrifice the rest of his battalion. He accepted the inevitable—that he could not now capture Maleme. He had to withdraw his companies from their exposed positions to higher ground inland.

Runners had to go out to the companies, telling them where to assemble, the points to make for in the hills. But it was a question how many messages would get through. There was no contact with either D or B Companies out near the sea. They could not be left there. Somehow word had to be got through to them, even though the man who took the message would run a very gauntlet of fire. All the radios were out.

Number 15 Platoon of C Company was close by Battalion Headquarters. Burrows moved over to them, found Upham behind a wall. He told him the position, said that word had to get across to the companies on the beach. He wanted Upham's platoon to do it.

'Send two very good men, Charlie,' he advised. 'They'll have their work cut out to get through.'

'Right,' Upham replied shortly. 'We'll fix it.' He peered cautiously over the wall, looking at the expanse of open ground stretching between his positions and where D and B Companies were thought to be over towards the 'drome. It would be about half a mile across to them, and under fire the whole way. Whom would he send?

Burrows said later that he knew this was a hazardous mission. But it had to be done. The enemy were everywhere, the exact location of our own men uncertain.

Upham crawled over to Sergeant Dave Kirk. ('The finest soldier I ever knew,' Upham described him.) He told Kirk what was required. They discussed the best route. Any route was as dangerous as another.

Then Kirk said: 'Who's going, boss?'

Upham was busy checking his pistol, seeing how many grenades he
F

had left. His reply was almost absent-minded. 'I'm going myself, of course, Dave,' he said. 'It's a bit dicey for anyone else, though. Don't know who to send.'

'Let's get started,' Kirk suggested.

Upham looked at him and grinned. 'I thought you'd say that.'

The two men set off from Pirgos, striking north-west towards the 'drome. They were both highly skilled in the art of movement and use of ground. They needed every ounce of it. Through the vines and the trees, dashing across the gaps, darting from cover to cover as the bullets came at them from all directions, they dodged and crawled their way forward. The countryside seemed to be whipped with fire.

They saw two of the enemy crouched in a ditch a little distance ahead. They had to go along that ditch. They had brought a Bren with them. With one long burst they cleared the way.

On and on across this no man's land, until at last they broke out of the bushes and found the airstrip beneath their feet. There, right on the edge, two New Zealanders lay dead, mute proof that some of the Kiwis had penetrated to the limit.

They skirted the edge of the field, right out to the beach. They found some B Company men there and passed on the orders. But D Company, under Maxwell, had already realized the hopelessness of the position and had wisely retired back along the coastline already.

Mortar and machine-gun fire was all around them, planes were zooming down on to the 'drome, and there was great enemy activity.

They started the journey back.

8

Valour in Defeat

BY MIDDAY on 22nd May the stricken 20th had fallen back into a perimeter in the hills where the disappointed Maoris had also taken up defensive positions. There they sat within sight of the aerodrome, but unable to reach it with fire, watching the troop-carriers running a shuttle service between Maleme and Greece. Thousands more men were landed on Crete that day.

Twice during the morning Upham, Kirk, and others of the platoon crept back to the village to rescue their own wounded boys, carrying several out on doors or improvised stretchers. But by noon all movement was stilled by the German gunners, while aircraft weaved overhead and roared down on any sign of activity.

During the afternoon the enemy pressed hard against the New Zealanders, searching for a gap in the line. C Company was in an advanced position and several times Upham's platoon was hotly engaged. From one ill-advised enemy attack his men captured a German machine-gun which they promptly put to good use.

Night came with the whole of 5th Brigade, and 20th Battalion, astride the hills two or three miles from Maleme airfield, with the ground in between now a mass of Germans.

With darkness, Upham's platoon heard the Germans moving around them on three sides, machine-gun belts rattling. It had been a grim day—the early-morning drama of the attack on the 'drome, the bitter thought that only daylight had defeated them, the fall back into the hills; then the mounting German pressure of arms against them, with clashes and more casualties. Upham's platoon sergeant, Bert Wallace, was killed that day, and Kirk stepped into the position.

Kirk and McKegney listened to the German preparations in the darkness out front. This would be a hopeless spot to be in when morning came, they argued. And then it wouldn't be possible to get out of it. So they edged over to Upham.

'I reckon we're too far out on a limb here, boss,' McKegney

suggested. 'We'd stand a better show if we dropped back in line with the others, don't you think?'

'What do you think, Dave?' Upham asked.

'Look around,' Kirk answered. 'There are only seven of the old platoon left. I don't know if these odd one or two chaps who've joined up with us will be any good.'

'Why not? They're 20th chaps, aren't they? Not their fault they've lost their companies.'

'Well . . . no.' Kirk hesitated. Then he grinned. 'But some of them saw you in the village this morning. . . . I think you put the wind up them. And I don't wonder.'

Upham frowned for a moment, as if trying to understand Kirk's meaning. Then he looked out over the ridge again and, changing the subject, said: 'We'll stay here. I don't think it'll get worse. But I'll tell you what I'll do.'

'Find a better 'ole,' McKegney suggested.

'No,' Upham answered. 'But when we get back to Egypt I'll turn on a slap-up dinner at Shepheard's for every man in the platoon who can make it.'

'Cheap round,' Keg murmured unsympathetically. A meal at Shepheard's seemed very far away.

Le Gros came crawling up. 'I got you some milk, boss,' he whispered. 'How're you feeling?'

Upham thanked him. 'Got some tucker for yourself, Leggy-boy?' he asked. He didn't say how he was feeling, but he was weaker than ever.

Meanwhile, Colonel Burrows was waiting anxiously for the night to pass. He couldn't see that he could last another day in this position. Casualties were too high, enemy fire too strong. There were not enough dressings for the wounded. He wasn't surprised when about five in the morning he received orders to pull the battalion out and withdraw eastwards towards its original reserve area near Canea. Move at once. They would retire in groups to Platanias, then re-form to complete the withdrawal to the final rendezvous.

With dawn soon upon them, Upham and the rest of the 20th clambered along the ridges towards safer territory.

*   *   *   *

But before the 20th completed its retirement to the Canea area enemy pressure became so intense that most of the battalion had to be stopped half-way in the region of the Platanias Bridge and turned round to face battle again. By 10 a.m. this temporary line was manned.

There followed a torrid day. There was brisk action around the Platanias Bridge, the Germans being held off by mortars and some artillery fire, and by sallies from our infantry.

From the bridge out to the sea was 300 to 400 yards. Into position there Upham and his platoon were rushed. Enemy attempts to get through along the beach were beaten back, but the defenders came under heavy fire from German mortars. The line was 'thin as tissue paper', as Colonel Burrows described it, but something had to be thrown in to delay the aggressiveness of a successful advancing army.

About 4 p.m. Upham heard the last whirr of the mortar bomb above him. He dropped full-length into the ditch alongside, seeing as he dived the body of the man next to him being lifted and shattered by the blast. Something bit into the back of his left shoulder, as if he had been punched.

He climbed shakily out of the ditch. The man he had been speaking to a moment before was dead.

The next bomb crashed down and he flung himself to earth again. But nothing more hit him.

He had a feeling of surprise as the blood began to soak from his shoulder and pain began. The thought of being wounded hadn't occurred to him.

He crawled over to McKegney. 'How are things, Keg?'

McKegney shrugged. 'Hickey's wounded. Getting hot, isn't it?'

A voice broke in. 'I'm wounded too.' It was Leggy.

Upham was all concern. 'Sure it's all right, Leggy-boy? Here, let's have a look. . . .'

'Or-r, 'tisn't much,' Leggy said. 'But these ruddy mortars . . .'

The rest of what Leggy said was drowned as another mortar bomb seemed to burst all around them, and he was heard to declare ever after that it was like a ball of fire dropping into his lap.

There was something still stuck in Upham's shoulder. He could feel it there. A mortar fragment. He moved over to Dave Kirk.

'I've got a bit of shell in my shoulder, Dave. Here . . . dig it out, will you?' And he handed Kirk an open pocket-knife.

'Eh?' said Kirk. 'Dig it out with a pocket-knife? Hell, I'm not a surgeon. Get on back to the R.A.P.'

Upham's face was thin and drawn with days of dysentery. But the way he looked at Kirk showed that his determination was as stern as ever.

'Take it out!' he repeated sharply.

Kirk shrugged and took the knife.

'There are two pieces in there,' he said, looking at Upham's bare shoulder.

'Go on, get on with it,' Charles retorted.

So Kirk tentatively prodded at the wound with the knife, apologizing profusely for the pain he knew he must be causing. Out came one piece of metal.

'I can't do the other bit,' he declared. 'You'd better get back and have it done properly.'

Upham thanked him for the homespun surgery, ignored the other suggestion.

So Kirk didn't argue. He went off and found Den Fountaine. Fountaine came up, promptly ordered Upham to the R.A.P.

The M.O. dressed it quickly. 'That'll fix it,' he said. 'But there's no transport back for you. You'll be walking wounded. You'll have to foot-slog it back to the A.D.S.'

'Walking wounded?' snapped Upham. 'Like hell—I've got a platoon down the road there.'

He stumped off angrily, went back to the remnants of his platoon overlooking the Platanias.

The long day drew to its end. Maleme airfield was now securely in the enemy's grasp. At other points in the island he was not bothering to engage in battle. Maleme would do. Crete could be won from there. A twelve-mile advance eastwards from Maleme would see him in Canea and the harbour of Suda. That was all that was necessary.

At nine o'clock that night orders came to C Company to leave the Platanias and complete the retirement to the old reserve area east of Galatas, not far out of Canea. Under cover of darkness the line thinned out, and exhausted men silently and thankfully withdrew.

*   *   *   *

The next day—the fifth day of the invasion—was moderately quiet. There was a continuation of heavy mortar attacks, aggressive enemy patrolling, and the usual air bombing and strafing that stopped all movement by day. Canea itself was by now almost in ruins.

Freyberg, reporting to Middle East H.Q., said that the scale of air attack had been far worse than anything he had visualized. This, combined with the exhaustion of his ill-equipped men, told him that the end was near. If there had been deep, well-sited defence-works in a dozen strategic positions, with enough men to hold them in depth, the defenders might have withstood the savagery of the air assaults. But fighting in the open, with poor equipment and food, few digging tools, broken communications, and the enemy possessing unchallenged use of the air, left men with only their doggedness and courage.

Fortunately for New Zealand, Prime Minister Fraser was at this moment in Cairo. He watched the development of the battle with growing anxiety. To any but the blind, the total extinction of our forces, or their evacuation, was only a matter of time. He had some reason to believe that few people outside Crete appreciated the gravity of the situation. He cabled Churchill:

'In the name of the New Zealand Government I would strongly urge that all possible additional support by air and sea be immediately provided, and especially the full air assistance that can be released from all other quarters, including the United Kingdom.'

Churchill replied:

'Although I sympathize and share your feelings of anxiety I cannot accept the implications of the final sentence of your telegram. The suggestion that we are holding back air assistance for the sake of the United Kingdom is really quite unfounded. . . .'

It is easy to understand Churchill's touchiness. He of all people would have known by then that both the Greece and Crete episodes had been, in the almost total absence of air support, futile and hopeless from the very beginning, and that inspiring words and moral pride were little consolation to troops cowering behind rocks and in ditches while an unopposed enemy air force smashed at them without respite.

*   *   *   *

The sixth day, 25th May, was a day that is remembered; remembered for its dramatic contrasts of quietness and fury, of collapse and defiance, of great heroism amidst exhausted defeat.

Early in the day all troops were warned that a massive enemy attack must be expected. The front line was held by the 18th Battalion, its right flank resting on the beach, joined on its left by some spare units who formed a bridge across to the 19th, lying a little to the rear. As a second line behind the 18th, a Composite Battalion lay in anxious wait, its motley gunners and truck drivers ill at ease with the weapons of the infantry.

The morning passed quietly—almost peacefully—if one excludes the steady bombardment from German mortars, machine-guns, and aircraft. As the day wore on, the weight of fire became heavier, and attack became imminent.

To provide a force ready for counter-attack, two companies from the 20th Battalion were sent forward from their reserve area. These comprised the remnants of the former B, C, and D Companies. Upham and his platoon were among them. They were held in the olive trees just north of Galatas, their commanders Fountaine and O'Callaghan waiting alongside the Brigade Commander Kippenberger for the orders that would assuredly come. Planes found them there, and for an hour they were heavily bombed and strafed.

By four o'clock in the afternoon the Germans were ready to make their assault. The mortar fire increased, hundreds of bombs crashing down on the thin New Zealand lines. And into the dust and torn air thirty Stukas came screaming, adding their dive-bombing to the onslaught.

Forward then came the German infantry, into the ranks of Kiwis who were already dazed and shattered. Under sheer pressure of lead and fire the right flank of the 18th was overwhelmed.

Now Kippenberger had to move fast. With his line broken, he had to call on the two reserve companies from the 20th to prevent a complete break-through. Fountaine and O'Callaghan were ready for their orders. Out they raced from the olive trees with their men, directing them into position as they ran. They found the right of the line all but gone. Dashing into whatever cover was available, the men opened fire.

Grimly they held their places during the remainder of that vital afternoon, while the German forces beat against them.

By now Upham's arm was in a sling. His shoulder wound was painful, his dysentery no better. But he refused to yield. He knew now that a stand had to be made, that somehow they had to hold off an enemy who scented the first serious crack in the New Zealand defences.

He had to hold a ridge. Leaving his men below the brow, he crawled forward alone to the top, and studied the confident advance of the enemy.

He waved back, waited while Kirk brought up the rest of the platoon. Then into position.

Now he received his second wound. From a machine-gun burst an almost spent bullet plunked into his right leg, low down, passing through the anklets he was wearing.

He bent down, tore the anklet away, saw that the bullet had not gone in far. Better leave it there, he thought. Help stop the bleeding.

It wasn't till a fortnight later, back in Egypt, that the festering wound forced itself on his attention. Then he bent down, squeezed at the flesh each side of the wound and prised the bullet out.

The attack was not long in coming.

These Germans were from the 5th Mountain Division. Good troops. Well trained and efficient, they moved steadily towards the New Zealanders. They had seen the way the line had cracked near the beach —there should be no trouble with the handful of men manning the ridge ahead. . . .

Half an hour later they reeled back, every attack beaten down by the shaggy remnants of the 20th. In front of Upham's withered platoon they left forty dead.

But the others made their way round the flanks and the Kiwis began to suffer, not only from fire in front, but even from behind. The Germans besieged Galatas village, deep behind the front line.

Upham now was in a state of exhilarated defiance. The enemy machine-guns, firing from close range, were the main trouble. He had to detect them, point them out to his riflemen, have them destroyed.

So in an audacious game he paraded up and down, exposing himself long enough to draw enemy fire, enabling him to pin-point each gun that began firing at him. One by one his men shot them out of the battle.

'There Charlie was,' McKegney said later, 'telling us to keep down, keep down, and all the time standing there in the open himself, his arm in a sling. Most of the boys thought it was too hot for us to stay there, but they couldn't do much about it, with Charlie wandering around as if it didn't matter, lead flying everywhere. You'd have thought he was planning to stay a couple of months. Charlie knew, I suppose, that if we didn't stick it out for a few hours the whole div might have gone west.'

Meanwhile Brigadier Inglis, commanding 4th Brigade further back, realized that the New Zealanders were being engulfed. Acting swiftly, he sent up all the reinforcements he could lay hands on. As soon as Kippenberger received them, they were rushed into gaps in the front, taking up positions in ditches, behind walls, wherever cover could be found.

Scraping the bottom of the barrel, Inglis sent forward signallers,

the Kiwi Concert Party, and even the 4th Brigade Band, all to act as
riflemen. Here, indeed, was resolution in desperation.

Up amongst the olive groves a signals officer hesitated as he saw
the front he was given to hold. He would have been in his element if he
had been asked to establish a Brigade Signals Centre on the spot, or a
radio transmission link; but to dispose a platoon for infantry defence
was rather deep water for him. To his relief he espied another officer
through the trees, an officer wearing the red patch of an infantry-
man.

Hastening to him he said: 'Here, you take command of my men
and put them into position. I'm only a sigs officer. I don't know infantry
tactics. You take over.'

The other officer, likewise a lieutenant, looked at the signaller with
an expression of polite astonishment. 'Me take over?' he repeated.
'Do you know who I am?'

'No,' the signaller replied. 'But you know more about this business
than I do.'

'You think so?' the other queried, and now there was a grin spread-
ing on his face. 'Well, I'll tell you something. You say you're only a
sigs officer. Well, I'm only a ruddy bandmaster!'

So they went into the line together.

Just on dusk another strong attack was made by the Germans
in an effort to capture the village of Galatas. This brought them so far
forward that the two companies of the 20th under Fountaine and
O'Callaghan were in danger of being cut off. They had to be pulled
back to maintain a line with the others.

The orders came through to Upham. He could withdraw his
men all right, though it would mean fighting part of the way. But
there were other troops in the line beside him whom he would have
to warn.

So he ordered Kirk to take the platoon out, and himself went
across to the others to warn them that they might be cut off unless they,
too, pulled back.

Kirk, however, found the way out was all but closed. So, taking
the fight to the enemy, he vigorously counter-attacked, inflicting sharp
casualties and making good his ground to the rear. Even then, he
found himself out of touch with the rest of the company, and joined
in spiritedly in the famous counter-attack on Galatas that took place
soon after. Kirk and his men rejoined their company early next morning
after holding an advanced salient right through the night.

Kirk won the D.C.M. Upham said of him: 'He was the really
superb fighting man. A crack shot, he always carried a Bren gun and

used it with deadly effect, and was one of the few men who could fire it accurately at close range like a Tommy-gun. . . .'

Meantime Upham had returned from warning the other front-line troops to find that Kirk had safely disengaged the platoon and was piloting them back across the ridges. Upham was alone, and now had to find his own way back to the new defence line.

He began picking his way. The Germans were already infiltrating forward and it was obvious there were some of the enemy between him and safety.

He came out from a grove of trees to find that he would have to cross a hundred yards of open ground. That was dangerous. He paused, looked back.

At that second the shots came.

In an instant he saw the two Germans. They were moving towards him through the trees, just two men on their own. But if he ducked and ran he'd never make it across the open. Yet he couldn't stay and fight it out on the edge of the olive grove.

Two more shots cracked at him.

Back on the far side of the clearing one of Upham's platoon was watching. He heard the shots, saw Upham twist round to look, then . . .

'Charlie . . . the boss . . . he's copped it!'

He saw Upham reel, collapse to the ground, one arm flung above his head as he fell.

The two Germans must have seen it also. Satisfied, they continued moving carefully forward, looking for the New Zealander's body.

But Upham had only tripped over a tree-root. He lay there in the grass, thinking it couldn't have happened at a better time. But he needed safer cover.

He squirmed his way through the grass to the nearest tree, noticed with satisfaction that there was a low fork in the trunk.

He had a rifle again. But with his arm in a sling it was a heavy, almost useless weapon for a one-armed man. In the fork of the tree, though . . .

Cautiously he raised his head, peered through the fork. He could see the Germans moving steadily towards him, about thirty yards away.

With his good arm he lifted the rifle, rested the barrel gently in the fork, made sure it was cocked, the safety-catch off.

Two of them to get. . . .

Only one hand to hold the rifle, to pull the trigger, then work the bolt after the first shot and bring the second round into the chamber.

Would he have time for the second shot? If he fired his first shot too soon, the second German would know he had been shamming, would drop into cover and scout him out. He'd never get across the clearing then.

They came closer. They looked good men—they were moving carefully, not exposing themselves unnecessarily. They had sub-machine-guns.

He had to be sure of killing one of them with his first shot, but leaving it so late that the other man couldn't get away. But then would there be time to work the bolt and get in his second shot?

One mistake would be finish.

He waited, his wounded arm in its sling, the other elbow clutched round the stock of the rifle, finger on trigger. Would he have time to aim again before he would have to fire the second time?

They came closer. Twenty yards . . . fifteen . . . ten. And they were cautious now, because they could see the clearing ahead. They were peering into the grass, looking for his body.

Closer . . . closer. . . .

Eight yards . . . seven . . . six.

He lay dead still, hardly breathing.

Close enough.

He squeezed the trigger. The crack of the gun seemed to shout back from the trees. He saw his man pitch forward.

Like lightning he shifted his hand to the bolt . . . a moment's fumbling would be fatal . . . seized it, drew it back, pushed it home again . . . with the other man looming over him.

When he shot the second German the man's body fell against the muzzle of his rifle.

. . . Close enough.

*   *   *   *

The same attack that nearly cut off Upham's men saw the Germans sweep into Galatas. Their pressure in this area indicated that they wanted possession of the town by nightfall, and they rapidly swarmed into its little houses and set up their guns around the town square. Here was a dangerous lodgment which Kippenberger recognized increased the predicament of the New Zealand Division. It was too late now to attempt merely to patch the line; the risk before him was that everything might crumble away if the enemy were left in Galatas.

Kippenberger decided that he must strike, and strike boldly. Two

British tanks were handy, one commanded by the notable Roy Farran, and two companies of the 23rd Battalion came up, tired but in good heart.

Farran clattered into Galatas, spitting fire, and returned to report that the town was 'stiff with Jerries'.

Kippenberger told the two companies that there was no time for reconnaissance; the tanks would move in, the infantry would follow in behind the tanks, single file on each side of the road, and take everything with them.

Then Farran said: 'I've got two wounded men inside. Could any of your New Zealanders take their places in my tank?'

Volunteers were called for. Farran says: 'About three hundred volunteered,' which is a pleasant but inaccurate exaggeration. However, two men were quickly found who could fire Vickers guns. They were sent up the road for a rapid lesson in tank fighting, while the infantry waited silently by the roadside.

Now there were odd stragglers also joining in, glad to be given the chance of hitting back, linking themselves up to the two queues waiting on the roadside.

There were groups from the 20th, some men of supply units, a few British officers, and all sorts of scattered remnants who refused to be left behind. In the very face of collapse and near-disaster, with men broken and exhausted, here was an example of resilience that was an inspiration.

Ten minutes sufficed for the men to learn their jobs in the tank. They returned. Then with barely another word the infantry moved off, tanks in front, Galatas in the dusk ahead.

Beginning at a walk, soon the men broke into a run to keep up with the tanks. And then, as the buildings of Galatas loomed up 200 yards ahead, there suddenly arose a clamour from the throats of men that still rings in the minds of those who heard it.

'The whole line seemed to break spontaneously into the most blood-curdling shouts and battle-cries . . . our chaps charging and yelling. . . .'

'One felt one's blood rising swiftly above fear and uncertainty until only an inexplicable exhilaration quite beyond description surpassed all else, and we moved as one man into the outskirts.'

So wrote the men who took part in this remarkable episode.

Into the town they charged, along the lanes, over the walls, through the gardens, in and out of the buildings, shouting, fighting, and always

driving forward. They were fired on from all sides, from roofs, doorways, and windows. They died quickly and freely, but the rest forged
on. The noise was overwhelming.

The enemy drew back, darting out of the houses and shops, trying
to re-form on the far side of the village square. But there, even with
our two tanks knocked out, another charge was thrown in. The
Germans broke and ran.

There were scenes of great gallantry. Men raced straight into the
face of enemy guns, plunging into the horrors of bayonet fighting with
reckless heat, routing out the Germans with a fury that comes to those
who have had to defend too long.

There are many who say that this hour was the fiercest fought by
New Zealanders in the whole war. There could surely be no other hour
to match it in the superb rallying of men to a desperate call; no other
engagement could share its spirit of sudden bold retaliation, crowned
as it was by complete success. For Galatas was swept clean of the
enemy, and men with the hot surge of battle still coursing through them
were disposed in defensive positions to hold it.

*   *   *   *

But by early morning the implacable logic of wider strategy had
ruled that Galatas would have to be yielded anyhow. Broken as the
line was, a withdrawal to a shorter defensive position was essential,
one that the available fit troops would have a chance of holding.

A final massive counter-attack against the Germans was discussed
during the night hours. But there were no fresh troops to make it, none
who could be spared from the necessary task of merely delaying the
inevitable. Crete was already lost. The commanders now had to prevent
disaster.

So from courageous Galatas, out on a lonely but defiant limb,
the men were spirited away before daylight, and brought back to the
ridges just east of Karatsos, where they turned again, their backs now
barely a mile from Canea. Here they would fight again.

Fight they did next day—the 26th May—against an enemy who
kept pushing forward with confident aggression. The Germans made
no bold assault, and seemed to be building up strength for another
major attack to come. But all day there were probing forays, and all
day came the rain of mortars, the unremitting air bombing and strafing,
the scream of Stukas.

To Freyberg the end was in sight. Only eight artillery pieces left,
communications gone, his battalions still resisting doggedly, but cut

to shreds, exhausted and disorganized, a prey to any enemy plane that cared to look for a target and spray it with fire. He signalled Wavell:

> 'The troops under my command here have reached the limit of endurance. No matter what decision is taken by the Commanders-in-Chief, from a military point of view our position here is hopeless. A small, ill-equipped, and immobile force such as ours cannot stand up against the concentrated bombing that we have been faced with during the last seven days . . . the troops we have are past any offensive action.'

In London Churchill's sources of information were so ill-informed that he permitted himself to cable Wavell that victory was '*essential and reinforcements must continue to be hurled in*'. Churchill probably had a few hot words later for those who failed to tell him that the situation was already too far gone for any reinforcing operations, let alone victory. Wavell had done his best with what scanty forces he had —but they had never been enough.

But to the Germans it was still no easy matter. In the War Diary of the 5th German Mountain Division this was found: 'The enemy is offering fierce resistance everywhere. He makes very skilful use of the country and of every method of warfare. . . .'

That night saw our men falling back again, forming a new line at what became known as 42nd Street. An attractive name for a place of war, 42nd Street saw yet another demonstration of what men are capable of, despite weariness and the smell of disintegration and defeat.

The chain of command from Force Headquarters through to the lower echelons had by now almost completely broken down. Commanders wandered around searching for their commands; orders took hours to reach their destinations, if at all; units could not find the officers from whom they expected orders. Men on the spot had to make decisions.

It was such a decision that led to the affair at 42nd Street. Two brigades—the 5th New Zealand and an Australian brigade—found themselves alongside each other, holding a line that followed the road called 42nd Street. They thought they were in a reserve area and that other troops were out in front between them and the enemy.

But as the day advanced—and it was now 27th May, the eighth day of the battle—the two brigade commanders came to realize that there was nothing out front. All forward opposition had been trampled down.

Soon enemy forces made their appearance, driving swiftly eastwards. On the spot, the unit commanders decided that there was no
future in quietly letting the enemy build up in front, and that it was
futile thinking they could stem an enemy assault. No—the decision
was made that when the enemy came to close quarters the defenders
would open fire and charge forward. Counsel of desperation? But how
often has such a straightforward bold decision succeeded. It had worked
at Galatas. It relies for its success not on weapons and weight of fire-
power; it relies on the spirit and courage of individual men. Commanders have to know that their men, however exhausted, still possess
the determination and dash to carry it forward.

There was no concerted zero hour, no elaborate orders as to which
units would counter-attack first, which would follow through, or what
supporting fire would be given. The hour was too late for that kind of
battle.

The Maoris of 28th Battalion began it, most witnesses agree. They
had watched the Germans coming, the efficient, almost contemptuous,
drive of a victorious army.

Bayonets fixed, they waited behind the walls and in the ditches.

Then from a man who could contain himself no longer there came
a shout. In an instant it was echoed by a score of others and a line of
men suddenly leapt into the open.

Forward went the Maoris 'with an élan almost incredible in men
who had already endured so much' (so wrote one historian). Within
seconds they were followed by the 21st Battalion, the 19th, the 22nd,
the 23rd—such of them as still remained.

Here was something that baffles description. Men who were battered
into defeat and exhaustion, with nothing left but rifles and bayonets,
almost as one rising to their feet, hearing the shouts of their comrades,
and taking the battle straight into the face of the enemy.

Men could not be restrained. Companies and platoons told to wait
behind to make sure of a reserve could not resist. It was a scene of
mass reaction—like the way a hush will suddenly fall over a huge
crowd or the emotions of a thousand men will suddenly and simultaneously erupt as if spiritually controlled.

They all went forward, walking grimly at first, then running, firing
at the grey uniforms in the grass, behind the trees and hedges, using
the bayonet ruthlessly on those who resisted. It was no panic charge of a
distraught rabble. Officers kept the men to their senses, keeping interval
to save casualties; but on and on they went. The uproar swelled over
the peaceful fields of Crete.

For the enemy, the sight of troops advancing into the fire with such

THE FACE OF A SOLDIER

Upham photographed after the campaigns in Greece and Crete

BATTLE OF MINQAR QAIM

Surrounded by the enemy, New Zealanders build their sangars on the open slopes of the ridge

The battle opens with an artillery duel

sharp pugnacity was too much. They fought for a moment, wavered, then fled. And they were destroyed as they ran.

In a spirit of exhilaration for which there can be no words, our men swept the Germans back from 42nd Street nearly half a mile.

Our own casualties were surprisingly light. For the enemy it was a sad day. The 1st Battalion of 141st Regiment, fighting its first engagement, was all but eliminated, and other units were sharply cut about.

Out of defeat and adversity, history tells us again and again that the greatest deeds are born. There had been the ill-fated counter-attack on the Maleme 'drome, born to failure from the start, but carried to the very brink of success by the courage of determined men. Then Galatas—the evening when crisis loomed—when beaten soldiers turned and swept back into the village. And now 42nd Street—little wonder that Churchill later referred to the New Zealand Division as 'that ball of fire'.

In all the annals of warfare have men behaved more nobly?

*   *   *   *

Charles Upham would have been in his element at 42nd Street, allowing even for his one useless arm, his wounds, and his dysentery. But, with the rest of the 20th, he was already further south, marching into the interior of the island to protect the escape route that all Allied forces now had to follow.

Evacuation had been ordered. A little fishing village on the south coast, called Sfakia, was the only place left from which the Navy could take men away. It was to be another Greece—another race between ships and enemy—another gamble as to how many men could be lifted from the beaches at night before the Germans arrived. It is a humiliating business.

It was a march of some forty miles to the south coast. The road seemed to lead upward all the way, with interminable zigzags, hairpin bends, and over mountain ridges reaching 3000 feet. To men who were fresh and fit this would have been a physical effort of some magnitude. But to the Kiwis, Australians, and British troops who were exhausted from lack of sleep, short of food and water, defeated by the weight and shock of never-ending air attack, whose courage had been futile in the absence of adequate fighting equipment, here was the culminating ordeal.

To fall behind was to be taken prisoner. To continue ahead was to drive the body to unattainable lengths of endurance.

G

Units whose commanders had managed to keep them organized made the march in grim, plodding stubbornness. Friends helped each other, gained strength from the company of their mates. At halts they fell to the ground, had to be forcibly awakened when the march was due to start again.

Over the whole nightmare road was a mass of disorganized stragglers, men who had lost or left their units, painfully fighting their way southwards, trying to attach themselves to organized parties. For it was soon known that parties who were still armed and organized would receive priority in evacuation.

The road was littered with abandoned equipment of all kinds. The dead lay there too. The wounded, the weak, the ones who fell out, lay with them. Some even struggled onwards on hands and knees.

While amidst the horror there was still beauty, and nobility of character shone alongside degradation.

No more moving description of those terrible few days could be given than that of D. M. Davin, in his official New Zealand history of the campaign in Crete. He sums up the agony, the courage, and the despair of it all in these words:

'Trucks would pass ruthlessly along the column, ignoring the appeals of wounded men who would not fall out while their legs assured them that they might still be free. Or sometimes a truck would stop and one of its occupants would gruffly get out to make room for a man on foot whose condition was so bad that the passenger could not bear to ride while he walked. And of those who marched some went stonily on, ignoring the appeals of companions who could go no further; while others showed an awareness of something greater than their own exhaustion and did their best to struggle forwards, a wounded companion slung on a blanket or a wooden stretcher between them. And time and again the sight of a man stumbling along with an arm around the neck of each of two comrades who took turns carrying his rifle stressed its echo of Calvary.'

Alas, there were few trucks, and a premature demolition at one point of the road made wheeled transport a luxury for a very favoured few. Even at the end of the journey, on the hills looking far down to Sfakia on the coast, the road petered out entirely, and goat-tracks had to be followed down the hillsides for the last few miles.

Kippenberger watched his 20th trudge past him. They were still together, still organized, the product of firm but tolerant leadership.

His men had gone hours without water, many had no water-bottles to fill even when the rare wells were reached.

He looked with some concern as the Battalion Padre, Spence, came past. Spence had several water-bottles hanging around his belt.

'I see you are well equipped with water-bottles, Padre,' the Colonel said, trying hard to keep the sarcasm out of his voice.

'Oh yes,' came the reply. 'I just carry one or two in case any of the boys are short.'

And Kippenberger noticed then that the Padre's own lips were cracked and parched and his face grey with fatigue. And the voice of the Padre was the thin gritty voice of a man who had not touched water for a long time.

Kippenberger later wrote: 'I think it was the most Christ-like thing I ever saw.'

       *   *   *   *

So in the course of several days thousands of the beaten Allies converged on Sfakia. While the Navy worked like demons to take them off, necessarily by night, they lay up in the caves and the stony gullies that ran sharply down to the rocky coast. As they waited their turn, the enemy came closer and closer, pressing on the outer ring of defenders, forcing the line to be contracted shorter and shorter, and the men in the hills packed tighter around the tiny village.

On 30th May two companies of the 20th were carrying rations from the beach up to the rearguard forces. They were close to the lower end of a long ravine known as 'Rhododendron Valley', hard by Force Headquarters. Inglis and Kippenberger were standing there talking, discussing the orders for the embarkation of troops that coming night.

With startling suddenness, the sound of firing came to them from the direction of the ravine, only a few hundred yards away.

Inglis ran to a knoll, raised his binoculars, and saw Germans advancing down the ravine.

Here indeed was trouble. The Allied rearguard was out holding the main approach road to Sfakia, some miles away. But now the enemy were within the perimeter, almost on top of Force Headquarters itself. Obviously a determined enemy patrol had penetrated the defences, no doubt by an unguarded route over the hills. Or perhaps it was the vanguard of a massive enemy assault.

The briskness of the firing gave some at Force Headquarters the impression that a general attack was upon them.

'They're here!' a senior officer shouted.

'Well, we've had it now,' muttered a man of higher rank still. 'They've caught us. This looks like the finish.'

But Inglis and Kippenberger had moved into action. The former rushed orders to 18th Battalion to mount men on the eastern slopes of the ravine. Kippenberger told A Company of the 20th to block the mouth of the ravine, and ordered Fountaine of C Company to get men up the cliffs on the western side.

Fountaine ran over to Upham.

'Get your men up there, Charlie!' he called, pointing to the precipitous hills. 'Get on top of them. And you'd better move fast. They're in a hell of a flap at Force H.Q.'

Upham looked at him. He was shrunken with illness, weary beyond description, still unable to eat, his wounds a dull heavy drag on his determination. But there was a shadow of a grin on his face as he said: 'Oh, tell 'em to go to hell and not get excited.' He turned to Dave Kirk beside him. 'Get the boys moving, Dave. And tell 'em it's a five-minute job.'

Upham led his men to the foot of the cliffs and they started climbing. They had been on their feet day after day; they had marched over the mountain passes, and now, at the last, the sheer walls of the ravine were so much torture.

With his men worn out, himself driven by little more than will-power, Upham led the way up the face of the hill, upward and upward, every step an effort of concentration. It was steep, the going brutally hard.

Slowly they inched their way up the 600-foot walls of the ravine. It became apparent to the watchers below that Upham intended to get right on top of the Germans, to be able to fire down directly from overhead.

They toiled wearily on. Some of the party were disposed in positions on the hillside; then Upham pushed further ahead with three other men. For another half-mile his small group crawled on, clambering painfully ever higher. It seemed to the men that he would never stop.

'Won't this do, boss?' they pleaded. But he plodded on remorselessly. It was no use, he thought, firing on the enemy from a position which would allow them to retire the way they had come. He was determined to go so far that no retreat for the enemy was possible. Meantime the Germans were pinned down by the frontal fire of Washbourn's A Company blocking off the lower end of the ravine.

General Freyberg was watching also. It seemed to him they were climbing very slowly. An hour had gone by; an hour and a half; it was nearly two hours now since the first outbreak of firing.

After the war Freyberg returned to his battlegrounds on Crete and looked closer at the cliffs Upham's men had scaled. 'I can understand now,' he said, 'why they seemed to take so long.'

But finally the group of gasping battle-worn men came to a spot where Upham said: 'This'll do. Now use tracer. Got to see where you're striking.'

With legs trembling, almost at the end of their resources, they slumped into position on the cliffside.

They got the Bren ready.

Far down below they could see the Germans moving from cover to cover in the ravine. They were right on top of them. The hillside was so steep that Brown, who had the Bren, had to be held by the legs so that he could lean over far enough to fire.

'Right, let her go!' Upham said.

Brown began firing.

Hopelessly caught by the plunging fire, the Germans ran desperately about, but they were doomed. One after another they fell to the fire sweeping down on them from overhead.

'Here, give me a turn!' Upham shouted excitedly. He took the Bren, saw that there were still a few left to account for. He aimed carefully, fired, and picked off all of the enemy who still survived.

For a minute they were silent, watching for signs of any further movement.

Then Upham said laconically: 'That's the lot.'

It was. Of the fifty Germans who came down the ravine that day, twenty-two were killed by Upham's men. The rest were mopped up by other troops surrounding the valley.

The slow, aching climb down the hillside began.

And when they reached the bottom again, reeling like drunken men, there was Burrows.

He was waiting to tell the officers about embarkation that night. His news brought a sigh—one officer and forty men of the 20th would have to stay behind. There was not room in the boats for all.

Fountaine assembled his company, told them the story, and asked for any volunteers to form part of the forty to stay behind.

The men who had climbed the cliffs, still hot, weary beyond words, their legs weak and shaking, paused. Then Grooby, the C.S.M., stepped forward. At once Fraser, the C.Q.M.S., followed, along with Kirk and Vincent. And then Fountaine's company, barely forty in number all told, shuffled forward in line with their N.C.O.s. They would all volunteer to stay.

It had to be done by drawing lots.

Fountaine went back to Battalion H.Q. with the names of the men.

Burrows met him. 'I suppose Charlie Upham wants to stay too?' he asked.

Fountaine nodded. 'Doesn't think it's right to go off himself while some of his men are left behind. He'll stay with them if he gets half a chance.'

Burrows looked serious. 'Watch him, Den. Make sure yourself that he embarks. I didn't tell you before, but Kip's given me special orders about Charlie. He said Charlie must go off tonight; *he's not to be allowed to remain under any circumstances.* So keep your eye on him.'

Fountaine understood. He knew that, already, wherever men gathered in small groups and talked quietly about the last ten days, Upham's name was being mentioned. And one man would have seen this, and another man would have heard something else. And so quickly had the word spread that a legend was already in the making.

Afternoon drew into evening. Men who were embarking handed their water-bottles and their rations to those staying behind. There were unhappy, strained farewells. Fountaine was never far from his company, and he kept his eye on Charlie Upham.

There was a time when he thought he had been outwitted. Upham disappeared.

But not for long. He was back soon, feet dragging, his wounded shoulder hurting abominably. But he felt pleased with what he had done. Because he had always loved animals, and couldn't bear to see them suffer.

In the midst of all this human ordeal Charles had noticed that the Cretans, who had wisely deserted their village, had left behind a few mules, still closely tethered. They had no food. They would soon die.

He stumbled over the broken ridges to the mules, untethered them, set them free to forage in the grass. Then he made his way painfully back to his men.

*   *   *   *

Night came. An armed cordon ringed off the beach, allowing through only those who were to be evacuated that night.

The hours passed. Then out of the dark came the ships' boats and the landing craft, and men began to clamber aboard.

Kippenberger stood and counted his men of the 20th as they passed through the cordon. He saw Upham come through, a 'walking skeleton', he described him later. Upham was weeping, in a medley of utter exhaustion and illness, and from bitter frustration at not being allowed to stay for another crack at the enemy. To have to leave some of his own men behind, and go off to safety himself when he felt he could still fight, was galling to him. That he was already physically far past the point of effective soldiering he did not accept.

Den Fountaine said: 'I actually had to hold Charlie and literally drag him off.'

Upham had built up such a cold fury against the enemy, and such an implacable determination, that his mind could still dominate his battered body.

9

The Victoria Cross

THERE were new huts at Helwan for the New Zealanders, there was accrued pay, and there was a week's leave—survivors' leave, they called it. Off they went to Luxor, to Palestine, to Alex. While they were away reinforcements came marching in.

For Charles Upham, he did not forget the promise he had made on the hillside overlooking Maleme, just after the failure of the counter-attack on the 'drome. A slap-up meal at Shepheard's, he had said. So he kept his word. He turned on a worthy feast for his boys—but, alas, there were only five of them: Kirk, Le Gros, 'Shorty' Christian, and two others. The remainder of his band were left on Crete or were in hospital.

Meantime Kippenberger collected eye-witness accounts of Upham's conduct on Crete. One report from a captain of the 20th said: 'He showed a total disregard for his own safety, very seldom using cover, and always moving around his platoon cheering his men on. . . . Coolness, leadership, and unremitting attention to his men. . . .'

And a corporal wrote: 'After being wounded on the third day he carried his arm in a sling and was in constant pain. . . .'

Another said later: 'I was with him at Maleme and history will tell how magnificent he was. Some people are under the impression that he was foolhardy and reckless, but in my opinion he wasn't. There was method and cool reasoning in all his actions, he summed up the situation quickly, and his courage and determination ensured success.'

Yet another opinion was: 'He seemed to have a battle sense and to work by instinct. He never took useless risks and seemed to know just how much he could accomplish. . . . He was able to move faster and march with less fatigue than any of the men ten years younger.'

Worn out after the campaigns in Greece and Crete, Upham was in hospital for some time, with sinus trouble adding to his burdens. He was finally discharged, to find that the battalion was toiling through a series of ambitious manœuvres, along with many other units, in the Nile Valley, watched by great numbers of men of high rank.

It would be inconvenient for him to rejoin his platoon immediately, it was said, so they seized on him to act as one of the umpires of the exercises.

Part of his task was to approach a New Zealand brigade with the news that an enemy tank force was advancing on them in great strength. What would be the New Zealand Brigadier's orders?

Upham thought his duties as an impartial umpire should not override his loyalties to the New Zealand Division. So before delivering his news he prudently ferreted out the 'school' solution. *Withdraw*—that's what the New Zealand Brigadier would be expected to order.

Thus, when the imaginary tanks hove into sight, and Upham stood alongside the New Zealand commander to ask for the Brigadier's orders, he got some satisfaction out of telling him in advance what the mighty ones said should be done.

'Withdraw?' the Brigadier expostulated. 'Not on your life!' And he didn't.

That night, as the great ones gathered in solemn conference to debate the lessons of the exercise, Upham arrived to take his seat as the most humble of the umpires. Somehow he arrived at the wrong door, for, as he entered, he found himself alongside the microphone that was to be used by the speakers. Glancing over the parade, Charles paused a moment at the sight of so much rank—he had never seen so many generals and brigadiers in one place. He couldn't repress the involuntary remark: 'My oath, what a galaxy of bloody talent!'

In an instant all the noble heads turned on him, and he realized more than ever how lowly is the lot of the second lieutenant. For too late he knew what had happened. The microphone had been switched on, and Upham's cheery remark had gone booming down the hall, a diverting introduction to the evening's business.

Some weeks later the division was sent to do amphibious training at Kabrit, in the Canal Zone. Enemy air-raids on the Canal were increasing, culminating on 8th September with an attack that had the authorities expecting a parachute landing. It was battle stations for everyone.

Some of C Company of the 20th were hardly prepared for it. There had been something of a party, heads were unsteady, and the air-raid alert caught men confused between the necessity of getting out of certain clothes and into others. These things are very difficult to work out in some circumstances.

One of those who found it difficult that night was Fanny Hill of 15 Platoon. He staggered from his bed of confusion to the assembly point, oblivious to the fact that he was clad only in his boots and identity disc.

Upham saw him, swallowed hard, then moved up to him and put his mouth close by Fanny's ear.

'What the hell are you going to do to the paratroops?' he shouted distinctly. '*Kick them to death?*'

*   *   *   *

From Kabrit the division moved out into the Western Desert again, there to improve the defences of the Baggush Box, 160 miles west of Alexandria. There was battle training in the sand, swimming in the Mediterranean, digging in the stones, each company living a self-contained life in a manner where men really came to know their fellows.

More exercises were held there early in October, watched, it was said, by every brass hat in the Middle East.

During a pause in the manœuvres Upham slipped off his web gear and laid it on the running-board of an A.S.C. truck. He moved away a few yards to attend to something else, turned back, found that the truck was gone. With it went his Army pistol and binoculars.

This is serious, the Army always says to such an occurrence. That's what they told him now when he privately mentioned his loss, though he delayed putting in an official report.

Upham frothed and fumed, pointing out how absurd it was to worry over it so much when he had seen literally millions of pounds worth of equipment readily cast aside on Greece and Crete. Anyway, he argued hotly with anyone who cared to discuss the subject with him, if he *had* to produce a pistol and binoculars he'd get them soon enough the next time he was in action. Couldn't they wait till then? His pride was hurt.

Rather sheepishly he asked the men of his platoon if they would help him look.

Not merely the platoon but the whole company volunteered, and a good part of the following day was spent in an emu parade up and down a large area of the nearby desert. It was amazing what things actually were discovered, including some ancient Roman coins, so it is said, a broken Grecian urn, and a sheet of paper containing some Cairo addresses. But no sign of the pistol and binoculars.

'The driver pinched them,' was the general verdict. And so upset was Charles over the whole trivial incident that a meeting was held and the suggestion put forward that, to save Charlie's face, a volunteer would have to pinch a pistol and binoculars from some *other* officer in some *other* unit. Because otherwise a court of inquiry would have to be set up.

Eventually, all hope gone, Charles had to make an official report admitting his loss. He wrote it out that evening, handed it in, and roamed around like a bear with a sore head. He was too annoyed with himself to bother listening to the mess radio when the news from London came over.

But at 9 p.m. those listening heard a news item that had them leaping from their seats.

In the warmly modulated tones of the B.B.C. came the announcement:

'*The Victoria Cross has been awarded to an officer of the New Zealand Military Forces, Second Lieutenant Charles Hazlitt Upham, for gallantry in Crete.*'

*   *   *   *

There were several officers present when Charles was first told he had won the V.C. The news seemed not to register immediately on his mind—like the way a man acts and looks when he thinks people are talking of someone else. There was no expression of surprise. He seemed neither excited nor overcome. Just a slightly puzzled, almost defensive, attitude. And after a silence that seemed to indicate distrust and disbelief he at last spoke.

'It's meant for the men,' he said harshly. 'My men—by God they could fight! You know, those chaps can do anything. . . .' and he continued talking rapidly, almost wildly, about the merits of his platoon, as if trying to postpone the fact that he himself had been singled out.

Yet deep in his mind he knew it all on the instant. He knew immediately that his life now would be different, that he would be constantly trying to escape from a position of fame; and he knew that he was going to be hurt by the belief that the Victoria Cross was being awarded for something that was no more than a man's ordinary duty. 'He had done nothing . . . nothing. An officer must lead . . . an officer must urge them on . . . but it is the men who do it . . . he hadn't won anything . . . his men had won it . . . yet he would have to suffer the humiliation of receiving an award that belonged to his men, not to him. . . .'

So ran his thoughts in those first few hours, and Charles Upham has never really overcome that first feeling of embarrassed defensiveness. It has remained with him throughout the years.

Out in the desert that first night Charles withdrew into himself, worried more over the prospect of a court of inquiry than over his V.C. He made one excuse after another for not going to the officers' mess to join the general celebration. Shyness drove him underground. Finally Evan Wilson, a fellow-subaltern, had almost to bludgeon him into a reluctant and timid appearance.

It is doubtful if Upham was ever less happy.

Then only three days later came another announcement. The Victoria Cross was awarded to Sergeant Jack Hinton for bravery at Kalamata, in Greece, where he had been captured in the final resistance. It was not enough coincidence that both Upham and Hinton were from the 20th Battalion, but both belonged to C Company. And then to C Company came a D.C.M. for Dave Kirk, and an M.C. (Greek) for Major Wilson, the officer commanding C Company who lost his life on Crete while temporarily leading a Greek battalion.

Up went a notice in the lines: 'Join the 20th and win a V.C.', and Colonel Burrows, now doing a tour of duty at Base, wrote an amusing letter to Kippenberger concluding: 'It would be a convenience if in future the names of members of the 20th Battalion who win Victoria Crosses be published in one list and not on different days as appears to be the present practice.'

Meantime, the 20th were having military competitions—tactics, drill, weapons, grenade throwing, etc., and this engendered a brisk enthusiasm.

Platoon drill would be one of the hard ones for Upham's 15 Platoon, for they couldn't trust him to give the orders at the right time. On the morning of the drill competition he stood talking with Bob May, rather glumly thinking that he didn't stand much chance. He would let Bob take as much of the drill as possible. He said: 'Well, Bob, we'd better get going . . . and—Bob . . .'

May looked at him enquiringly. 'Yes?' he asked.

'I think, Bob, you'd better salute me this morning.'

And May solemnly agreed.

But in the culminating competition for a platoon attack Upham's clumsiness with drill was of no account. With great vim he led his platoon against the imaginary enemy and the obstacles that the umpires threw in his way. He won easily, with a clear margin over the rest of the battalion.

To those who may have wondered if Charles Upham was merely a brave individual there now came the realization that he was also a shrewd, quick, and determined tactician. He seemed to know the right thing instinctively.

But something worse than military tactics faced him on 25th

October. Into the desert came the New Zealand Mobile Broadcasting Unit, intent on recording an interview with the new V.C. to send back to New Zealand. Norman Johnston, a prominent post-war advertising man, was in charge.

Perhaps forewarned, Upham was in his dug-out and had placed Eric Le Gros on guard outside. 'No, he'll see no one,' Le Gros firmly said to Johnston, in the best manner of the millionaire's butler. 'He doesn't want to talk about the V.C. Of course, if there's anything you want to know . . . ?'

Johnston assured him that it was only Upham they wanted. But it needed Colonel Kippenberger's active assistance before Charles was persuaded to even talk with Johnston.

There was a long argument. Upham was like a rock, feeling that to broadcast a message would be a form of self-aggrandizement.

Kippenberger played a major part in the argument, deftly translating Johnston's suggestions into language that might appeal to Upham's feelings.

'You see, Charlie, this might be the only chance you'll get of paying a tribute to the men you fought with. Johnston's not asking you to say anything about yourself—talk about your men if you'd like to."

It was that sort of argument that finally, very reluctantly, won him round. He agreed to broadcast a message. If they left him alone he would write it out.

Johnston and Kippenberger left him to it.

Upham fished around in his dug-out and collected a few sheets of Y.M.C.A. paper and began to write hesitantly. Then he crossed out this word and that, substituted new ones, wrote along the side and on the back, all the time muttering darkly beneath his breath.

Johnston came back a couple of hours later. By that time Charles was in a fever of nervousness and distress. The sheets of Y.M.C.A. paper looked as if they had been through a washing machine.

The microphone was set up. Upham began the first take.

It wasn't long before he let slip one of his more powerful expletives. Johnston grinned, said: 'Let's try it again.' They did.

On the third try they made a success of it.

And the words that thousands of New Zealanders heard over the air a few weeks later, the words that Upham slowly put together at Baggush in the desert, were these:

'I wish to thank all those who have sent me cables from New Zealand and England. I have been very fortunate indeed, having the very best of commanders above me and the very best of N.C.O.s and men in my own platoon, as well as right throughout the New Zealand

Division. It was very easy to do any job under those circumstances. It was the men in my own battalion, not myself, who earned the distinction. Their morale was the highest in the whole army. Nothing could stop them.

'We left many friends killed over there. Men we will never forget. I will mention the names of some of our own company—Major Wilson, Sergeant Wallace, Sergeant Mussen, Corporal Herbert, Corporal Malloch, Lance-Corporal Skilton, Privates Allen, Atkins, Boyd, Burns, Brown-Pride, Gilligan, Hislop, Watson, and Woods; not to mention Sergeant Hinton and hundreds of others left wounded in Greece and Crete. I hope the people in New Zealand remember them, lying in hospitals and prisons all over Europe. Do all you can to send them food and clothing. These men were not captured whole and unharmed like the Italians we ourselves took, but were wounded and sick men who struggled and fought right on to the last.

'After the war we must do all in our power to help the Greeks with food and clothing and stud stock to help build up their country again. The Greeks were very staunch friends of the New Zealand soldiers and hundreds of us owe our lives to the big-heartedness of these people.

'The division over here is going from strength to strength and the morale of our own troops is unsurpassed. You will hear more from us again. We have a great little army up here in the sandhills.

'I would like the New Zealand Government to know that it is impossible to send over too much New Zealand tobacco to the troops. It is very much appreciated here. Kia Ora.'

The men of my battalion . . . the men who had died . . . send food to the prisoners . . . help the Greeks . . . tobacco for the troops.

It was no artifice of construction. Upham simply was not capable of mentioning himself. In or out of action, his thoughts were constantly of other people. His modesty was almost an obsession.

Johnston packed up his equipment, well satisfied in a rather awed way, for this had not turned out to be the kind of talk he had expected. He went back to Battalion H.Q. and asked Kippenberger to say a few words as a postscript to the broadcast.

Kippenberger agreed, made some notes, and recorded the following:

'I am speaking as Upham's Commanding Officer. Upham is the first New Zealand *officer* to get the award of the Victoria Cross probably since the Maori Wars. He is very distressed, genuinely distressed, that he has been singled out for this award, as he has the idea that a great many men who served well and gallantly deserved to get it instead of himself.

'Nevertheless every man in the company and every man in the battalion is satisfied that the award was made to the right man. He was unquestionably the paladin of the battalion, unquestionably the finest fighting soldier that it had throughout the operations. The exploits for which he has been awarded the Cross—a whole series of dazzling exploits—any one of them deserve an award. . . . During the whole affair he was suffering from dysentery very badly indeed. He had contracted it some five weeks before in Greece. He was unable to eat bully beef and biscuits, which were the only ration in Crete. He lived simply on milk which the men of his platoon found for him. He was a walking skeleton when the affair ended.'[1]

*   *   *   *

Nine days later the whole of 4th Brigade was astir early. This was to be a spit-and-polish day. The Commander-in-Chief Middle East, General Sir Claude Auchinleck, would review the brigade in a ceremonial march past, and the feature of the day would be the presentation of high awards won on Greece and Crete.

Charles Upham was tense and tight-lipped as he began dressing for the parade. Le Gros was helping him.

'We've got to do this right, Leggy-boy,' he said nervously. 'All the top-hatters are going to be there. Make sure again all that gear's ready.'

'Everything's jake, boss,' Le Gros said cheerily. 'You don't look too bad. And I've cleaned those boots about six times . . . they're *your own* boots, you know.'

'My own boots, eh?' Upham said, looking down at them. 'Well, I suppose that's something to be thankful for. Come on, Leggy, I've got to get moving.'

'What about a brandy before you go?' Le Gros suggested.

'No, Leggy-boy, not today. But you have it. Do you good.'

'Well . . . I dunno, boss,' he said innocently. And he watched as Upham began walking over to Company Headquarters.

'And tell that Auchinleck,' he called out after him, 'that we don't want any more shambles like that last show. Give 'im the works.'

Upham waved back absent-mindedly.

Then into the dug-out that formed the Company Orderly Room, where a number of officers and N.C.O.s were waiting. Terry Madsen, the C Company clerk, watched Upham sympathetically. Fancy a man

[1] Both broadcast talks reproduced by permission of the New Zealand Broadcasting Corporation.

like that being in such a state of jitters, he thought. Upham was pacing up and down, highly strung, thoroughly miserable.

Madsen tried to soothe him. 'Take it easy, sir. Give it an hour and it'll be all over.'

Upham grunted, went on fretting.

Then the message came in: *'Ceremonial parade postponed twenty-four hours.'*

It was all Madsen and the others could do to save Upham from becoming a casualty then and there.

But next day saw it through.

Looking spruce and somewhat better composed, Charles paraded with the rest of the brigade. It was a day of brilliant sunshine. On a small plateau overlooking the sea the troops were drawn up, their guns in a protective ring outside. Overhead a screen of fighter planes banked and wheeled, guarding what would have been a very tempting target for any aggressive enemy. The ceremony attracted the largest assembly of war correspondents, photographers, radio and film men yet seen together in North Africa.

First there was an inspection by Auchinleck, accompanied by General Freyberg. Then, with the troops lined up in formation, three names were announced: Kippenberger, to receive the D.S.O.; Lynch, to receive the M.C.; Upham the Victoria Cross.

The three officers marched out, lined up in front of the Commander-in-Chief.

Auchinleck handed the official citations to General Freyberg. 'You read them,' he said.

There was a brisk wind blowing. The citations were long.

So Freyberg turned to Brigadier Inglis. 'You read them,' Freyberg said.

Inglis condensed the citations quickly, read out a neatly turned précis.

Then, as each man stood to attention before him, Auchinleck bestowed the awards. He talked quietly with each man.

'Congratulations, Upham,' he said. 'New Zealand will be very proud that you've won this decoration.'

Upham fought his battle to the last.

He said: 'I didn't win it, sir.'

Auchinleck's eyes smiled. 'Then if you didn't, Upham, I don't know who did.'

And that was that.

Retiring from position in front of the C.-in-C. Upham retreated twenty paces before recollecting that he was required to salute. He promptly, if belatedly, did so, to the great relief of his senior officers, who at the same time noticed that under his puttees he was displaying a pair of yellow socks.

Yellow socks! Shades of Sandhurst. What a mixture of a man, they thought. On one hand an intense desire to do the correct thing militarily and to fight the war to his utmost; at the same time an innocent indifference to many of the traditions and formalities of military life.

The answer was—some things really matter; some things really don't. Upham always sharply classified things into one division or the other.

*   *   *   *

That night in his dug-out Kippenberger thought over the events of the day and decided to write a letter to the Headmaster of Charles's old school, Christ's College. He said:

'Dear Mr. Richards,
          I would like to congratulate your college on Upham's V.C. We are extremely proud and pleased that he belongs to this battalion, as does Hinton, and nothing in my service has given me such pleasure as the preparation of the recommendation and citation. The latter was really a masterpiece of understatement.

Quite apart from having won this decoration, Upham is an outstanding officer of whom you may justly be proud. His head is not in any way turned, nor likely to be. It really has been rather pathetic watching him meet the attacks of photographers and reporters. He did it very well, though with desperate reluctance. I only induced him to speak for the wireless by pointing out that it gave the opportunity to mention some of his men who had died. . . .

I am sure you will not think it a presumption on my part to congratulate College on this decoration, which General Freyberg told me was about the best earned he had ever known.
                              With kindest regards,
                                   Yours sincerely,
                                   H. K. Kippenberger

Elsewhere throughout the world, as tales of heroism in defeat began to be announced, tributes appeared in the Press.

The *Daily Herald* of London wrote of the exploits of Upham and of Hulme, another New Zealand V.C. winner. The headline was: 'NO HEADLINE CAN TELL THE HEROISM OF THESE MEN'.

H

But from *The Times* of London came a tribute which quickens the blood, makes men humble and ashamed of their own unworthiness, and at the same time grateful that qualities of such nobility do exist in others, to the wonderment and awe of those who can profess none of it.

When noble words join to applaud noble deeds we have something worth treasuring, and *The Times*, in its third leader of 15th October 1941, produced a piece of treasure.

'FOR VALOUR

In the Baghdad of the Arabian Nights it used to be ordered that the story of any notable achievement should be written down in letters of gold. Is gold good enough, we can but ask, for the achievements of the two New Zealanders who have been awarded the Victoria Cross for valour? The story of Second Lieutenant Upham covers nine days. During the whole time he was suffering from dysentery and could eat very little. The ordinary mortal, who knows to his shame how a little indigestion can upset both his eye and his nerve on the golf course, will feel that on the least eventful of those nine days Mr. Upham's courage was superhuman. Courage moreover, in this case, meant something far more complex and intellectual than was demanded, say, of even the officers in the charge of the Light Brigade. All the time, and not only on the fifth of those nine days when, painfully wounded, bruised and starved, he bagged his brace by shamming dead, or . . . when by exposing himself he tricked the enemy into doing the like, he was thinking, planning, pitting his wits against the German strength. We all like to think that in the excitement of battle we should be able to do deeds of which the mere thought turns us cold in repose; but the story of those nine days includes not only the hour after hour of silent endurance through which discipline helps to fortify the least heroic, but also the deliberate courting of danger in cold blood for the sake of the platoon, of the Army, of New Zealand, of the British Empire, and the free world. And Sergeant Hulme, that deadly stalker of snipers, he too has won his V.C. as much by his brains as by his contempt for danger.

These deeds were done in Crete. Deeds as brave and as ingenious are still being done in Crete by Britons, by Cretans and others, though few or none can be told to exalt us with the honours that they deserve. Deeds that can only be done through the highest forms of intellectual and physical courage are being done on all sides in this war-stricken world; and, perhaps for the first time in history, civilians have been free to reveal the same combination of initiative, endurance, and self-forgetfulness even unto death which is the constant glory of our sailors, our soldiers, and our airmen. The men of Talavera and of Waterloo were heroically brave; but there may be some excuse for asking whether the nature of modern warfare has not raised the standard of courage to heights unknown before. If it should be so, and if brainpower, initiative, and resourcefulness are necessary to courage of the highest order, it may be surmised that the free peoples are more likely to produce that order of courage than any others. The forces of the whole Empire, from every continent, of every race, know that they are fighting for freedom, with their own home-people passionately in support of them. Out of all this devotion to an ideal, this rivalry in the service of a sacred cause, there must grow a great glory of courage, before which all men and women of good will must feel as proud as they are humble.'

The citation upon which the King approved the award of the Cross read as follows:

'8077 Second Lieutenant Charles Hazlitt Upham.
    During the operations in Crete this officer performed a series of remarkable exploits, showing outstanding leadership, tactical skill, and utter indifference to danger.
    He commanded a forward platoon in the attack on Maleme on 22nd May and fought his way forward for over 3000 yards unsupported by any other arms and against a defence strongly organized in depth. During this operation his platoon destroyed numerous enemy posts but on three occasions sections were temporarily held up.
    In the first case, under a heavy fire from an M.G. nest, he advanced to close quarters with pistol and grenades, so demoralizing the occupants that his section was able to "mop up" with ease.
    Another of his sections was then held up by two M.G.s in a house. He went in and placed a grenade through a window, destroying the crew of one M.G. and several others, the other M.G. being silenced by the fire of his sections.
    In the third case he crawled to within fifteen yards of an M.G. post and killed the gunners with a grenade.
    When his company withdrew from Maleme he helped to carry

a wounded man out under fire, and together with another officer rallied more men together to carry other wounded men out.

He was then sent to bring in a company which had become isolated. With a corporal he went through enemy territory over 600 yards, killing two Germans on the way, found the company, and brought it back to the battalion's new position. But for this action it would have been completely cut off.

During the following two days his platoon occupied an exposed position on forward slopes and was continuously under fire. Second Lieutenant Upham was blown over by one mortar shell and painfully wounded by a piece of shrapnel behind the left shoulder by another. He disregarded this wound and remained on duty. He also received a bullet in the foot which he later removed in Egypt.

At Galatas on 25th May his platoon was heavily engaged when troops in front gave way and came under severe mortar and M.G. fire. While his platoon stopped under cover of a ridge Second Lieutenant Upham went forward, observed the enemy, and brought the platoon forward when the Germans advanced. They killed over forty with fire and grenades and forced the remainder to fall back.

When his platoon was ordered to retire he sent it back under the platoon sergeant and he went back to warn other troops that they were being cut off. When he came out himself he was fired on by two Germans. He fell and shammed dead, then crawled into a position and having the use of only one arm he rested his rifle in the fork of a tree and as the Germans came forward he killed them both. The second to fall actually hit the muzzle of the rifle as he fell.

On 30th May at Sfakia his platoon was ordered to deal with a party of the enemy which had advanced down a ravine to near Force Headquarters. Though in an exhausted condition, he climbed the steep hill to the west of the ravine, placed his men in positions on the slope overlooking the ravine and himself went to the top with a Bren gun and two riflemen. By clever tactics he induced the enemy party to expose itself and then at a range of 500 yards shot twenty-two and caused the remainder to disperse in panic.

During the whole of the operations he suffered from diarrhoea and was able to eat very little, in addition to being wounded and bruised.

He showed superb coolness, great skill and dash, and complete disregard of danger. His conduct and leadership inspired his whole platoon to fight magnificently throughout, and in fact was an inspiration to the battalion.'

*   *   *   *

Back in the desert Charles was fighting a losing battle against the legend growing up about him. Men who had helped dig the defences at Riakia in Greece, or had clung to the ground under the bombs that plastered Hellfire Corner in the Servia Pass, talked about him in the evenings, when there was little to do but commune with one's fellows. They told the stories of the counter-attack on Maleme 'drome, the defiant resistance on the hills, the grudging withdrawals, the price the Germans paid for every advance, and the final drama around Sfakia. And throughout the whole division conversation never went far before Upham's name was mentioned, and the stories about him exchanged, to be told again the next night, and the next.

Upham shrank from it all. Notable people came to see him, and he avoided them whenever he could.

New Zealand's High Commissioner in London, William Jordan, visited the New Zealand forces in the Middle East. He went out to the Western Desert to the 20th Battalion, and then with the C.O. on to C Company.

Upham glimpsed them in the distance.

'Oh, look who's coming!' he exclaimed in dismay, and promptly disappeared.

The official party arrived. 'They want to see Lieutenant Upham,' came the word. Actually Jordan wanted more than that. He hoped to arrange to take Upham back with him to England.

Platoon Sergeant Bob May paraded 15 Platoon, but with no appearance of the platoon commander himself. May kept an impassive face. He knew Upham had gone to earth in his dug-out, hoping that May could handle the situation and see the visitors politely off the premises.

May handled it nicely, telling some persuasive white lies in the process.

Later, when Kip discovered that Charles had been close at hand the whole time, he sent a warning to his over-sensitive V.C.: 'Next time I'll charge you with cowardice.'

It was inevitable that Charles would receive congratulations whenever he met new people. At first embarrassed, he soon developed a technique of his own which did not give offence to the well-wisher, but nevertheless indicated that the subject of the V.C. was not welcome. In reply to the congratulations, Upham would give as short a 'Thank you' as he could and immediately embark on a rapid discussion of the weather, or the state of farming in New Zealand, or any other topic that would serve to divert attention from the subject of himself. He became expert at changing the conversation.

When his own V.C. ribbon arrived he made no effort to attach it to his uniform. It lay around his dug-out unused.

This didn't suit Eric Le Gros, who gained a good deal of reflected glory from his boss's distinction.

'What'll I stick this on?' he asked one day. 'No good leaving it lying around.'

Charles shook his head.

'Go on, you've got to wear it, boss,' he insisted. 'Chaps'll think it funny if you don't.'

'No, Leggy.'

'You won't? All right, if you won't, *I'll wear it myself.*' And there is reasonable ground for believing that he might have done so had not Kip taken a hand at this time.

Upham was shy, and he hated being conspicuous, Kip explained later. 'He was inclined to be careless about dress and I had to speak to him several times about that. He always seemed surprised to hear that anyone thought he wasn't properly turned out. Anyway, as soon as I ordered him to wear his ribbon he immediately did so.'

But it was only half a victory. The V.C. ribbon must be worn on the inner side of all other ribbons, that is, nearest to the centre of the chest. Charles found in this a sufficient excuse for mounting his ribbon so far to the inside that it was mostly covered by the lapel of his jacket.

He never wished to give the impression that he was ashamed of his decoration, or that he did not regard it as a great honour. Far from it. But his reluctance stemmed from his acute loathing of self-importance, an almost obsessive desire to be inconspicuous.

For Molly McTamney the V.C. was, of course, something that any fiancée might well dream of. Perhaps it gave cause for fear, for men of that kind were liable to be where the bullets flew thickest and death was close at hand. But, along with men who climb great mountains, explore continents, or achieve other pinnacles attainable only by human beings of the greatest resolution, the winner of the Victoria Cross is for ever singled out from his fellows.

But Charles gave her few crumbs from his own plate of memories. Not once in all his war-time letters to her did he refer to the deeds that won him the Cross, and on only one occasion did he ever refer to the V.C. or to the fact that he had won it. On that single occasion he wrote to her saying: 'Please don't put V.C. on your envelopes.'

A man who adopts that attitude through life usually acquires a reputation for being unconventional, even odd. There are so few people who understand what it is to be completely mentally honest.

Freyberg once chided him for not wearing the ribbon on one of his uniforms. 'Put it up immediately!' he ordered. 'It is an insult to the King not to wear it.' Upham thought that over, came to see there was some point in it.

A week later he was guest at a dinner, where he met the General again.

'Pleased to see you've got your ribbon up,' Freyberg remarked.

Charles looked at him with a rather malicious twinkle. 'Yes, sir; and you've got yours up too, sir; but mine at least is in the right place.'

Freyberg looked down, then laughed as he saw, with amused chagrin, that his batman had mounted his own V.C. ribbon the wrong way.

War heroes can be a great inspiration to people on the home front, and it was inevitable that plans were mooted for sending Upham back to New Zealand for a tour of duty.

One day the Acting Military Secretary, Captain Guy Rhodes, received a visit from Upham. They knew each other well. Rhodes was one of the original officers of the 20th, had gone through Greece and Crete with it, had become its Adjutant, and was now relieving in a Base appointment while convalescing from a spell in hospital.

He was astonished to see the state Charles was in. The man looked worried to death and thoroughly nervy and upset.

'They tell me the Military Secretary is arranging to send me back to New Zealand,' Charles said miserably, coming straight to the point of his visit.

Rhodes nodded. He understood that was in the wind.

Tears actually came to Upham's eyes. Almost like a frightened boy, he pleaded with Rhodes that they shouldn't do it to him, that he be left in peace with his platoon in the desert. He was appalled at the thought of missing the next campaign. Rhodes explained that it was out of his hands. But Upham pleaded his case in other ears also, and it wasn't long before Rhodes received official word that Second Lieutenant Upham would remain with the division after all.

His platoon were glad to keep him, not only for his example and his toughness, but also for his kindness. Upham could be kind to the point of softness. He was always an easy 'touch' for any hard-luck story.

He scrounged hard for his men, intent on getting them the best of everything. He gave them presents that he received from home, rushed hotly to the defence of any of his men in trouble. One man who injured his knee during training had cause to appreciate his officer's loyalty. It was a hospital injury, and a man back in hospital, away from the desert, quickly loses touch with his friends. Circumstances suggested to a suspicious mind back in Base that the injury was self-inflicted, and the ominous Army routine went into action. Held in what amounted to a state of arrest, the poor chap, seeing medical evidence being prepared against him, wrote a letter out to Upham, hoping that it might reach him in time.

It fortunately did. Upham leapt to pen and paper, and, with his own distinctive brand of strong language, dashed off a hot, furious letter. He never spared the feelings of superior officers and, strangely enough, they never seemed to mind.

*   *   *   *

By November 1941 the newly named 8th Army was ready for another offensive in the desert. While Wavell's forces had been engaged in the fruitless campaigns in Greece and Crete, Rommel had become well established in North Africa. But now it was the Allies' turn to take the offensive.

Every unit organized its men for the campaign. As always happens, a group of men had to be left out of battle so that if disaster occurred there would be a kernel of experienced men around which the unit could be re-formed. It is never a happy occasion for a commander to name the officers who must remain behind, and for the officers in turn to tell off the men who must stay with them.

Kippenberger of the 20th chose his officers to be L.O.B.—six of them. Amongst them were Maxwell, prominent for his performance in Crete, and—to the surprise of many—Charles Upham himself.

'I left him out,' Kip explained later, 'because of the mood he was in. From his experiences in Greece and Crete he had developed a hatred for the enemy. He was bitter about Army shortcomings and about the two miserable withdrawals. Yet he believed that his men were superior to the Germans in fighting ability. He was fretting for more action. He was really too anxious to get at the enemy again. I thought his mood was too dangerous. I left him out because I thought he would get himself killed too quickly.'

Upham's reception of this news was unbelieving, then bitterly hostile.

When he finally knew it was true, his face flamed, he grabbed his equipment and threw it on to the ground, exclaiming: 'What the hell am I doing here anyway?' He could not understand that Kippenberger was doing it not only for his own good, but for the good of the men he would lead into action.

But Howard Kippenberger, one of the most thoughtful and able military leaders New Zealand ever had, judged his man right. He knew Upham's courage, his ruthless singleness of purpose. He wanted him to have time to add a life-saving share of sober cunning to his other attributes. But at this point of time Upham was not temperamentally ripe for acting soberly. Kippenberger's wisdom was manifested in fighting that came later, when Charles emerged as a leader of shrewdness as well as fiery courage.

But at the time it made Upham thoroughly sore and bad-tempered. He was moody and unapproachable.

However, when the first disappointment wore off, his disposition improved. He set to work preparing for the return of the battalion, improving the dug-outs, making sure that when his boys came out of the battle they would find as much comfort as reasonable ingenuity could provide for them.

On 11th November the division moved forward to battle. 'We felt like runners, tense for the pistol,' graphically wrote Kippenberger.

Sidi Azeiz, Fort Capuzzo, Sollum—it was all success at first. But then, against well-prepared opposition, Point 175, Sidi Rezegh, Belhamed—names that still ring in chill memory—were taken by the New Zealanders only after heavy fighting. These battles opened up one of the main objectives of the campaign—the relief of Tobruk—and on 27th November 1941 the 19th Battalion found its way through, joining up with men from the Essex Regiment patrolling out from the town.

The relief of Tobruk is now merely an incident of history. And hardly had it been accomplished before Rommel's tanks, returning from a useless foray towards the Nile, threw themselves at the Allied infantry standing on those desert ridges.

One by one the New Zealand battalions were engulfed, the corridor to Tobruk was broken again, and all the successes of the previous few weeks seemed lost. Out of the battle zone the New Zealanders withdrew, proud, it seemed, of their successes, bewildered by the turn of events that had reduced several battalions to mere shells, bitter at the thought that so much sacrifice had been suffered for so little gain. There were hard criticisms of Allied command, whose policy had committed the infantry to battle in isolated groups, without adequate tank support.

But in the end it seemed that Rommel lost most. While cutting deep into our infantry, he nevertheless saw score upon score of his own precious tanks succumb to point-blank artillery fire, saw them fight with less than equal success against the British armour until, at the end, he had a bare forty tanks left. He couldn't hold Cyrenaica with that; so back from Belhamed, from Sidi Rezegh, from Tobruk, he retreated, and left the field to the battered opposition, who hardly realized they had won a victory.

Upham's long, restless wait with the other L.O.B.s came to an end. He saw the pitifully few remnants of the 20th come back, looked almost in vain for any men of his precious 15 Platoon and of C Company.

Those that returned Charles met warmly, showed them to their quarters like the manager of a hotel. He had worked hard to have the dug-outs in good order, to have all possible comforts laid on ready for them. He moved several of the men in the ranks into the comparative grandeur of the former sergeants' mess—and that was luxury.

They told him the story of the campaign as they sat in the cool evening air. He sympathized, and he scowled, and he shared their pride and their anger. And, with an almost dog-like affection and respect for his leadership, some went away saying: 'It wouldn't have happened if Charlie had been there.' Great as Upham's mana might have been, it was expecting a bit too much to imagine that his presence would have altered the fate of the 2nd Libyan Campaign. But expressions like that were, and were meant to be, merely symbolic. Upham's own platoon had been led into action by Sergeant Bob May, and it is doubtful if Charles himself could have done better. May was a first-class soldier.

Thousands of reinforcements came up from the Nile Delta to fill the ranks of the division. Seven out of the ten battalions required new commanding officers. Upham became Company Commander of C Company.

Amongst the new officers was Pat Barton. This is his story: 'I had had a commission for about eighteen months while serving in Fiji and had never seen a shot fired, so I was viewing with considerable trepidation joining a line battalion with many old hands from Greece, Crete, and Libya. When I heard I was posted to the 20th my fervent wish was that I would not be allocated to Charlie Upham's company— that would be the last straw and my greenness shown up to the full. Imagine my feelings when I stepped out of the train at Baggush to be told I was posted to C Company. I had hardly time to gulp in dismay when a small wiry man with a pipe jutting from his mouth came over eagerly, thrust out his hand, and said: "I'm Upham; how are you? By jove, we're damned pleased to see you. We need you badly." I need not have worried over my reception.'

That was Upham all over. Warm, generous, and trusting towards the other man; curt and impatient with him if he failed to measure up to standard.

But between Charles and his batman Eric Le Gros things were always the same. It was pure vaudeville. Sturdily independent, Le Gros treated Upham as something less than an equal, but with a sort of irreverent respect. He wheedled, and he wangled, with a skill that bordered on the unscrupulous—highly desirable attributes in a batman.

Sometimes Upham showed his appreciation by leaving an extra pound note in a pair of boots put out for cleaning. But if Leggy didn't feel like cleaning the boots that day he would quietly trade them for some other officer's boots, and Upham never seemed to know the difference.

Leggy, moreover, had a peculiar appreciation of the Army system. Unreliable at times, an expert dodger if he felt like it, nevertheless his loyalty to Upham was so intense as to be almost an embarrassment. In the Company Officers' Mess the batmen took turns acting as mess orderly. Whenever it was Leggy's turn the attention he paid to the other officers was so scant that they might just as well have got their own meals. But behind Upham's shoulder Leggy hovered like an alert bodyguard, pressing on his boss second helpings of any delicacies before the others even set eyes on the dish, flipping the jam or the beer from their reaching hands on the mere suspicion that 'his' officer might be needing it.

He took orders from no one; no one, that is, except Upham. 'He's my only boss,' Leggy declared categorically, in amiable defiance of all other Army discipline. Whenever anyone else tried to give him orders Leggy became hard of hearing in a most exasperating way. And to all the other officers of the Commonwealth Forces he displayed a lack of respect and an acid tongue that somehow never got him into trouble. It was nothing to accost a group of visiting officers who might have arrived in the lines with the words: 'What do you bastards think you're doing here? There's no one around. Get to hell out of it!'

Upham took Leggy with him everywhere; and if that meant going into places reserved for officers Leggy was taken in too. Upham turned his icy-blue eyes very coldly on anyone who suggested that this was not a proper thing to do.

*   *   *   *

The Baggush Box was surrounded by mine-fields, measured by the square mile and by tens of thousands. One mine-field lay close to C Company, necessitating a long detour to Battalion H.Q. and to the main supply road.

Upham asked the new Battalion Commander, Colonel Burrows,

for permission to open up a route through the mine-field to gain better access. Kippenberger had now become a brigadier.

Burrows said: 'It's a dangerous job. Get the engineers.'

'No,' Charles replied. 'We can do it. There are a few experienced miners in my company.'

'All right. But be careful. You haven't any mine detectors. What'll you use?'

'We'll prod for them with bayonets,' Upham said.

Burrows went over later to see how Upham's miners were getting on with the job. He found the rest of the company keeping a safe distance away. Working on the mines was Charles himself, assisted by two men.

It made Burrows think back to the day at Maleme when he wanted Upham to send someone through the German fire to warn D and B Companies. Upham went himself. Here again he chose to do the dangerous work himself. That was his nature.

Upham and Dave Kirk were finishing the lane a few days later. A call came through for Charles to go to Battalion to pick up three new junior officers. So he left Kirk to finish off, jumped in the company pick-up, and drove himself over to meet the new men.

Coming back with them, instead of travelling round by the road, he drove straight across the desert to where Kirk was finishing lifting the mines.

'Finished the track, Dave?' he called out.

'Yes, but we'd better have another check.'

'I'll soon check it,' Upham said.

He promptly installed one of the new officers in the driver's seat, pointed out the supposedly cleared lane, and told him to drive the pick-up through it to Company H.Q. beyond.

The truck moved off gingerly, the three new officers facing the realities of war rather earlier than they had expected.

'You're a bit tough on them, aren't you?' Kirk suggested. 'They're so new they might blow themselves up.'

'If you say the track's cleared, Dave, that's good enough for me,' Upham replied. Then he added tartly: 'They've had it safe long enough. This won't be the only mine-field they'll have to drive through.'

Kirk shrugged. He knew his officer well, but there was a hard streak that he could never penetrate.

With his obstinacy, Charles would never let up once he started on anything. One evening near Christmas 1941 he set out with a friend to walk to another unit about half a mile away. It was very dark. They walked for twenty minutes, then for an hour. Two hours passed—and still the destination eluded them. With a persistent dogged fury at his own failure, Charles insisted on walking and walking; and it was not till 3 a.m. that his friend persuaded him to rest till daylight.

Then he got pneumonia and jaundice. Feltham, the Battalion M.O., found him lying in his dug-out with all the right symptoms. 'I'll get an ambulance over,' he said.

'I'll go by *truck*,' Upham said, with complete absence of logic. And he refused to be evacuated unless he went by truck. Perhaps he regarded the ambulance as a symbol of defeat.

Jaundice victims have to avoid anything fatty and greasy. Doc Feltham warned him clearly about that.

He called on his patient a few days later. He found Upham sitting up in bed devouring a New Zealand mutton-bird—and it is doubtful if there is a fattier, greasier dish in the whole world of gastronomy. Upham would never acknowledge weakness, or accept the symbols of it.

*   *   *   *

In January 1942 the New Zealanders were having more amphibious training at Kabrit, in the Suez Canal area. There Upham rejoined his company after his sojourn in hospital.

One thing he had to straighten out immediately. Some transport drivers, past masters at this sort of thing, were living in a cave. Headquarters Company, to whom they really belonged, thought they were under control of C Company. C Company thought they were back where they belonged. But Upham soon put that right. 'We knew all good things come to an end when we heard you were back,' they said ruefully.

Next, an Army film unit wanted to make a propaganda film showing the slickness and efficiency of our Middle East infantry in rapid debussing. The way a well-trained section could leap from its truck and dash into battle positions would make a good film.

It was not unexpected when Upham's C Company at Kabrit was called upon to provide the men for the film.

He had moved cautiously into the job of Company Commander. At Kabrit the Company Orderly Room consisted of a small tent in which the company clerk Terry Madsen slept. There was just room, in addition, for a primus, a tin or two of coffee, and the telephone. One day, soon after arriving at Kabrit, Charles happened to be in B Company lines.

He returned to his own headquarters looking rather worried.

'Terry,' he said, 'I've just been to B Company. You know, for

Company Headquarters they've got a ruddy big E.P.I.P. tent, with tables and chairs. They've got trays marked "In" and "Out"; and they've got papers clipped together hanging on nails with names on them like "Returns" and "Action Pending". We don't seem to have any of that. Do you keep any files, Terry? If you do where in the hell are they?'

Madsen grinned cheerily. 'Right here, Mr. Upham,' he said, and dived under the pillow on his bed. Everything was neatly filed inside a rubber band.

'What about "Ins" and "Outs", and "Action Pending", and that sort of thing? Don't you need a bit of a system?'

'It's all here,' Madsen said blandly, tapping the rubber band.

'Well, look, Terry. Don't say what you're going for, but make some excuse to wander over to B Company. Have a look round their orderly room—make sure there's nothing you're overlooking.'

Madsen shook his head patiently, but went over and had a look nevertheless. When he returned he reported that B Company didn't do anything he didn't do.

'Ask yourself who'll be ready first to move in a hurry,' he pointed out to Upham. 'You see, it all gets bunged into this old ammo box and shoved on the truck; and then I wait around for you others to get packed up.'

Upham's face suddenly cleared. 'Well, that's just how it should be, Terry. You just carry on the way you like it. To hell with "Actions Pending"!'

That suited Terry.

10

In Syria

THIS is the Djedeide Box. In Syria. It is astride the Bekaa Valley and will stop the Germans from penetrating south down the valley. The enemy may come swiftly through Turkey and sweep into Syria. He will find a number of sympathizers here. Once through Syria he is at large in the Middle East and can put an intolerable squeeze on the Suez Canal.

Inside the Djedeide Box three brigades will sit, complete with supporting arms and all their supplies. If the enemy by-passes them they can debouch and attack him on the flanks or in the rear. To stop him driving through the Box it will be a mass of concrete emplacements and dug-outs, heavily wired and mined, bristling with armament. It will need a lot of work to make it ready.

On the eastern slopes of the valley the 20th Battalion began its digging. There was hard rock, necessitating much help from the engineers with their explosives; but there was plenty of cement, with paint and camouflage material to follow, and no enemy in sight. As a result the defensive positions were well done.

Upham, commanding C Company—and now a captain—was almost fanatical over the siting and digging of his defences. But to his previous abilities as an aggressive platoon commander there now seemed to be added a more mature shrewdness. Cunning was added to courage. To the task of laying out his company positions he brought a cool-headed wisdom that others had not suspected in him.

What was good for other companies appeared not good enough for him. He insisted on his positions being prepared with even greater care. They had to be finished off to perfection; then meticulously camouflaged. Colonel Burrows said: 'He had a very shrewd eye indeed for infantry positions. He believed in the vital necessity for camouflage and did it very carefully. Not only did he site his positions perfectly, but he planned out very fully how he would fight from them.'

Kippenberger, Brigadier of 5th Brigade, saw them too. 'Perfectly constructed,' he said. And after the war he told an interviewer that

they were the best and most skilfully prepared company positions
he had ever seen.

Over his diggings Upham presided like a mother hen with chickens.
There must be no tell-tale tracks, not even footprints, leading to his
dug-outs, except down the hard lanes where they wouldn't show. No
aerial photos would give him away.

One day Burrows and his Adjutant were walking down to C Company. They missed the proper track and were making straight across
the slopes towards Upham's Company Headquarters. In the distance
they saw Charles look up, peer at them deliberately across the hill.

Then they heard his voice suddenly ring out. 'Sergeant-Major!'
he shouted. 'Tell those two stupid bastards up the hill to get away
from my positions, whoever they are. They aren't going to leave tracks
around here.'

'Do you hear that?' the Adjutant said to Burrows. 'Are you going
to let Charlie get away with talk like that? He can see it's you.'

Burrows paused. Then he grinned. 'Of course Charlie knows it's
me, but he's pretending he doesn't. He *meant* us to hear him. Come
on . . . we'll turn round and go back. . . .'

Charles stood and watched them off the premises, like a game-
keeper eyeing a suspected poacher.

With a man of less quality than Jim Burrows—'Gentleman Jim'
they called him—Upham might not have got away with it.

*   *   *   *

Free from the acute pressure of war, the New Zealanders expectedly
got themselves into a little trouble. Bob May, now C Company's
sergeant-major, found Upham a doubtful quantity in the conduct of
orderly-room trials.

'What am I supposed to give this joker, Bob?' he would ask.
'What's the usual thing?'

May would read out the passage from the book. 'A fortnight's
pay is the maximum.'

'Now look here,' Upham would say to the miscreant in front of
him, 'you're a good soldier. What's gone wrong with you since you
came up here? Walking away from your post; getting shikker. Look—
if I let you off with a warning, what about giving me your word of
honour that you'll play the game for the next three weeks?'

The word-of-honour method worked all right out in the field.
But when the troops were close to Baalbek, doing guard duties, tempta-
tions were too great. However, Upham found that few men let him

down once they realized that the contempt of the boss was more effective a punishment than his fines. To have a V.C. despise you often hurts.

But then, while Charles was still concerned over the number of his men going A.W.L., who should completely disappear without trace but Eric Le Gros himself. 'Araq' Le Gros, some called him, because Leggy was a connoisseur in Middle East beverages and knew what ticked and what didn't.

'I beat it for six days,' Leggy explained. 'I holed up in a tent in the 26th Battalion lines and they never found me. There was a bit of a party on there—and it never stopped. I couldn't have got home if I'd tried. Then I heard that the M.P.s were searching every tent. Well, by this time I'd got hold of a dog. So I started off back to the 20th with the dog. I didn't want those M.P.s to catch me.'

Upham was standing by his tent when Le Gros' bedraggled figure came slowly into view. He watched him approach.

'Where have you been, Le Gros?' he asked stonily.

Leggy pointed vaguely in the direction of the 26th.

Upham looked him up and down. 'My God, you look terrible,' he said. 'You'd better——'

But at that moment Le Gros' newly acquired dog rushed forward, jumped up, and deposited its muddy paws on Upham's stomach.

Leggy thought this wasn't a very tactful homecoming.

'Don't hand me on to Burrows,' he pleaded when he came up on charge. 'Burrows will slaughter me.'

'I'll put you down for fourteen days C.B., Le Gros,' Upham said sternly. 'But I don't know what'll happen to my boots. Who's going to clean them? And after this . . . you'll have to go out on parades like all the rest. That'll keep you off the plonk.'

*   *   *   *

Some solid drinking went on in Syria. Saturday night was always the night of the big do. Sunday mornings were greeted with many mournful eyes. But on Sundays there was Church Parade, and some sort of turn-out was expected. Charles himself took charge of the 'Other Denominations' parade. The Roman Catholics paraded elsewhere for their own service and no questions were asked about which service a man chose to attend.

One particularly heavy Sunday morning saw Sergeant Beechey line up the parade of 'Other Denominations'. Upham arrived to take over, looked with astonishment on the pitifully thin muster of 'Other Denominations'—barely enough to comply with the Prayer Book's promise—'where two or three are gathered together . . .'

I

Charles apparently felt that some kind of public apology should be made to the unseen hosts of Christian spirits present in the Syrian atmosphere. So he eyed his tiny squad confidently, returned Beechey's smart salute, and announced loudly: 'Must be a hell of a lot of R.C.s this morning, Sergeant.'

Upham was not a religious man in the sense of being an ardent churchman. His religion was a way of living—a respect and awe for things of nature, a personal morality based on honesty and trust, and a hatred of badness. But he conformed to, and respected, the rituals of religious worship.

Padre Spence said to him, preparatory to taking a Church Parade of C Company: 'What hymns do your boys like, Charlie?'

Upham knew the answer. 'You know that one . . . dah dee dah dee . . .' he hummed unmusically.

'How do the words go?' Spence enquired tactfully.

'Oh, you know . . . "when the whips are cracking up yonder, I'll be there".'

Spence gulped hurriedly. 'Ah yes, Charlie . . . I know the one you *mean.*'

Charles had a profound respect for all ministers of religion, regardless of their denomination. A difference in dogma meant little to him. Perhaps his belief in the efficacy of the cloth stemmed from the time at Christ's College when girls from the Christchurch Girls' High School were invited to the college dance. They were allowed to come, but had to be chaperoned.

'I'll be chaperone,' Charles announced confidently to his schoolmates. Sure enough, when the taxi called for the girls, there sitting in the front seat was the very guarantee of respectability—a figure in clerical vest and dog-collar.

Charles found that by reversing his college waistcoat, and turning his stiff white collar round, he could quite well pass for a clergyman in the dim light of the taxi. It worked all right. The girls made it to the dance.

Colonel Burrows knew Charles probably better than anyone else: Upham, with his outspoken attitude towards most things military, a mixture of shyness and truculence; Burrows, All Black footballer and first-class cricketer, a model of tolerance and determined wisdom. Upham would do anything in the world for two people—one was Kippenberger, the other Burrows. His belief in their judgment was almost as strong as his hatred of the enemy.

Burrows says: 'I remember only one occasion when Charlie was drunk. That was in Syria.'

So it was. Peter Maxwell, John Phillips, and Charles had decided
to visit the 18th Battalion mess. Things went swimmingly there.
Brigadier Inglis was present and in top form. There was a ditch they
fell into when they started for home, and by the time they reached the
20th lines it seemed a crying shame that the rest of the battalion should
be sleeping and not joining in the general fun.

'Let's wake up old Ralph,' someone suggested, and with a little
difficulty they identified the Nissen hut in which Ralph Patterson, the
battalion second-in-command at the time, was sleeping. 'Here, get
some stones.'

With the enthusiasm of small boys they began throwing stones on
the tin roof of the hut. This made a very satisfactory clatter.

The fact that no one seemed to be wakened by the din served only
to increase their efforts, and a veritable rain of stones thundered
joyously over the head of the second-in-command. Then they extended
their activities to the huts of other officers.

'What's wrong with them?' Upham shouted thickly in disbelief.
'Come on, we'll go *inside* and wake 'em.'

But by this time the clamour had begun to worry the camp guards
—was it a raid by a few daring Syrian bandits—a fifth-columnist
trying some sabotage perhaps? And in the end a sentry decided he
needed help from his sleeping comrades in the guard-tent. Raising his
rifle, he fired a shot into the air.

'Garn!' Upham roared. 'Couldn't hit us if you tried!' So they
trooped inside the huts and made themselves thoroughly unpopular.

Then the Colonel arrived on the scene. Prepared to be tolerant of a
drunken frolic, nevertheless the fact that the guard had become involved demanded some action. . . . All three would report in the
morning, and a fair matting it promised to be. Upham's only excuse
at the time was a somewhat unsteady claim that 'You couldn't do that
in *my* lines, sir'—as a kind of complaint that anyone could sleep
through such a shower of metal on the roof.

The morning came. Phillips and Maxwell made their way sorrow-
fully to Battalion Headquarters by the usual track. But Charles now
realized how silly he had been. Rather than risk any other officer of
the battalion seeing him, he made his solitary way to Headquarters
by a circuitous route. Throughout the wigging that followed he stood
looking at the floor—utterly mortified, pathetically ashamed.

Burrows, a school-teacher by profession, told them that the incident was on the level of the pranks he expected from his twelve-year-
old boys. If they were going to behave like that when they took too
much liquor then they'd better watch their liquor.

In a spirit of shamed self-denial, all three voluntarily promised to go on the water-wagon for several weeks ahead. Burrows accepted that promise curtly, dismissed them, then rose from his chair and shepherded them across to the officers' mess. There was a mess rule that no one could shout a drink. Burrows thought the occasion allowed him to break the rule, and he restored their self-confidence by a quick round. So much for their self-denial—but this was an order.

Resolution and hardness on the one hand; shyness and intelligence on the other. With such a mixture of human qualities Upham was always something of a character. His response was always unpredictable. And amongst his worst qualities was his often unreasonable pig-headedness. Once he formed an opinion, or categorically stated some fact, nothing in heaven or on earth would shake him from it.

'Rum tastes better mixed with something else,' he declared, when the company received its rum ration. 'In tea, for example,' he stated firmly.

'In tea?' his junior officers gasped. 'Oh no, not in tea, sir.'

'Yes, in tea,' he repeated. 'Rum's *best* in tea.'

With horror that mounted every minute they argued with him. Even the cooks and the C.Q.M.S. joined in. Rum in tea is simply appalling, they said. The men liked it neat.

'Have you *tried* it in tea?' they asked him in despair, because once he got this bee stuck in his bonnet there'd be no stopping him.

'No,' he replied doggedly. 'But *it's best in tea.*'

So the whole rum ration was poured into the tea urn.

The fearful result was all that the pessimists predicted. But Upham said there must have been something wrong with the tea.

Then for a time he was in charge of the battalion rum store. Stocks had sunk low and he had to leave the battalion for a few days. 'You take charge of this rum, Leggy,' he said. 'And keep your eye on it.'

Le Gros politely acknowledged the order, perhaps too politely.

On his return Charles looked around quickly. 'Well, Leggy-boy, how did the rum go? How much did you drink?'

With some forebodings Leggy produced the one remaining bottle.

'My oath, is that all? One bottle! Have you been shouting the whole ruddy battalion? I suppose you batmen have been grogged up the whole time. Anyway, let's taste it.'

With even more foreboding, Le Gros handed over the surviving bottle, saw Upham pour one for himself, raise the cup and take a good draught.

A pause.

'Leggy, you utter bastard. This rum's diluted. It's half water, isn't it?'

Le Gros nodded glumly. 'There was only half a bottle left,' he said, as if that explained everything. 'I thought it would look better if we built it up a bit.'

'You did, eh? All right, I suppose there's nothing we can do about it. But look—B Company are next on the distribution list. Cork it up again, Leggy, then take this bottle along to B Company Officers' Mess. They'll never know the difference.'

*   *   *   *

As he always had been, Upham continued to be a thorough pest to the Q.M. staff. By constant arguing he obtained for his men the best of what was offering, always pressing for more and for something better. So keen was he to see his men equipped with more grenades that he offered to pay out of his own pocket a reward for every extra grenade his men could acquire from other sources.

He was keen like that on vital equipment, yet casual and rough in matters of personal appearance. As for shaving, for example, he could have won the title of the fastest and worst shaver in the British Commonwealth. He appeared to use four strokes—two violent ones down the left side of the face, then two on the right side. Finish. He was too impatient to bother about the odd tufts that sprouted in between the beaten lanes.

For variety, company commanders inspected one another's companies. Peter Maxwell of D Company came over to inspect Upham's.

Maxwell stopped disapprovingly in front of one C Company stalwart. 'Did you shave, soldier?' he demanded, looking at the stubbly chin.

The soldier shifted uncomfortably. Then his guilty eyes turned slowly and became riveted on Upham's jowl, with its stalks paralleling the mown tracks like a tornado's swath through a forest.

Maxwell followed his eyes, swallowed slightly, then turned back to inspect the man's rifle.

'Humph. Must have spent your time cleaning your rifle.' And he passed on.

There was a message waiting at the orderly room when this inspection was over. Upham was to report at Battalion Headquarters.

There Colonel Burrows said to him: 'Charlie, the Brigade is sending two officers to inspect some defences in the Lebanon. They are being dug by an artillery regiment, but they want some New Zealand infantry officers to report on them, and make any suggestions. Brigadier Inglis has chosen Johansen of the 27th as one. You're the other. You'll be in pretty classy company, I dare say, so watch your step. You're going the day after tomorrow.'

Late one afternoon Johansen and Upham reported to the headquarters of their artillery hosts. They were rather surprised that first evening when, on entering the mess, they noticed a bottle of Scotch on a sideboard bearing the label 'The Colonel'.

The Colonel himself arrived soon after. It had apparently become the unit tradition that the Colonel's entrance should be solemn. It was indeed. With all standing at attention, the C.O. walked slowly down the length of the ante-room in dramatic silence.

After mess Upham and Johansen were beckoned to join him, and the labelled whisky bottle was uncorked. Under the balm of good spirit the chill of exaggerated formality began to thaw. But it was inevitable that the talk should turn to Singapore, which had fallen to the Japanese only a few weeks before.

Drinking freely, Charles became more and more talkative over the subject of Singapore. He had strong opinions about it. But the Colonel, after analysing the reasons for the capitulation, just as strongly declared that no other course had been possible.

Then Upham blurted: 'There can be only one man to blame for the fall of Singapore, one man only, and that's the one at the top.'

'Oh?' said the Colonel icily. 'And how do you make that out?'

'Because all the evidence points to it,' Upham retorted. 'And I reckon the men in charge there can't have known a bee from a bull's foot.'

The C.O.'s face flushed. 'I'll have you know, Upham, that the commander at Singapore is a personal friend of mine.'

'I don't care,' Upham shot back, 'if he's your favourite uncle.'

'Then I'll have an apology from you, Upham, forthwith!'

'That'll be the day!' Upham flashed, and he banged his glass down on the table.

The Colonel stood up abruptly. 'Leave the mess at once!' he ordered.

'And you!' Upham snapped, his temper aflame. He rose sharply, turned, and marched out. Inside, everyone in the room sat in stunned silence.

Johansen, distressed by the sudden clash, stood up and said steadily: 'I'm afraid I must withdraw also.'

But the Colonel took him by the arm, guided him back into a chair saying: 'Perhaps we've had too much to drink. Let's forget about it.'

It was some time before Johansen could get away. Then, to his surprise, he found Charles outside their tent, leaning on the tail-board of the truck they had brought with them, and inside the truck all their gear, ready packed for home. Batman and driver were there too, fully dressed, roused out of bed by Upham and given orders to prepare to leave.

'About bloody time,' Upham growled at Johansen. 'We're off home. What have you been doing—sucking up to that bastard?'

Johansen took no notice. He was senior to Upham. Quietly he told the batman and the driver to return to their quarters and go back to bed. They wouldn't be leaving that night, after all.

Finally he produced another bottle. 'Now come on, Charlie. We'll have this in our tent. What the hell do you think the Brig would say if we beetled off home without making our report?'

It took some time, and a fair part of the bottle, to mollify Charles, but in the end his anger died and he agreed that they would stay to complete their task. But it was asking too much to expect him to be civil to the Colonel. Rank did not enter into a matter like that, he considered.

Next day they began work. The Colonel ignored them. Just as well, perhaps, for it wasn't long before Upham's forbearance was strained too far. He agreed with Johansen that it wasn't fair to expect artillery-men to construct sound positions, as if they were infantrymen. But as they tramped from one position to the next his patience grew thinner.

For the whole defensive area was a complete and utter failure. Whatever mistakes were possible to make were made. The concrete could be seen miles away; most of the positions were hopelessly sited. 'And as for camouflage,' Upham said, 'you might as well have painted red, white, and blue flags all over them.'

Then they made their first report to the officer appointed to receive it. There were two stages in their task—first to report on the existing positions; second, to peg out better ones. They decided to report first, do the pegging-out later.

They said what they thought.

And then, to their amazement, the officer said: 'Look . . . don't bother to do any more. Just put in a report that everything's satisfactory and forget about it.'

Now it wasn't only Upham who rushed to the lines and ordered the batman and driver to pack up for home. Johansen piled into the truck in a spirit of cold fury. He, too, wasn't going to have any more of this. Off they set for the New Zealand Division again.

'You're the senior,' Charlie said, as they arrived in their old brigade area. 'You'll have to tell the Brig. But I'll have the drinks ready for you when you come out.'

Johansen did the best he could with Brigadier Inglis, but there was a limit to what he felt he could say. He didn't feel happier when Inglis told him that, whatever the circumstances, his job was to get the proper positions pegged out. He and Upham would return and complete their assignment.

So back they went and, keeping their tongues well in check, worked day and night on the defences, marking and pegging, until at last the artillery regiment, and its Colonel, could expect to survive for a time if the invasion came.

The few days' special leave in Beirut that followed were like nectar.

*   *   *   *

Upham and Johansen had not been lightly chosen for the inspection job in the Lebanon. Already both of them had acquired a reputation for the skill of their defence work. Their ideas were a little different at times from the conventional, but the results were outstanding.

As good luck had it, Johansen had a few of his machine-guns emplaced in Upham's company area at Djedeide. So they co-operated on their schemes and together felt rather proud of their combined efforts.

General Holmes, commander of 9th Army in Syria, came on a tour of inspection of the Djedeide Box. Followed by the inevitable retinue, he came striding down to Upham's area, where Charles and Johansen waited in some apprehension. They stood at attention on top of one of their best-concealed posts.

Then, after introductions, the General said: 'Well, Upham, I'm told you have some really first-rate positions to show me. Where's the first one?'

'Right here, sir,' said Upham.

'Oh yes,' said the General, 'but where, man? I haven't all day, you know.'

Upham bridled. 'I said *right here*, sir, In fact, you're standing on the bloody thing!'

*   *   *   *

The New Zealanders learned about mules in Syria. To carry supplies to troops stationed on trackless mountain ridges mule units were attached to the division.

The mules arrived with strict trade-union rules about them. They were not to be used for more than so many miles per day, nor were they to carry more than a certain weight. Charlie Upham thought a man could carry that weight himself.

To the officer delivering the mules Charles said: 'What's the use of a mule if it won't carry more than a man?'

The officer began patiently to explain that it wasn't so much what they carried but what they saved a man from having to carry. To Upham, with his remarkable stamina, that was no argument.

He launched into a long description of what he thought the mules ought to carry. The argument developed hotly, the visiting officer stoutly defending his animals. It ended up with Charles claiming, with no justification whatever, that the man didn't know anything about the ruddy mules and 'Anyway, they're too damned fat!'

This put the mule officer into a towering rage and he threatened court-martial and other awful things.

Upham, however, did know and understand animals. He loved them. During most of his stay in Syria he owned a dog. And when one night in the Western Desert he returned to his dug-out and found that a cat had had a batch of kittens on his bed, where they were all happily snoozing, he undressed silently and slept on the sand outside rather than disturb them. It was a love born of years in the open, living with his horse and dogs in the outback of New Zealand.

For several days a number of the officers were away from their units doing tactical exercises without troops, the officers themselves forming platoons and taking turns in assuming command. These were live-ammunition exercises, not mere paper battles.

It came Upham's turn to command a fighting approach through the foothills and up a valley. Then, at night, the mules would be used as they moved into steeper country.

The advance began in the afternoon, Upham leading the way, with Johnny Sullivan, the 20th's Intelligence Officer, alongside him. Sullivan had to point out the route.

The platoon had been going two hours, and had made its way well up the valley, before Sullivan came back to Upham with a worried expression. He said: 'Charlie, I'm sorry. . . .'

'What's the matter, Johnny?'

'Charlie, I'm afraid I've made a mistake. I've guided you up the wrong valley. We can't get up here any further; we'll have to go back nearly to the start line, then head off to the left a bit to bring us on to the proper route.'

Upham said: 'That's a pity, Johnny. But don't worry. We're not going to turn back. There's no time for that. We'll go straight ahead, up over the ridge and down into the proper valley the other side.'

Sullivan told him he didn't think it could be done. He thought it was impossible. The hills were like precipices.

'But that's what we'll do,' Upham said quietly. 'We won't go back. We'll get there somehow.'

He led them on and on; and later Sullivan acknowledged that what he had thought impossible Upham was able to accomplish. While the platoon followed in exhausted distress, Upham climbed on unfalteringly. As one man later described him: 'He was unique from a physical and temperamental viewpoint. I do not know of any other New Zealand soldier with his powers of endurance.'

It was one more example of the man's single-mindedness, a refusal to let anything turn him from a single objective.

As night came the mules were brought up and assembled for the next move forward. But this had to be a silent move. So Upham issued orders to the other officers to muffle the hooves of the mules with sandbag material. It was a more difficult job than it sounded, and Upham watched indulgently as his officer-troops struggled to make any progress.

Finally he smiled knowingly and said: 'Hold it. Hold it. You townies just haven't got *any idea*. I'll do the job myself.'

So, watched by the officers, he called up all his skill in animal handling and began wrapping up the hooves one by one. It was hard work, and it seemed to get harder. But rather than let them see that he, too, found it difficult, he worked with increasing determination and vigour.

He was breathing heavily by the time it was finished. He tried not to show that the job had all but beaten him too.

'It's a matter of understanding animals,' he explained in a kindly way. 'You've got to keep the beggars still. Now, if we're all ready, we'll get started.'

It was true that the mules had kept still. Whether that was a tribute to Upham's powers no one knows. But the stoical animals had stood fast, had reluctantly allowed the mufflers to be put on, and continued standing immobile until the job was finished.

But now, as Upham's triumph was about to be demonstrated, and the mules to advance silently over the rocky paths, a telepathic signal must have passed from one beast to another.

Almost as one, they started squirming and twisting, pawing at their own hooves, scraping and rubbing.

In horror and distress Upham watched the awful spectacle. For within a minute every muffler lay loose on the ground, tattered and stripped, and the uncovered mules stepped delicately away from them in quiet satisfaction.

Upham's fury was nearly catastrophic.

*   *   *   *

Back with the company soon afterwards, Charles found Leggy becoming a bit more trying. Leggy had too many independent qualities to make the perfect batman. It requires a good deal of self-restraint to find that your batman has gone on leave and taken your boots, so that you cannot appear on parade. And it requires something more than self-restraint for an officer to make a cup of early-morning tea for his own batman when the latter has returned late from leave the previous night with more araq than is wise. But Eric Le Gros and Charles Upham were both unusual people.

Due to his earlier indiscretions, Le Gros found he had to suffer the indignities of going on manœuvres and on sentry. But he was a distressingly poor sentry. He became a member of a small guard that occupied a tent near a bridge. Le Gros was placed on sentry duty on the bridge. The remainder of the men slept in the tent nearby. Unfortunately Leggy went to sleep also, and while he slept the tent was neatly unpegged and removed from over the heads of the unconscious guards.

Leggy would have been court-martialled for this, but somehow the authorities accepted the version that the tent had fallen out of the back of a truck. It would never do to probe the matter too far, or even to ask Upham if he knew anything about the real facts.

As May 1942 came round, all battalions went out eastwards to the Syrian desert to conduct manœuvres. Those units who were near the frontier at Aleppo performed with more enthusiasm than discretion, and an international incident, with interesting possibilities, was narrowly averted when the Kiwis advanced cheerfully across the frontier into Turkey.

Charles's men of C Company had the task of advancing along an oil pipe-line to hold it against imaginary enemy forces who would be seeking to cut the line. It was a hard march out, the men moving all night on foot, with the imaginary enemy certain to be defeated in the imaginary battle next morning. But whether or not the enemy were defeated, certainly one would expect some interesting re-deployment, flanking movements, platoons in attack, forming a rapid box, etc., when the end of the march was reached.

Morning came with the troops tired but expectant.

There appeared a liaison officer in a car, complete with map showing the last-known battle positions. Upham studied it.

'Well, what will your orders be?' the liaison officer asked.

'You tell me first what the school solution is,' countered Upham. 'Then I'll give my orders.'

'The school solution is to withdraw,' the liaison officer said brightly.

'Withdraw!' exclaimed Charles, his jaw dropping. 'After marching out all night—now we march back?'

'That's right,' came the cheerful reply. 'That's the school solution.'

'Well I'll be . . . !'

Upham had a remarkable flow of language, very apt for an occasion like this.

It was while battalions were on manoeuvres that word came to return rapidly to camp. Back they went, and packing up began. New Zealand? The Pacific? India? Or the Western Desert again?

Wishful thinking clouded judgment, but there was certainly the example of the Australians, who had already packed one division back home to meet the threat of the Japanese.

Terry Madsen, C Company clerk, said to Upham: 'What do I do? If we're going home I'll want these files, these 347Bs, and all this junk. But if we get sent up into action they'll be a damned nuisance. How do they expect me to pack up the orderly room if they don't say where we're going?'

Upham looked at him solemnly with his serious deep-fire eyes. 'You pack for action, Terry,' he advised.

As they struck camp, and men packed their gear in battle order, Upham found he wouldn't need both pairs of boots. 'We won't want these, Leggy,' he said.

That was enough. Rapidly locating his particular crony at the time, Leggy said: 'We're on to a good thing here—the officers can take only one pair of boots. Now this is what we'll do. . . .'

How many officers parted with their second pair of boots to Leggy and his mate is not clear; nor is it clear if Le Gros actually told them it was an order from Captain Upham that they discard one pair.

But as the convoys moved off to the south, Upham took his pipe from his mouth and asked in amused despair: 'How much did you get for all the boots, Leggy-boy?'

11

Break-out from Minqar Qaim

ROMMEL was to blame. Having been driven out of Cyrenaica in January 1942, he had edged back to a position near Gazala and Bir Hacheim, but then both sides had lain dormant for several months.

On 27th May he struck fiercely.

Within eight weeks 8th Army was decisively defeated, despite outnumbering Rommel's forces almost two to one, despite numerical superiority in tanks and artillery. The German commander did it by concentrating superior forces against the isolated Allied groups that were thrown in piecemeal against him.

Over the mountains and down the valleys of Syria the New Zealand convoys roared out, through the orchards of Palestine, the sand-wastes of Sinai, past Cairo, the Delta, and on to Mersa Matruh, far west of Alexandria. And as they moved into the desert they encountered 8th Army in retreat, thousands of vehicles crowding the road as they all poured eastwards. Around Matruh the division spread out into defensive positions, and there waited for the enemy.

But anxious that his division should not become a beleaguered garrison force in Matruh, Freyberg urged that he should be given a more fluid role. This was done, and the division was ordered to hand over the defence of Matruh to other troops and to move south into the desert to the area of Minqar Qaim. There it was to operate as a mobile force to hold the low ridges in that region, and wherever possible to use its mobility to attack and delay the enemy.

While this move was in progress the 20th was given the task of guarding a party of New Zealand engineers who were laying 9000 mines in the path of Rommel's advance. They would follow the division to Minqar Qaim later.

The mines were to be laid on the site of an old mine-field for which no plans existed. There would be risks, there might be casualties from the old mines. But this gap in the line had to be closed.

The engineers, assisted by Indian troops, laid their mines. Protecting them sat the 20th, with Charles Upham tensioned like a spring in anticipation of the action that all knew was impending.

He reconnoitred quickly round his company area, with Leggy alongside. Then he started walking back to the group of slit trenches that were his temporary headquarters.

'Hold on, boss,' said Leggy. 'This is where the old mines are, isn't it? The sappers haven't been over this yet. Let's go back the way we came.'

'You go if you like, Leggy. I want to get back quickly.'

'But the ruddy mines . . . ?'

'Blast the mines! They're old. Most of them will be duds by now. Anyway, the sappers have to risk it; why shouldn't we? But you go on, Leggy. You go round the long way. I'm in a hurry.'

Leggy swallowed hard. 'It's O.K., boss. I'm coming.' And he paced warily alongside Upham, right across the old field, treading the ground with the delicacy of a ballet dancer.

After helping with the mines the 20th rejoined the division at Minqar Qaim, but was almost immediately ordered to embus again and move northwards. As the men were climbing into the trucks, a drone came from the skies. Eyes turned upwards. Then a flare floated down.

Charles was away from his company at that moment, but in the light of the flare he came racing back, shouting to his men to run for a wadi some yards away. They fled there as the bombs came tumbling down. More than twenty Stukas pounded the column.

Upham and Sergeant Monteath of Battalion Intelligence found themselves diving for the same slit trench. Monteath won.

'You young devil!' Charles shouted good-humouredly, his face alight with the sharp drama of the dive-bombing attack.

But Monteath wondered why Upham was bothering about a slit trench, for next second he was standing up, searching the wadi for his men, and shouting at the top of his voice for them to engage the planes with small-arms fire. Charles's voice on the battlefield became high-pitched with excitement and carried great distance over the noise of firing and exploding bombs.

Spending the night northwards of the division, the 20th returned to Minqar Qaim early on the morning of 27th June. Everybody then dug in as well as they could amidst the hard rock and stones. Here now was almost the whole division, lying along the Minqar Qaim ridge, with its artillery and trucks hard by. The 4th Brigade, with the 20th, was out on the flat ground east of the main ridge.

It was at this stage that the division learnt that the commander of

8th Army had been relieved of his post and Auchinleck, Commander-in-Chief Middle East, had assumed personal control. There were orders to make a stand in the Mersa Matruh area; orders to retire to Alamein; orders to retire but only after offering stubborn resistance. It is still a matter of doubt which orders were finally given to all formations.

All that the New Zealand Division appreciated as dawn came on 27th June was that they were on an 'island' in the desert, with few battle-worthy troops near, and Rommel's flood was about to pour upon them.

At 7.30 that morning the 21st Panzer Division began its advance from its overnight positions. The German 90th Light Division moved ahead also. Within the hour the enemy had run against the spikes of the New Zealand Division sitting astride Minqar Qaim. Artillery on both sides opened the battle, the Kiwi twenty-five-pounders effectively keeping at a distance a screen of tanks that ushered the panzers on to the battlefield.

With the gunners running the battle so far, more ominous signs appeared at 10.30 a.m. when a patrol from the Maori Battalion sighted an enemy column moving into position some three miles away. It was advancing on a front a mile wide, led by its tanks, behind them up to a thousand trucks laden with infantry. Almost leisurely its artillery came into action, then its mortars, while the New Zealanders answered in kind with a steady, watchful enthusiasm.

The exchange of high-explosive shells continued the rest of the morning, while the infantry in their slit trenches or stone sangars watched and waited. Towards midday it was apparent that a great mass of the enemy was passing across the north front of the division and there were signs that some of it was then turning southwards so as to cut off the New Zealanders from the east.

By early afternoon Rommel had four armoured divisions in the Minqar Qaim area. The New Zealanders were obviously in for a warm time, but they wondered, as the day advanced, why the Germans were so reluctant to move in to the attack. It was a reluctance born of knowledge that by nightfall they would have the New Zealanders completely surrounded.

*　　　*　　　*　　　*

There had been a lull in the shelling, but about two o'clock the enemy guns broke into fresh life, followed by the mortars. Whereas earlier in the day the New Zealand guns had been the target, now the Germans began shelling the infantry positions as well.

Charles Upham had one of the company's three-ton trucks and had driven it from the escarpment down towards his company lines. He was sitting on the bonnet looking out over the desert.

'Bob,' he called to C.S.M. May, who was near him. 'There's a primus in the back. What about boiling up? I reckon we won't have time later on.'

May climbed into the back of the truck to get the primus.

There was a sudden crash, the sound of breaking glass, and the truck gave a convulsive lurch. Bob May found himself leaping for safety out of the back of the truck.

'What was it?' he asked.

Upham, still sitting on the bonnet, said casually: 'An eighty-eight went right through the back, out through the windscreen. But where the hell is that primus? Come on, get a move on, Bob.'

May thought the two matters hardly compared in importance. He started towards the truck again.

The next shot smashed the tail-board.

'This is getting a bit hot, isn't it?' he suggested. 'We're the target, I think.'

Upham shrugged. 'Near misses don't hurt. . . . Come on, Bob, get that primus cracking or we won't get a cup of tea before the damned show starts.'

But now tanks suddenly appeared through the dust, and all along the front German troop-carrying trucks came heading in. Here now came the attack—infantry jumping down, like ugly flowers suddenly sprouting all over the desert, mortars and machine-guns being mounted and beginning to fire.

'Hold it! Hold it!' Upham was shouting, with his men itching to fire.

They waited till the enemy trucks closed to a range of 400 yards; only then did the New Zealand infantry and anti-tank gunners open up.

Out swarmed the Germans, racing for cover in the low desert scrub. They were good men, too, men of the Panzer Grenadiers. Like well-trained campaigners, they dropped swiftly to earth, began returning the New Zealand fire spiritedly. The clamour of battle rose quickly to a crescendo over the desert hills and flats of Minqar Qaim.

The Kiwis clung tight to their slit trenches. If one merely put a hand up above ground level it felt as if the Germans were all firing at that. The whole battlefield seemed to be alight, the air thick with fire.

And then, to the stupefaction of his company, there was Upham above ground, running from post to post in the open. 'Don't waste your ammo!' he was shouting. 'Ease up on it. Keep it till they come in!'

And across the flat to the next group of slitties . . . a few shouted words
. . . then running on to the next. . . .

'Keep watching! You'll never kill a German like that, son,' he called
to a new hand lying deep in his trench with his face buried in the sand.
And as he raced around, from one section to another, the mortars
seemed to follow him, and the small-arms fire tore at the stones around
his feet.

'That's Upham,' the gunner said to his mates as they rammed round
after round of twenty-five-pounder ammunition into the gun. They were
firing over open sights now, at lowest trajectory, their shells screaming
out straight over the heads of the C Company infantry. They could see
that infantry officer running around the field right in front of their
gun, crouching as he dashed through the haze of smoke, dust, and
fire.

'Blast him—he'll cop one from us in a minute,' they complained.

Out on the exposed front a platoon thought the pressure was
becoming too severe. They started singling out, falling back towards
the main company position. Upham rushed over towards them.

'What the hell are you doing? How many casualties have you had?'
They told him.

'Hold on here!' he ordered. 'Let me know when you have thirty
per cent casualties. Then I'll see about it. But we've got to stay put in
this show. We mustn't budge an inch.' Then he ran back across the sand
to his other platoons.

Runners were needed to take messages out to the front, across to
companies on the flanks. Upham went himself, rather than ask his
men to face the fire in the open. And if he saw one of his men unnecessarily exposed to the fire he sharply reprimanded him.

'Keep your rump down, you fool. Do you want to sleep on your
stomach the rest of your life?' He lashed at them with his tongue for
taking risks. They in their turn looked on uncomprehending, as they
saw him running backwards and forwards over the battlefield, apparently immune and unconcerned.

But from early in the engagement Upham had made a discovery.
The enemy fire was well disciplined, but it was inaccurate. A man
might be hit by mischance, but unless he stood still the risk of being
hit was worth taking, when morale and control needed someone prepared to move around.

His company mortars ran low in ammunition. Rather than have
his men seen coming back from the firing line, he ran back himself,
ferried fresh supplies out to the mortar-men.

'He was always a hard man to get on the phone,' Colonel Burrows
K

said. 'He never seemed to be at Company H.Q. Someone would go for him. Then he would come on the line breathless, as if he had been running.'

Lieutenant Moodie with his anti-tank guns had earlier sent his batman to Upham's Company H.Q. to act as liaison with the rifle platoons. As the battle grew more torrid he looked over towards C Company, expecting to see his man come crawling back with any necessary information. He didn't envy the man his job. The air was too deathly.

Then across the flats Moodie saw Upham coming in person. The German fire was heavy. Upham was wearing a soft hat and, as he ran, he leant to one side, holding his hat down on an angle as if to keep out the bullets, like a man battling against the wind.

In the midst of Moodie winning his own M.C. that afternoon, he did not cease to wonder at the spectacle of Charles Upham moving continuously around the field, spending more time above ground level than below it, shouting, running, encouraging, swearing, working like a beaver.

Bob May was now out on the right flank with one of the platoons. There was a machine-gun out beyond the mine-field giving them a bad time. Try as they might they could not locate it. He sent a message in to Company H.Q. to ask if anything could be done about it.

Upham peered into the sun. The desert was trembling with heat, and the ground itself was lost in a mirage-like haze. Trust the Huns to pick the right angle to attack from. You couldn't tell what was what out there. That glassy shimmering spot way out—was it a truck, a tank, a group of men, a big gun, just a patch of scrub? But out of the haze the Germans were steadily coming. He had to try to identity something. And where was that blasted machine-gun that was worrying Bob May's boys?

A truck driver named Falconer was standing near him. 'Come on, Scotty,' Upham called suddenly. 'Get your truck going. Take her down there by Company H.Q.'

So Falconer gingerly manœuvred his big three-tonner into a spot near the slit trenches that formed the headquarters. What a spot for a truck! Out there in the open, in plain sight of the enemy, Falconer thought that he wouldn't have a truck to drive much longer.

And then, as the men of Company H.Q. watched from the shelter of their slitties, up on to the truck Upham began climbing. Up on to the step, on to the edge of the tray, then with a squirm to the very top of the cab, and Upham drew himself upright, standing on top of the cab with his legs apart.

Deliberately he raised his binoculars and gazed steadily towards the advancing Germans.

Terry Madsen looked up at him in dismay. No time for politeness. 'Get down, you idiot!' he shouted. For Upham stood there motionless, a veritable monument overlooking the battlefield of Minqar Qaim.

'Get down, boss! Get down!' they yelled to him. 'They'll hit you.'

Upham, his eyes glued to his binoculars, called back to them: 'They've been trying all day. Haven't hit me yet.'

There was a pause, while they shrank into their trenches as a burst of machine-gun fire seemed to whistle only inches over their heads. And then Upham's voice came clearly down to them again. 'Half right, near that black rock—it's a tank, about twelve hundred yards. Four fingers left—two more tanks and one truck. Jerries getting a gun into action. About a span to the left again—looks like a mortar, moving in closer, about six hundred yards. . . .'

And when he had calmly seen all he wanted he climbed down steadily.

They looked at him in anger rather than awe. The boss had no right to do a thing like that. Brave if you like, but that sort of bravery went too far.

But did it? No. Because Upham had more than one thought in his mind as he mounted to the top of Falconer's truck. The first thought was his knowledge of the inaccurate shooting by the Germans. He could rely on that. But another feature of the enemy fire was the low trajectory of it—as if the Germans were deliberately trying to keep the New Zealanders deep in their slitties. It seemed to be only inches above ground level. All right—if the fire was low he could be out of danger if he climbed high.

But those were only passing thoughts. His main thought was simply that someone had to see what was happening out front. He was the best man to do it.

So he stood up like a lighthouse, a target for all, but not a bullet went near him.

Once more he had weighed the risks, grave ones this time, against the needs of the moment.

Anyway, he was having a lucky day, he told himself.

*   *   *   *

The afternoon drew on to evening. Nowhere did the enemy break through the steady, controlled fire of the New Zealand infantry. Nor did they risk throwing their tanks into the muzzles of our guns. It was a duel of bullets and shell, not a personal conflict. German infantry who tried to come to grips were beaten back.

But the events of the day were no comfort to the New Zealanders. They were now attacked on three sides; artillery ammunition was down to thirty-five rounds a gun; they had no tanks; and the evidence grew ominously that during the day the Germans had thrown a ring right around Minqar Qaim. The line of retreat to the east was cut. The Germans did not need to make a frontal attack. Next day, with all their divisions in position, they would chew up the New Zealanders piece by piece.

Freyberg realized that to save his division he would have to break out of the circle. It would be a gamble, but there was little choice. But he had barely given the preliminary orders before he himself was wounded, and Brigadier Inglis took command of the division. Burrows moved up to become Brigade Commander.

Inglis directed that the break-out should be done half an hour after midnight. It would have to be a surprise affair, with no warning, no artillery preparation. The whole division would have to withdraw furtively from its battle positions, assemble in the darkness, then wait for zero hour.

Then the chosen infantry would make a silent approach against the Germans lying directly to the east. As soon as they were detected, they would charge ahead with bullet and bayonet. They would punch a hole right through the enemy line.

Behind them the transport would have been formed up waiting, with the rest of the division sitting silently in the trucks. And when the assaulting infantry signalled that a breach had been made, the trucks, the guns, the ambulances, everything would pour through the gap.

It had the one merit of simplicity. To think of it even now is chilling —the division surrounded by Germans, with their tanks, just waiting for dawn to move in and destroy. The plan—simply to throw themselves bodily against one spot in the ring; to disregard the fire, the tanks, the casualties; to burst right through; and to hope that enough destruction would be done on the way to allow the mass of the division's transport to race through as well.

It could be a holocaust. It could be an epic.

The infantry of 4th Brigade would punch the hole, 19th Battalion leading in the centre, 20th on the left, the Maoris on the right.

Once the transport escaped through, the attackers would embus and the whole division move far eastward to the defences at Alamein.

*   *   *   *

Night came, and a clear moon rose like a ghost over the desert.

4th Brigade assembled in the dark, pulling back from their slit trenches out in the open, forming up in silence on the start line, their transport drawn in tight behind them.

Two battalions were late reaching the start line and the clock had advanced to 1.45 a.m. before everyone was ready. For the commanders this delay was a period of anxiety. Once before, at Maleme, Burrows had had to make an attack when his troops had not arrived in time. The delay spelt failure on that occasion. Now at Minqar Qaim, with Burrows commanding 4th Brigade, he had to wait and wait till all were ready.

But to the men in the ranks, who nevertheless knew what was ahead of them, the delay was just another excuse for sleeping. They dozed where they lay, and when they felt the nudge in the ribs from their section-leader they woke calmly and quietly, knowing that the time had come. Each man knew that the test of his own manhood was at hand.

But it was not all grim. There was the spectacle of big 'Snowy' Smith of the 20th, a soft-spoken, likeable giant of over six feet, who was gravely concerned because the rim of his tin hat was very shiny and conspicuous. With some glee he unearthed a desert topee, anchored it firmly *on top* of his tin hat, and thereby made himself about seven feet tall. It certainly hid the shiny rim of his helmet. In such fashion he prepared to advance against the enemy—a most impressive sight, an excellent landmark to steer by, and no doubt a formidable and startling apparition to the unsuspecting Afrika Korps.

And when at last they were all ready Burrows said quietly: 'All right. Let's get started.'

J. L. Scoullar, author of the official New Zealand war history *Battle for Egypt*, graphically wrote:

'As soon as the Maoris reached their start line, 4th Brigade advanced. Probably definite orders to move were received by the companies poised on their lines. No one remembers them. The start seemed to be automatic, as if a familiar spirit had whispered that there was a rendezvous to keep and it was time to be on the way.'

There was bright moonlight over the field, but the night seemed dark. It was all silence, just the rhythmic chuffing of men's boots against the sand and the stones, rifles held high, men walking forward with fear and hope in their hearts, wondering when the earth in front of them would awake and blaze. They were walking towards the enemy, to punch the hole right through the line, to make the gap through which the New Zealand Division must escape.

The fabled spirit that exists between soldiers is born at times like this; not in the frenzy of the encounter, in the violence of the battle, but in the moments when men walk together into danger, steady and deliberate, each man alone, but bound together in some invisible way with his neighbour walking forward a few yards to his right or left.

They walked 200 yards . . . 500 . . . 1000 yards. And still no sign of the enemy.

Then a single shot came . . . another . . . and in a moment the whole front erupted into flame.

Ahead of the advancing troops a thick curtain of fire was flung up, the interlocking tracer forming an impenetrable screen. Would we still attempt to break through it? How many would succeed?

'Any delay at this stage must have been fatal, but a most amazing and thrilling thing happened. To a man the whole brigade charged forward. No orders were given; no urging forward by officers and N.C.O.s. With shouting, cheering, and war-cries every man broke into a run as if he knew exactly what was expected of him.'

So wrote Burrows afterwards.

Into the teeth of the fire the New Zealanders flung themselves. For the 19th, in the van, it was not so difficult at first, for they found only light opposition straight ahead of them. But on the left the 20th, charging down into a gully, ran into the thick of the German defences. Into there the 19th turned also to help their friends.

Here in this wadi war was fought savagely.

Germans in slit trenches were bayoneted or shot. Men following behind did the same to their bodies, for fear that a German might be shamming and would fire on them from the rear. German trucks burst into flame. Others were used in desperate efforts to escape the ruthless New Zealanders.

Through the wadi they poured, shooting, grenading, bayoneting, shouting, and yelling.

With the 20th rushed Charles Upham. Those who saw him at the start noticed the huge load of grenades he carried, some said in a sand-bag, but certainly in a stuffed haversack slung around his shoulders. Charging into the wadi in the very front of his men, he left the bayoneting to the others, concentrated on the trucks and other vehicles with his arsenal of grenades.

The weirdness and drama of that night is still fresh in the minds of those who took part. The sheer audacity of the plan . . . the chatter of machine-guns in the darkness . . . the lines of tracer that men seemed just to ignore . . . the leaping fires of burning trucks . . . the shouts and screams . . . the chilling sounds of close conflict . . . and the indescribable din of a confused battle.

While through all the noise the men of C Company could hear Upham's voice, shouting and calling as he led them on, his voice a beacon and a rallying point for the whole company.

Not for him the role of the company commander to merely co-ordinate the attack, to watch and to guide. He was at one time the commander as well as the foremost combatant.

They watched him with his bag of grenades, tossing them at every target he saw, regardless of the risk of wounding himself from the explosion of his own bombs. It was throw . . . throw . . . rush in . . . another truck—throw . . . rush.

There were many who saw him that night. But none can say for sure how often he dashed in against the enemy vehicles, heedless of the fire pouring at him, and flung his grenades at them. ('Perhaps six or seven,' Upham grudgingly acknowledged after the war—but there were more than that.)

He was fired at by German Tommy-gunners from the back of one truck as it strove to escape. He yelled at them, rushed in with a grenade, and destroyed them all. The Germans were desperately trying to get their vehicles moving, to escape from the terror that had so unexpectedly been loosed upon them. Time and again Upham leapt upon their trucks as they were getting under way, bombing them into wrecks or setting them afire.

There were German staff cars too, for it seemed that the 20th had crashed right into a German headquarters. Upham was seen with his pistol, firing into the cars as they lurched away, few of them escaping; and as he raced up alongside one laden car he wrenched the door open, flung in a grenade, and slammed the door shut on its hapless passengers.

Through to the other side of the German lines the battalions fought, leaving behind chaos and destruction. They emerged into clear ground, and suddenly all was still. Up went the flare signal that the gap had been made, and towards the gap poured the transport that had been waiting at Minqar Qaim.

The 20th emerged from the battle all fiercely excited and stimulated. They saw Upham, his voice still high with tension. Fraser, the C.Q.M.S., looked at him in amazement. 'What's happened to you?' he asked.

For Upham was covered in blood.

Not then, not till the following night, did he report for medical treatment for his wounds. From the grenades he had been distributing on the enemy he had at the same time peppered himself with grenade fragments.

All he said was: 'This show tonight will make bloody history.'

It did for him, but he didn't mean it that way.

But to mention Upham is but to name one man whose exploits in the break-out were dramatic. There were dozens of men whose courage and dash were unseen in the darkness, where heroism burst and flamed in moments of mad confusion, where men singly and in concert performed one of the epics of World War II.

But meantime Inglis had had to make a change of plan for the mass of the division's transport. The 4th Brigade trucks rushed through the gap successfully but Inglis decided that the opportunity of pushing the rest of the transport through the same hole had gone. It was too late. The enemy was reorganizing on the flanks. So he turned the rest of the division south-eastwards and a wheeled break-out was attempted in that direction.

They ran headlong into a body of German tanks. There were a few desperate minutes then, with trucks caught in the tank fire. Freyberg, lying on a stretcher in his vehicle, lifted his head to see the fiery gauntlet that the convoy had to run. It looked grim. 'Another Balaclava,' he commented.

But it wasn't. There were quick decisions needed, and given. The column split. Some went east, some west. But with few losses the great majority finally made good their ground to safe territory in the east.

Back with the 20th, the foot-soldiers welcomed the arrival through the gap of their trucks, gladly embussed, and moved rapidly eastwards. Several times they detoured to avoid clashes with advanced enemy forces. But as the hours passed and their tempers cooled, their exhilaration was replaced with a feeling of amazement that the break-out had been accomplished with such little loss. Casualties were light. And to the enemy . . . ?

The diary of Afrika Korps said:

> '1st Battalion Panzer Grenadiers has suffered very heavy casualties as the enemy succeeded in surprising the battalion and cutting it to pieces in a hand-to-hand fight.'

And when Hoppy Hopwood arrived with the C Company H.Q. truck, and Leggy suggested that everyone get cracking as fast as possible, Charles replied: 'It's all right, Leggy-boy. We've rocked the bastards this time.'

But it was not the effect on the Germans, or on the New Zealanders, that was the feature of Minqar Qaim. It was simply that, by a display of daring and fearlessness that has few equals, the division escaped annihilation. That was as good as a victory.

Minqar Qaim was a glorious feat of arms.

12

Disaster at Ruweisat

THOUGH delayed by rearguard actions like Minqar Qaim, Rommel's forces were now in full cry. Auchinleck's 8th Army was falling right back to its final defence line at Alamein, where the available route to the Nile Valley narrowed to a front of thirty-eight miles—the Mediterranean bounding it on the north, the Qattara Depression on the south. Along this front the Allied forces were strung thinly, gathered for the most part into a series of strong-points, but with few units other than the New Zealand Division in good fighting shape.

Given a mobile role in the defence line, the Kiwis now faced a long period of almost continuous movement and manœuvre. Ridges were occupied one day, abandoned the next, an attack mounted in the evening, the captured ground relinquished next morning. Few men knew what all the movements were about. Few had much confidence in the higher command of the Middle East forces.

It was a case of the defenders struggling to upset the balance of the enemy, who themselves were at the point of exhaustion and at the extreme end of their supply lines. Most attacks had little chance of success; but there was such weakness on both sides that almost by accident the battle for the Middle East might have been won and lost in a few fateful hours.

To those who saw or heard the official orders from on high, cynicism came easily. It might be a convenient Army expression, but civilian soldiers did not enjoy the hypocrisy of being ordered to '*take ground* to the eastwards'—when that was the direction of their own bases and rear units, and the enemy were still all in the west.

But on the other hand there was no fear of using the words 'withdrawal' and 'evacuation' in other contexts. 'The Chief has decided to save 8th Army' was the condescending message that emanated from the staff at Middle East H.Q., prefacing secret plans for the retreat to the Nile and for complete withdrawal from Egypt.

These were days when men in the ranks were confused, satisfied with their own performances when confronted with the enemy but, it seemed denied again and again the opportunity of joining battle in one significant, well-prepared encounter.

Weary beyond words, C Company of the 20th came one night to their latest defensive area. Upham pointed out to his platoon commanders the sector each was to occupy. The men began the chore of digging, just as they had done the previous night, and again early that morning. There were, as usual, not enough picks and shovels to go round.

Colonel Burrows was back again as Battalion Commander. He had a new car, too; and somehow Charles had managed to acquire the old one—a Ford V8 which his driver Hopgood greatly admired but which presented an attractive target to the enemy.

Burrows arrived in the company area, walked briskly over to Upham.

'You're in the wrong place, Charlie. This is part of D Company's ground.'

Thin and unkempt, Upham looked at him wearily. 'I'm in the right place,' he said doggedly.

'Charlie, I'm sorry, but you're in the *wrong* place. Your position is over there.'

Charles looked where the C.O. was pointing.

There was a pause, silent except for the sound of Upham's heavy breathing, and the ring of picks and shovels.

The ring of digging—the never-ending digging . . . always somewhere different . . . always when his men were at the end of their tether . . . dig here . . . dig there . . . then up tools and move a mile somewhere else . . . dig there . . . and just every now and then they saw the enemy.

When would they really fight? When would the brass hats learn that his men were getting more tired and sick every day? When would someone come out with a confident plan for a real showdown—a battle where his men could show their mettle? Never apparently—just dig and dig. . . .

And the frustration and exhaustion of the past few weeks suddenly boiled up inside of him. Not looking at Burrows, just staring into the desert, Upham began to swear, first softly, then with increasing venom. He swore at the Army, the war, the Germans, the 'higher-ups'; he swore at Burrows, he swore at the desert—in an outpouring of emotion that violent language seemed to relieve.

It was not for nothing that the other man was known as Gentleman Jim. Because Burrows just stood and listened gravely while the worn-out figure of Upham abused him, along with the rest of the world. He didn't interrupt. He was a great enough man to recognize that this was no time for sharp rebukes, but for sympathy. His silence indicated his sympathy.

And when the pot of emotion ran dry, and Upham just stood there glaring, Burrows looked at him in the desert twilight and said softly: 'I understand, Charlie. But I repeat—you're in the *wrong* place. You should be over there.'

Like an exhausted and sad schoolboy Upham muttered: 'Yes, sir,' and walked heavily away. He had been spoiling for a fight with anyone, even Burrows, but the soft words and the refusal to argue had turned his wrath to water.

*   *   *   *

Burrows continued on his way to see Kippenberger at 5th Brigade H.Q. He thought he might see Inglis there too. He hoped so, because there was something he wanted to say to both of them. Strange it should be about Charlie Upham, whom he had just left. But it had taken days to check up on all the facts, and to make sure that what he had to say to Inglis and Kip was the result of sober judgment. He had waited till the drama and excitement of Minqar Qaim had died down to make sure that his thoughts were not exaggerated by the stimulating events of those hours. He had had to speak to a few reliable witnesses, too.

He found Kippenberger there.

'It's about Charlie,' he explained.

'Yes, how is he?' Kip asked with quick interest, for Upham had always been a man he had watched carefully.

'Tired, like the rest of us; and savage. He wants a showdown. But I want to talk to you about Charlie at Minqar Qaim. You heard about him, I suppose?'

'Yes, who didn't?'

Burrows paused. Was it silly suggesting it? It had never happened to any combatant soldier before. Would the suggestion be scorned, politely disregarded, and Burrows's own sense of judgment doubted? But he was satisfied in his own mind about it.

He drew breath, then said soberly: 'Kip, Charlie's got to have *another* V.C.—for Minqar Qaim. . . .'

*   *   *   *

The 20th were moving east, exhausted after three simmering days of constant movement. Hoppy Hopwood drove Upham's V8 car. Upham, Le Gros, and Terry Madsen stretched out on the cushions asleep. Charles's last words had been: 'That's our convoy, Hoppy. Just follow it.'

Hoppy followed. But sleep bore him down too. He allowed the car to weave to a halt, slumped forward over the wheel. . . . When he awoke an hour later his own convoy was out of sight. But there was another going the same way. Starting up the engine again, he joined in the queue, then started to sweat.

He decided the best thing to do was to tell the boss as soon as possible. So he leaned over, shook Upham by the shoulder, till he stirred him into wakefulness.

'Captain Upham! Captain Upham! I've lost the convoy. I'm sorry, but I couldn't keep awake.'

'Wish way we goin', Hoppy?' Upham muttered.

'Towards Alamein. But I dunno where this convoy will take us to.'

'That'll do, Hoppy. Just keep going. I don't care a beggar where we are.'

When dawn came they found themselves very close to home, were soon in their own company lines.

Charles was wanted immediately at Battalion H.Q. He went with Hopgood in the car, left instructions for a group of slit trenches to be dug for his headquarters while he was away.

On his return the trenches were ready, the one for his own use being deep, well covered, comfortable. He looked at it appreciatively, complimented the men on a good, thoughtful job. Then, pointing to the trench, he turned to Hoppy and said: 'This one is for you, Hoppy.'

It was typical of him to insist on the best being given to the man who had had the least sleep.

He said to those around him: 'Now leave Hoppy alone. See that no one wakes him up today.'

Hoppy caught up on his sleep, dragged himself out late in the afternoon, and tidied up.

He was just finishing, and beginning to wonder what the night's move would be, when Upham shouted at him. 'Hoppy—over to Battalion, smartly!'

Hopgood thought this sounded like an emergency. He ran to the car, realizing that the radiator would be empty, because it always leaked right out in a few hours. It would take him five minutes to fill a tin with the brackish water from the water-point. No time for that. Grabbing a tin of pure drinking water from the back of the car he proceeded to fill the empty radiator hurriedly.

Then Upham shouted to him across the sand: 'Hoppy, if you're

too lazy to get ordinary water I'll bring it to you myself.' And, grabbing
a tin, he stumped away towards the water-point, filled it with brackish
water, and brought it back and deposited it under Hoppy's nose.

Hopgood blinked. 'But I thought you said we had to get to Battalion smartly?'

'Yes, we do. In about half an hour. Feeling awake now, Hoppy?'

Hoppy reluctantly acknowledged that he was now feeling very
alert indeed.

Just as well too, Upham thought; because the track over to Battalion wound through the mine-field. A driver had to be right on his
toes for that.

But Hopgood didn't mind very much, for they were hardly out of
sight of the company before Upham had him stop the car and opened
up a kit lying on the back seat.

'Here you are, Hoppy. Only one tin. This puts plenty of spunk into
you. Where's that opener?'

Together they sat and enjoyed the sheer ecstasy of a tin of New
Zealand oysters that Upham had been keeping for a day like this.

*   *   *   *

The company truck was well laden with sticky bombs, hand grenades, and bed-rolls.

Charles was some distance away when the truck caught fire. As
he raced towards it he could hear the bombs beginning to sizzle,
the flames starting to lick all around the boxes of ammunition and
grenades.

The driver, Ben Gurdon, was up on the back of it throwing off the
bed-rolls.

'Get off, you fool!' Upham shouted as he raced up. 'Those bombs
will go up. Get off, you bloody idiot, you . . . !'

But by the time his oaths had finished he was up on the truck
himself, throwing off the rolls, dashing sand over the flames, time after
time ordering Gurdon to jump off.

Ben Gurdon disregarded him. Together they cleared the truck,
subdued the fire.

At last they climbed down together, grimy, covered with sweat
and sand, the taste of burnt cordite still in their mouths.

'Well done, Ben,' Upham said quietly. And they went their separate
ways to get cleaned up.

*   *   *   *

11th July 1942. Midday

The New Zealand Division received orders to take part in an attack on Ruweisat Ridge, an important feature overlooking the battlefield of Alamein. It was held by the enemy, who were also believed to have advanced posts out on the flat, south of the Ridge, and across this flat the attack would have to be made.

The division would move forward to secure a start line within range of Ruweisat, and there await orders for the actual assault. When the time came it would be a night attack, the troops advancing in a north-westerly direction across the flat and on to the vital points of the Ridge.

Tanks would be needed to protect the western flank of the division as it moved forward, Inglis claimed. The enemy held all that ground to the west. They wouldn't let the New Zealanders move across their front towards Ruweisat unmolested. And when the infantry had captured the Ridge, and daylight came over the desert, they would need tanks to guard them while they sat on the exposed slopes and dug in.

'Strafer' Gott, commander of 13th Corps of which the New Zealand Division formed part, thought Inglis was seeing difficulties that did not exist. But he agreed that assistance was needed. So it was ordered that the tanks of the 1st Armoured Division would provide 'full fire support and flank protection'.

The division mounted its trucks and moved across the desert to the start line. The enemy picked up the mass movement, thumped shells at the trucks as they advanced, flailed them with artillery and mortars as the trucks stopped and disgorged their men.

The shells continued to fall, but in textbook fashion the infantry shook out into extended formation, began to plod steadily forward. They reached the wadi where they were to assemble for the main attack and disappeared into its safety. They dug in there. But there was no attack that night. Nor the next night; nor the next.

They all waited in the wadi. The shells continued to fall on them. And Inglis was disquieted to hear that the tanks would not now move forward with his men, would not protect his western flank during the advance. He demanded that the tanks be placed under his command. Gott refused. The tanks were not trained to operate like that, it was said.

At the very least, Inglis demanded, would the tanks advance at first light, following the infantry assault? By then his men should have captured and be sitting on Ruweisat Ridge. They'd be easy targets unless tanks moved in to protect them. They told him this would be done.

And the thousand and more New Zealanders who were to lose their lives or liberty at Ruweisat Ridge would have wished that Inglis could have received that promise in some signed water-tight legal document.

Then the word came: 'Attack to start at 11 p.m. this night, 14th July. Contact with the enemy expected at 1 a.m. Capture the Ridge by 4.30 a.m.' It would be *six miles* altogether.

The tanks are promised at first light, Inglis reminded himself again and again, as if to allay his feeling of uneasiness.

*   *   *   *

4th Brigade was on the left, 5th on the right. Each brigade had two battalions forward.

It was dark. There was hardly a sound other than the creak and clink of equipment as men rose to their feet, spread out into formation, silently accepted the orders to be moving.

For some reason C Company seemed disturbed just before zero hour. Intelligence Officer Johnny Sullivan was with them, showing them the start line, pointing out the axis of advance. They would have to wait, anyhow, until the 18th and 19th had moved off. The 20th were only in the second wave.

Sullivan came through the darkness to Peter Maxwell, standing silently with his men of D Company.

'What's the trouble over at C?' Maxwell asked.

'Oh, nothing really,' Sullivan shrugged. 'Only Charlie. Had his men in the wrong place. Then he went crook at me when I told him where he ought to be. He's just being difficult.'

Maxwell laughed softly. 'Charlie's always like that before a show. He needs something to get him annoyed. What happened, anyway?'

Sullivan grinned. 'He reckons he ought to be further forward. Doesn't like other people forming up ahead of him. Thinks they'll get in his road, I suppose. I had quite a job to convince him. Even now I don't expect he believes me.'

The leading battalions went two and a half miles before striking the first enemy posts. As the first volleys split the night air, they rushed out into line, then advanced on the enemy at the double. Grenades, bayonets, bullets, hand-to-hand fighting; and everywhere it was success. Some posts gave in quickly; others fought bitterly to the last. And as soon as one post was subdued, another straight ahead sprang to life, and they had to rush that; or maybe it was to the flank; and even some behind. The Kiwis tackled them all, charging in one direction and another, but always making ground forward to the main objective on the Ridge.

Within the first hour the company and platoon commanders were thinking: If these are only the outposts it's going to be pretty hot when we hit the main defence line on the Ridge. This is much thicker than we expected. But it's going famously. Very few casualties. The enemy being smashed up. We've lost touch with the platoon on our left—perhaps they went in the direction of that blazing truck; perhaps they veered off to that machine-gun far out on the left flank; and we haven't the faintest where Company H.Q. is now; but the Ridge ought to be straight ahead —another couple of miles perhaps.

And as they went on, capturing and destroying, wading through a very hot-bed of enemy resistance, the New Zealanders were thinking in terms of victory. Did it matter that communications were breaking down early? Companies were losing touch with their platoons and with their battalions. Battalions could not raise Brigade. Perhaps it did not matter, they thought, for the battle on the Ridge was still to come; these were just the furious preliminaries.

Onwards towards the Ridge they fought.

*   *   *   *

Moving off half an hour after the assault battalions, the 20th had the task of mopping up the 'left-over' opposition. They pressed forward quickly, urged on by the sound of the fire-fight crackling and exploding a mile ahead of them. Burrows, in command of 4th Brigade again, was travelling close by the 20th, and had to prevent them moving at the double in their anxiety to catch up with the war.

It was quiet going at first, but soon they came upon the relics of the fighting left behind by the assault units. They were surprised to find that the enemy's outposts had been so thick and formidable.

Now and then a stray enemy post, overlooked by the battalions in front, came to life, and the 20th had to engage and subdue it. The approach of New Zealand bayonets was usually sufficient, but once or twice Upham's men of C Company had to pause impatiently while the enemy were routed out with bayonets and grenades. D Company were also briskly engaged for a time, and then the whole battalion was pinned down for over half an hour by some accurate mortaring.

But Upham and his fellow-officers of the 20th became seriously worried. Things were not as they should be. The 18th and 19th had blazed ahead, smashed through the enemy apparently, and ought now to be in contact with the main defences somewhere about the Ridge. Yet out on the flat, short of the Ridge, there were more and more tightly held enemy posts, coming to life like a mass of erupting volcanoes in the very

L

middle of the New Zealand supporting arms. It shouldn't be. They were getting in the road of the main battle up front.

Then through the darkness Upham heard the distinctive clank of tanks. He called Bob May over to listen.

'Ours, I suppose,' Charles ventured.

'Hope so.'

'They'd better be,' Charles said grimly. 'If they're Jerries there'll be trouble in the morning unless they're cleaned out. They'll be in behind us.'

Brigadier Burrows was worried too. Concerned with the silence from his battalions up near the Ridge, and with the fact that the battle apparently still needed to be fought on the flat, he decided that he must get news from his forward units. The radios were out; telephone lines had failed; there was no communication except by personal contact. So he went over to Manson, C.O. of the 20th, and said: 'Ian, get someone to go forward and find out what's happened. Take this jeep.'

Manson decided C Company should send someone up. He went over to Upham and gave him the orders. 'Detail a good man, Charlie. The Brig wants the whole story from up front.'

Upham said shortly: 'I'll go.'

Manson and Burrows were not surprised. Charlie would always do a job like that himself. They saw him hand over his company to C.S.M. May, clamber aboard the jeep alongside the driver, then roar away into the desert battlefield ahead.

It was not long before the jeep came under fire. Annoyed at this interruption, Upham had the driver cruise round till shortly he came upon an enemy post that had been knocked out. There he obtained a German machine-gun complete with tripod and ammunition. He mounted it on the jeep, then continued forward.

There were still enemy posts in all directions, still actively hostile. He was amazed that so many had survived the onslaught of the attacking battalions. Shots came at them from all sides, but Upham swung the captured gun at them, firing pugnaciously at anything that seemed troublesome. He was tempted to run in to the attack, but he knew his first job was to get information, so he contented himself with short bursts of fire in retaliation, then veered away out of range.

Further and further ahead they went, weaving round enemy dug-outs and weapon-pits.

He came upon enemy tanks, looming up through the fading darkness. Sharply he detoured away.

The dim shadow of the Ridge was right in front of him when he saw his first New Zealander. It was Doug Green, commander of an artillery troop, who had gone forward with the 19th Battalion to observe for his guns.

'Where's the 19th?' Upham shouted.

Green told him they were only a short distance away.

'What about the 18th? How have they got on?'

Green had no idea, but he offered to help. He would like to know, too. So he climbed on board the jeep beside Upham and away they went together, touring the battlefield in search of the battalions.

But now things were much thicker. There were Germans and Italians everywhere around them, some in confusion, pulling guns out by hand and with ropes. Enemy tanks were moving around, trying to protect the infantry in their withdrawal. Flares were going up, tanks firing, red tracer bullets from machine-guns curling through the darkness.

Roaming backwards and forwards, Upham's jeep then ranged over all the battlefield worth mentioning. They did not come upon the 19th again, which by now was near its objective on the Ridge; they ran through elements of the 18th and 21st, both of which had become disorganized; and, although they were not aware of it at the time, they passed beyond the line of our forward troops and into the thick of the German and Italian masses that had now fallen back over the Ridge to safety beyond.

Several times their jeep stuck in the sand, and it needed their combined shoulders to heave it out again. The second time it stuck, Green realized with a sinking feeling that there were scores of enemy infantry within a few yards. They had blundered into a thick pocket of Axis troops.

Green silently indicated them to Upham, furtively cocking his Tommy-gun as he did so.

'Never mind,' was the reply. 'They're mostly Wops. Come on—let's get the jeep out.' And totally disregarding the Italians milling around, Upham put his shoulder to the back of the jeep and heaved.

Green put his gun down and lent his weight also. He said later: 'I expected a bullet in my back any moment. But Charlie didn't seem to care.'

They toured on. They would see a light in the distance. 'Let's try over there,' Charles would say, and they would scud off in that direction. It would turn out to be a German truck trying to tow out a gun; so they would swerve away and look for something else.

It was a fantastic adventure. They came upon few New Zealanders, but all over the field they were running into German and Italian troops, bursting in and out of them, often in a flurry of shots, then racing away in another direction.

They stuck again. More Italians this time, completely surrounding them. Out they clambered, began hurriedly pushing at the jeep.

Without a tin hat as usual, Upham was not a clearly identifiable figure in the gloom. Whether it was by some telepathic projection of his personality, or by a laughable mistake, it is hard to say; but within a few moments Green found that Charles was directing a few Italians to help free the jeep. They crowded around, seemingly anxious to assist, pushing and shoving willingly, until with a roar the wheels took up again, the New Zealanders jumped on board, and off they went with barely a wave to the lugubrious but obliging Italians in the patch of soft sand.

There was a tearing, scraping noise, and the jeep slowed down. They looked out. Trailing behind were yards of barbed wire, inextricably caught up in the axles underneath. They had to trail it the rest of the way around Ruweisat.

Next there was a sudden tilt, a slow slide, and in a moment the jeep was on its side. The right-hand wheels had subsided over the edge of a dug-out. And more Italians everywhere. These looked more belligerent.

Charles sized them up, then advanced suddenly towards them with angry gestures that left only one interpretation. In a jiffy a party of Italians pounced on the jeep, righted it, saw it rev off into the night, with Charles still waving his fist at them in mingled contempt and appreciation.

And, as they raced this way and that, the truth of the attack on Ruweisat began to dawn on Upham. From his extraordinary reconnaissance the facts began to emerge. They were unpalatable, but not yet dangerous.

The facts were these—that a grave miscalculation had been made as to where the New Zealanders would meet their main opposition. The main enemy line would be on the Ridge, or just short of it—so it was thought. That's where the battle would be. There would be mere outposts out on the flat. They would have to be rolled up during the march in, but the leading battalions would have to reserve their main effort for the big assault just near the Ridge.

But the truth was that the outposts, whose resistance so puzzled the Kiwis, were in fact *the main enemy defence line*. The New Zealanders had burst their way through them, fought on to the Ridge, and driven the enemy off it. That was victory. But out on the flat the so-called outposts, which had been treated rather off-handedly, had come to life again. They formed a fiery barrier between the battalions who had broken through and the supporting troops behind. Inside that barrier the enemy were as active as ever, and they had tanks coming in from the western flank to help them.

On the Ridge the battalions found themselves broken up, irretrievably in some cases. The nature of the fight on the flat, with sections dashing off in all directions, caused cohesion to be lost. The Ridge, a mere forty-foot elevation in the desert, was no landmark, and few troops found themselves on their true objective. But they were at the Ridge—that was what mattered most. The morning would see the sorting out.

Upham and his crew turned the jeep round and headed back towards the south, weaving its way through enemy ground as if in a snake-dance.

It was coming light when it plodded back to Burrows, its enemy machine-gun still mounted, enemy wire draped around it like a fancy dress. Upham told what he knew, then hurried back to rejoin his company.

The news was of great benefit, but no great comfort to Burrows. He had no alternative to pressing on. If his supporting units could make good their ground to the Ridge all might be well in the morning.

Then with tanks to hold off any counter-attack . . .

*　　　*　　　*　　　*

Almost full daylight. Closer to the Ridge. Only a shallow depression to cross before the short climb up the Ridge to the summit. The 20th were heading for a trig marked 'Point 63', but I.O. Johnny Sullivan had realized they were off the line, that Point 63 was a little distance away to the right. They would have to climb the Ridge first, then move along the top to the trig.

To the lip of the depression they came. Burrows was up with the 20th, still praying that his other battalions were safely dug in ahead. Once across the depression, then up to the Ridge, and all would be well.

And in a sudden moment it became all noise and fire, the red jets of tracer were leaping towards them, and the flashes and spits of flame were coming from half a dozen guns, down there on the left, in the depression, about 400 yards away.

They flung themselves to earth.

But not before they saw, only too clearly, that the enemy had armoured cars down there and, further back, almost in the shadow of those mounds, the unmistakable outline of the things they most dreaded —*tanks*.

Burrows summed up the situation instantly. It was serious—perhaps vitally serious. He shouted to Manson of the 20th to go in with the bayonet.

Manson looked at it quickly. He saw there was no time for fancy tactics. It had to be done on the run, straight into them.

He dashed over to Maxwell of D Company. 'Get straight on to the Ridge, Peter!' he called. The trig had to be taken as soon as possible. It was a commanding position.

He shouted to Washbourn's A Company to keep on the ground, await developments.

Then he was over at Upham's company, on the left flank, the fire pouring at them in a never-ending stream. He ordered Upham to detach from the rest of the battalion, wheel left, and make an assault on the German guns.

Just for a second, as his eye swept down the bare fire-whipped slope, Upham's face set. He could see what had to be done. He could see what was likely to happen.

And then that old exultation and burning feeling seemed to sweep up inside him. He was up on his feet, and his voice was ringing out: 'Come on, C Company! Come on! Come on!' and from the ground his men sprang up, swung left into line, and followed behind him, charging down the slope into the dip.

It was a long dash down the hillside. There could be no reconnaisance, no flanking movements. It had to be an assault into the very muzzle of the guns, straight down the lines of tracer, straight towards the German armour.

And as Upham ran, and he saw them all running with him, unhesitating and unflinching, a savage pride possessed him. What men they were! What bloody heroes!

But they were not thinking of themselves. They were looking at the fury ahead, and they were watching Upham as he ran out in front of them, and they were saying: 'Look at old Charlie!'

Now they were down into the hollow. Here were enemy trucks, guns, infantry. The fire came at them in vicious streams, the tracer like streaking red tennis balls.

'Come on now! Come on . . . into 'em!' Upham was shouting at the top of his voice as he ran forward. Hundreds of yards away, up on Point 63, all around the battlefield, they could hear his voice, rising above the din of battle as he roared his encouragement and his hate.

But a frontal attack is a brutal business. Ian Smith and Edwyn Shand—two of his platoon commanders—were killed in the first minute. Men were dropping all along the line. And with a wrench that threw him to the ground, Upham was hit in the left arm, a tearing wicked wound from machine-gun bullets that ripped through his biceps and smashed his arm at the elbow.

He got up and staggered on.

Now they were into a mass of slit trenches and in amongst the trucks and the guns. It was cold steel and grenade work. One of the machine-guns was silenced.

There were the tanks ahead. They were moving from one mound to another, sheltering hull down, firing from behind each one. German infantry were running back, seeking protection behind the tanks. And his men now were at the armoured cars, swarming over them.

Upham's mind was hazy with the shock and pain of his smashed arm. He told Bob May to take over command of the company, for he didn't know how much longer he could keep going. But he was still in front, shouting and exhorting, cursing at his arm, while from their position on the Ridge, men of D Company looked down and saw him with his grenades, and they marvelled as they watched him lead the rush against the remaining machine-gun post and destroy it with bombs and bayonets.

It was all smoke, noise, confusion. For five minutes his men seemed to be everywhere, running and firing and shouting, and the terrible sounds of close fighting were like bedlam.

Then all of a sudden it was still. It was suddenly all over, as if some weird signal had stopped it. The shots were still coming, but the fight had finished.

And as through a red curtain Upham looked around dazedly. He saw where they were. They were through the enemy, clear of the depression, up on its further slopes. And in the depression? Where the enemy had lain in wait for them? It was cleaned out—swept absolutely clear; everything in it was either destroyed or captive in our hands.

Even the tanks had gone—backing away furtively, keeping out of the ring, trying to shelter the infantry to the last, but now withdrawn well out of range.

Upham felt something like awe. He had thought it wasn't possible. Face taut with pain, he looked around wonderingly. They had two German officers on their hands and forty other German prisoners, and well over a hundred Italians; they had enemy guns, a German Intelligence truck full of battle-maps.

He looked at the stillness in the depression, at the long slopes they had come racing down, at the men working like doctors to salve the wounds of their friends; he saw the bodies of his boys lying back there in the sand.

Up on the Ridge he could see the other New Zealanders moving around, apparently secure on their target. He said slowly: 'This is the greatest victory yet.' Surely all enemy strength had now been broken.

He closed his eyes while Le Gros put a field dressing round the wound. It was a bad one this time, he knew, a really bad one.

Now Johnny Sullivan came hurrying over. He looked critically at the wound, realized instantly that Upham was in poor shape.

'You'll have to get to R.A.P. as soon as you can, Charlie. I'll try and jack up a truck.'

Upham looked up at him without speaking.

Sullivan went on: 'Like me to look after things for a while? We've got to push on up the Ridge, you know. What do you say, Charlie?'

Upham nodded heavily. 'You take over, Johnny, till I get my arm patched up. Then I'll be back.'

Sullivan looked at him silently. He thought it would be a long, long time before Charles would be 'back'. Be lucky if he didn't lose his whole arm.

Johnny Sullivan took over C Company, moved it into a stronger position on the Ridge. Then a small truck came on the scene and in it Charles Upham was taken away to the R.A.P., now established on the slopes of the Ridge further along. Le Gros would not leave his side.

Now it was daylight. From the Ridge there was the spectacle of masses of German trucks and men milling about to the north and west. Their guns were already bombarding the Ridge, where our men were finding that digging in was all but impossible. There was solid rock a few inches beneath the surface, so the best that could be done was to build sangars. They were little protection against air-bursts from the German artillery, a technique now being widely adopted.

Many commanders were desperately trying to find routes up to the Ridge from the original start line. Not only was the intervening area bristling with enemy who had survived the initial sweep by the New Zealanders, but now into that area more German tanks had moved. They edged up towards the rear of our positions on the Ridge.

Where was our own armour? Where were our tanks that were to be up at first light, protecting the New Zealanders on Ruweisat?

The question was asked at the first flush of dawn, again and again as the hours advanced. And men, with feats of gallantry too many to be chronicled, braved the no man's land that now separated the Ridge from the Kiwis' supporting arms, to appeal for the tanks to move up, as promised.

Nothing happened.

It was not long after dawn before those on the Ridge saw a long column of men marching westward, shepherded by tanks. At first they could not identify the marching column; then they didn't believe it; and when they finally knew it was true they couldn't understand how it could have happened. For the column of men was the bulk of 22nd Battalion, who had made good their ground to the foot of Ruweisat during the night (a mile or two to the east of the 20th) but now at dawn were surrounded by German tanks and left no choice but to surrender.

Brave men can attack tanks and achieve short-lived success. But once the anti-tank guns are blown out of the battle, and the enemy tanks hunt together, unprotected infantrymen can do nothing but rise from their sangars with arms raised. So it happened to the 22nd, to all but a few men on the flanks who managed to run and survive.

Thus came New Zealand's first disaster of this day, almost apologetically, and indeed it remained unknown to the brigade and divisional commanders until late in the afternoon, so complete was the disruption of communications.

The hot sun mounted over Ruweisat, and the men clung to the ground, divorced from the guns that could have helped them, proud of their success during the night, wondering hour after hour when the promised tanks would come forward to their aid. And hour by hour the shells and bullets poured in from the Germans reorganizing out on the plains.

They shelled the R.A.P. also. Already it was overcrowded. No casualties could be evacuated. Feltham, the 20th M.O., looked at Upham's arm. It was a horrible wound. He wanted to give him morphia. Upham refused, fearful that his usefulness might be affected. Feltham dressed it, then discussed with him how the R.A.P. could escape the shelling that was already causing wounded men there to suffer further wounds.

A white towel. One that already had a red stripe down the middle. 'Don't make it look like a white flag,' Charles said. Make it into a red cross. There was only one source of red colouring. Plenty of it. They collected some in a mug. Carefully they painted another large red stripe across the towel, forming a cross, then draped it in view of the enemy.

The gruesome but effective flag was honoured by Rommel's men during the rest of the day.

*　　　*　　　*　　　*

Fretting and impatient, his arm like red-hot steel, Upham could not rest quietly at the R.A.P. It was pitiful and frustrating there—more wounded than could be cared for lying around in the open, waiting with growing disillusionment for the arrival of ambulances and medical supplies. But, as the hours advanced, the exhilaration of the night attack was giving way to bitter realization that the infantry were isolated on Ruweisat Ridge, cut off from artillery, reinforcements, and supplies, communications lost, with the long-promised armour still somewhere over the horizon.

He got to his feet for the hundredth time and filled another pipe. It wasn't easy with one arm in a splint—and the pain of it made him giddy.

Then in a moment of sudden decision he was walking away, head down, shoulders hunched, walking away from the R.A.P. over the Ridge. He headed towards the area where he had left the remnants of his company. What good was it hanging around amongst the dead and wounded? He could still walk and think. He could fight them one-handed if he had to. He did it on Crete. Three hours at the R.A.P. were long enough.

Bob May saw Charles coming back unsteadily. By now C Company were so reduced by casualties that they had joined with A Company into a composite group. But the numbers were thinning all the time. Wounded men were leaving for the R.A.P. almost every minute. They were so vulnerable on the bare slopes of the Ridge, completely exposed to the enemy shells and mortars.

Upham walked in amongst the sangars, caught sight of a captured eighty-eight gun and walked over to it. With one hand he struggled with the breech mechanism, trying to disable a vital part so that it would be useless to the enemy again.

May walked over to him.

'What are you trying to do, boss?'

Upham scowled at him. 'Get back to the men!' he snapped. 'Keep under cover!'

'O.K., O.K.,' May said apologetically. (Why did Charlie always get so savage during action?) 'Just thought you might want some help.'

'Well . . . perhaps I do,' Charles replied in a milder tone. 'Here, Bob, give us a hand with this damned gun.'

And May helped him wreck the eighty-eight.

The German gun-crew were still lying nearby, all wounded.

'Those Nazi bastards don't look so clever now,' Upham said. He looked at the way their wounds had been neatly dressed. 'Our boys fix them up?'

May nodded. Then he caught his breath, for Upham had advanced towards the wounded men, was standing over them, looking down with contempt. May thought—he hates Germans so much he's capable of anything, but surely he's not going to abuse them now. He wouldn't hurt a wounded man.

Then May wondered if he had really ever understood Upham at all.

For Charles was bending over the wounded men, one after another, and was giving them each a long draught from his own water-bottle. The Germans drank gratefully.

Le Gros looked on open-mouthed. He had never expected to see his boss giving water to a German.

Bob May came up close to him, whispered: 'For Christ's sake, Leggy, take Charlie out. Get him back to the R.A.P. He's out on his feet.'

But Upham stayed with his men for a further hour before he allowed himself to be led away again, weak and groggy.

*   *   *   *

Meantime those in high command had become fully aware of the peril that beset the division. The night thrust had been almost too successful, the dash of the New Zealanders had carried them through the enemy lines on to Ruweisat, and all had seemed well.

But by day the ground between the Ridge and the start line had bristled with enemy guns again, forbidding any reinforcements, while enemy tanks had moved in and already swallowed up 22nd Battalion. Desperate measures were needed to save the rest of the infantry from the inevitable armoured counter-attack.

But it was after two o'clock in the afternoon before our tanks made any contact with New Zealand troops—even then only partial contact. Their advance into the battlefield was so timorous that by four o'clock requests to rush urgently to the rescue of 4th Brigade were met only by a proposal to send forward a 'reconnaissance' tank.

Let that heat-laden day drag round to 4 p.m. Exposed all day midst the gravel and the sand, with no supporting arms, no tanks, no supplies, few communications, the New Zealanders became more and more conscious that a victory was being slowly turned into defeat.

Consolidation must follow attack. But the enemy line, broken and dissolved into scattered elements, was being allowed to revive, those who had retreated were re-forming and hitting back, counter-attack was imminent. Why wasn't something being done? Where were the tanks?

The War Diary of the German 15th Panzer Division echoed their thoughts. It said: 'It was most astonishing that the enemy could not exploit his penetration into a break-through by pushing his tanks forward.'

At 4 p.m. the counter-attack came. The enemy had had all day to prepare it carefully.

Through the dust and smoke the tanks came heading in, heedless of the small-arms fire, singling out the handful of anti-tank guns and silencing them one by one.

Liaison officers raced back, urging our tanks forward. If they were coming forward at all it had to be now or it would be too late. Enemy guns were plastering the Ridge with their fire, the German tanks were looming up closer and closer, wondering why it was being made so easy for them.

Through the murk came armoured cars, manœuvring with skill and speed, racing on to the infantry posts with machine-guns spitting. In from the west rumbled the tanks, German infantry sheltering behind them.

Ruweisat Ridge was drenched with fire. Gone now were our own anti-tank guns, gone any means of defence against the enemy. There was no chance even of skulking below ground, for the men in their sangars lay only inches below the surface.

And as the guns of the tanks swivelled down on to them there was no more to be done, nothing more to be said. The tank commanders stood up in the turrets, waving the men up from the ground.

As the wave of enemy machines advanced on 20th Battalion, Charles Upham looked around the R.A.P. again. Half his company seemed to be lying there. He had never seen so many officer and N.C.O. casualties.

He began stumbling over the fire-torn Ridge towards the 20th again.

Peter Maxwell saw him heading towards the exposed slope where the remnants of C Company were awaiting the assault.

'Where're you going, Charlie?'

'If we're going to be cleaned up I'm going to be with my boys,' Upham replied, moving doggedly on.

'You bloody fool, Charlie. You'll stop it for good before you reach them. And if you do you won't get a doctor for hours. Stay with the R.A.P.'

'Like hell!'

He turned his back and stumped on.

He reached the broken rocks where his men lay, just as another mortar bomb seemed to burst all around him.

His leg crumpled under him as the shrapnel bit in. He went sprawling in the dirt. Now, if he wanted to fight any longer, he couldn't even walk. He lay there helplessly. But what did it matter now? All was lost.

Here now were the tanks and the cars, sweeping in amongst the 20th, rounding up the New Zealanders as they rose from their sangars, hands up sheepishly. Upham lay on the ground watching it coming closer, savouring the bitterness of it. One arm, one leg, one man for whom the war was ending in pain and humiliation.

Leggy was beside him.

'You've still got time, Leggy-boy. You can make it if you run for that little wadi. . . . Go on—you're not wounded—scram!'

'No, boss.'

'What are you going to do?'

'I'm staying with you, boss.'

'O.K., Leggy. But what about that truck? I told you and Jack Coyle to make a break for it in that truck. Why didn't you give that a go?'

'Jack did. Last thing I saw he was going great guns. But I didn't want to.'

Buck Carnachan edged over to the pair of them. It had been an unhappy day for signallers like him.

'What's the meaning of it all, boss? Looks like the biggest schemozzle of them all—and I've seen a few. What's gone wrong?'

'I'm sorry, Buck, really sorry.' Upham sounded apologetic, as if the disaster was all his doing.

'Well, have you got a spare fag you can give me? Might be the last I'll smoke for a while.'

Upham handed him a cigarette. They still had a minute or two before the tanks would reach them.

While Carnachan lit up Upham told him of the rules in P.O.W. camps. 'Promote yourself, Buck. Here, take two of my pips. Make yourself an officer. Then you'll come into camp with me—in an officers' camp. You won't have to work. Don't see why we should work for the bloody Hun. Take 'em.'

But Carnachan shook his head. 'Too late, thanks, boss. Truth is, I've just promoted myself to sergeant—I altered my pay-book just before I crawled over here to you chaps. Don't think I'd better try another forgery.'

Charles grinned weakly. 'Good on you, Buck. Now tell Leggy to try and scrounge me a cigarette, will you. That one was my last.'

Buck looked at the butt of the one Charles had given him. 'Oh Christ!' he said. 'Did I take your last ruddy fag? What a hell of a day!'

The leading tank loomed out of the dust, only fifty yards away, its guns swivelling towards them. The end was close at hand.

13

Valley of the Shadow

AN OVERNIGHT stop at Daba . . . hardly more than a few tents in the desert, surrounded by slit trenches and barbed wire. One night at Daba . . . just one more night of pain and exhaustion, of the spectacle of men whose spirits struggled more and more weakly against the growing tortures of the body.

The searing days in the jolting trucks when men's wounds and broken bones threatened to drive them crazy in the never-ending torment. Or were the nights worse? Nights when it was still, and the agony seemed to come flooding in with the darkness and the thirst.

It was better that first day after Ruweisat, when the wounded prisoners lay together in the open, the enemy trucks and tanks laagered around them, while the British guns shelled them all indiscriminately. Yes, they loved the twenty-five-pounder . . . a beautiful gun . . . they were proud of its pin-point accuracy. Yet when the twenty-five-pounders shelled the laager for an hour, unconscious of the fact that it held New Zealand prisoners, not a man was hurt.

Lying exposed in the open as the shells crashed around him, Charles Upham wondered if indeed there were a Providence protecting helpless men. Few of them could even move to find security in the trenches. They just had to lie there on the sand and listen and wait for the next shell.

Bursting and detonating all around them, the shells converted the laager into a place of sudden flame, ear-splitting noise, torn-up metal, and reeking, choking dust. But they lay there in resignation, and some great Hand kept them safe.

And now at Daba, on the slow journey westwards with the prisoner-of-war convoys. . . .

The tent was for wounded officers 'with no future'. Beau Cottrell, one of A Company's officers from the 20th, lay there crippled, his Achilles tendon shot away. No more for him the roar of the crowd as he ran on to the Rugby field in his All Black jersey. There were other New Zealanders in the tent beside him. They had little to do but endure

174

their sufferings, talk of the disaster at Ruweisat, and wonder how many of their friends had survived. Already they knew that no less than five New Zealand battalions had been cut to pieces.

A small man who seemed to be unwounded made his way into the tent and gently roused one of the officers. The wounded man turned over carefully, looked up and asked: 'Found them yet?'

'Yes, boss. All the boys are together.'

'Well, you hop back there, Leggy-boy. See how they're placed for water, will you?'

Leggy nodded, glad to get out of the tent again. The smell of death and badness in there was too strong. He went across to the other tents and dug-outs he had found, saw Bob May there with all the others, and enquired about the water situation.

He returned and reported to Upham.

Sitting up on his stretcher, Charles called loudly for attention. He demanded the chief medical officer. That, of course, was impossible, he was told.

So he shouted louder . . . and louder.

One of the wounded, tongue in cheek, called over to him: 'That's it, Charlie, throw your weight about. Flash your ribbon at them. They might take some notice then.'

Charles scowled. Because he hadn't got his ribbon. When the truck had picked him up off the battlefield, lying there helpless with one leg completely numbed, he had ripped the ribbon off and thrown it away in the sand. If he had kept it he would have received preferential treatment, he thought. He wanted no privileges, wanted no more than any other prisoner.

So he renewed his protests and finally made himself heard. There was enough water for the wounded officers—why not the men? They listened to him, and in the end agreed that it would be better to do what he demanded rather than put up with any more of his hectoring.

So the extra water ration went over to the wounded prisoners of the 20th.

But the arguing was a painful process. Every move now was an agony. His whole body seemed alight. His mind was often hot and wandering, and he knew that several times he had faded out into unconsciousness.

In between times he awoke and for a few minutes then his mind was sharp and vivid, turning over like an express train as if there was little time to lose.

*　　　*　　　*　　　*

It was inevitable for prisoners on both sides to be relieved of anything of value. But as Upham lay on his back, he protested volubly as the Italians looted the wounded prisoners. He knew that many of his own men would do the same, but he wouldn't countenance it himself. Apart from its illegality, he regarded it as degrading as much to the looter as to the victim.

Perhaps it was the force of his personality, or the cold flash of his peculiar eyes, or merely the vehemence of his protests, but the Italians shrank from robbing him. Not so lucky were the others.

Beau Cottrell found himself politely relieved of a beautiful watch that he treasured—a presentation to him back home. A young German took it from him. Cottrell lay suffering with his smashed heel, but grieving more at the loss of so prized a possession. Charles lay beside him.

Upham said suddenly: 'Here, Beau, you take *my* watch.'

Cottrell gave a short laugh. 'No, thanks, Charlie. Mine's gone, that's all that matters.'

'Go on,' Charles said irritably. 'I don't want this one of mine. And, anyhow, the bloody Ites will pinch it off me sooner or later. Go on, take it!'

'No, thank you, Charlie old man. I don't want your watch.'

The blue eyes flared. 'Well, if you don't want it they aren't going to get it.'

And Upham lifted his hand, flung the watch from him. It skidded into the sand a few inches from Cottrell's stretcher. He turned his back on Cottrell, satisfied now that neither was going to suffer more than the other. Beau would have no watch. Neither would he. And he would save himself the ignominy of having it filched from him later. Let it rot in the sand.

But before they shifted him Beau Cottrell rescued Charlie's watch. He kept it with him during the years of captivity that followed, brought it back to New Zealand, and to this day still produces it on demand, with its initials *C.H.U.* on the back. Charles has always point-blank refused its return.

*   *   *   *

Now it was Mersa Matruh. Or he thought it was. Things were not so clear. The men were different. They were all separated. Leggy had been taken off. Beau had gone. In fact, as Upham woke up this morning and looked dazedly around, he couldn't see anyone he knew. They all seemed to be Italians. No New Zealanders at all.

New Zealanders crossing the River Po. At the top of the embankment on the far side Charles Upham leaps from his prison truck and ran for the trees in the background

Upham's daylight escape attempt from Weinsberg prison camp. Still entangled in the barbed wire where he fell, Upham is smoking the cigarette that saved him from being shot only a few moments before

Upham receives his first V.C. from King George VI at Buckingham Palace.
Jack Hinton, another New Zealand V.C., waits his turn

They were on the concrete floor of a cellar; in an old stone barracks building in Matruh. How many times had this building changed hands, he wondered vaguely.

But what did he care? His head seemed like a detached balloon; his arm was living fire. It had had nothing done to it apart from the simplest field dressing. The stench of it was appalling. And the smashed bone was sticking out through the bandage in a way that seemed to tell him he had no hope. It was full of maggots, too.

The smell of blood and putrefaction in this place was overwhelming. Something was going on, some activity, but all he was conscious of was the pain, the presence of other twisted bodies, the terrible sounds of human agony. His mind went out and he lapsed into unconsciousness again. . . .

It was evening. Why was it that they all seemed to come awake now, everyone in this awful place, for the noise was increasing? He came sharply awake at the sound of screaming and looked around. In the dusk he saw the figures of them all, sprawled out across the floor. One look at the man next to him and he knew he was dead. He must have been dead for days, too. The sight and smell of it were unbelievable.

In a glance he could see that these were all badly wounded men— no 'walking wounded' here. They looked like the very worst cases.

Then as the night came more was added to their sufferings. For British planes came over, deluging the town with their bombs—severe, merciless bombing, more than these broken patients could stand. Many gave way to their terror, and screamed and thrashed about in agonized helplessness.

Even when it was over, and they managed to sleep, the fear poured from them again in uncontrollable nightmares, the shock and agony of their wounds making a pitiful blend with the mental torture of the falling bombs.

Next day came, and perhaps his mind was a little clearer. He could see around the cellar now—yes, they were all Italians. He was the only Allied prisoner there. They were all in a very bad way.

The scene in the cellar was indescribable. Even in his illness Upham found it staggering to his senses. For men lay dead in the rapid decomposition of the tropics. Clearly some had lain like that for days. Some orderlies came in and dragged their corpses across the floor, hauling them unconcernedly over the bodies of those still living.

Those alive had plumbed the depths of degradation, as many lay feebly in a mess of their own excreta, crying continuously for water and aid, while others burst suddenly and terrifyingly into the wildest screaming. A few, and a very few, lay like stoics as life ebbed from them.

M

Night came yet again after a day of alternating sleep and consciousness. Again the bombing, again the spectacle of men in the ultimate torments of mind and body. And on top of the bombs came shells from the Royal Navy, bombarding Mersa Matruh to destroy the few buildings that remained standing.

Hysteria, terror, and mortal agony reigned in this fearful cellar. And Charles Upham began to doubt his own sanity as he clung to the life which others were yielding without pride. A place of hideous unreality, yet he knew it was true, that it was all happening, for he was part of it. But he never knew it could be like this.

The pain of his arm was shocking. It would have to be amputated, he knew. And he came to realize that the reason for this ghastly underground pit was to assemble cases requiring amputation or the most drastic forms of surgery. He was resigned to it. Take the arm, he felt. In its present state it would soon lead to his death unless medical treatment was forthcoming.

And he found that down here was where the actual operations were done, too. There was no privacy. It was all just one filthy, communal operating theatre, where those waiting for the surgeon lay cheek by jowl beside those writhing fresh from the scalpel, and those for whom mercy had at last gratefully intervened. There were no drugs, no apparatus, little water. For the victims it was life or death, and it was mostly death.

The Continental doctor approached his amputation patients with a surgeon's knife, a little machine like a hinged paper-cutter, and a saw. As the orderlies closed around the victim, the dreadful details of the operation were spared those others who were looking on; but Upham saw, with cold horror, the blood-encrusted saw being wiped again and again across the doctor's trousers.

Upham's mind failed to register the passing of the next few days. How he himself survived is a mystery. All around him were the dead and dying, and probably only the iron core of his constitution saved him from joining that parade. But the screaming of those whose sufferings were too great for the body to endure, the squalor, the terror, and the appalling conditions he shared with the other wretches, left a mark in his mind that took years to erase. Only in recent times has he been free from periodic nightmares in which he has relived the scenes of human torment that he witnessed in that cellar at Matruh.

The clumping feet of the orderlies woke him. They were coming over towards him . . . the doctor behind them . . . and with them the saw, the thing like a paper-cutter, and the kit of instruments. He wondered hazily if this was his turn.

But no—not yet. It was for the man next to him, a twisted figure with both legs mangled, for whom there was no hope but double amputation.

The orderlies seized the poor fellow, prepared his body quickly, and held him firmly down. Only inches in front of his eyes, Upham stared aghast. The man struggled weakly, making pitiful sounds beneath the hand that was clapped over his mouth. His eyes bulged.

One . . . two . . . and as the cleaver went into the second leg an awful jet of blood spurted from him, straight on to Upham's chest. He recoiled in nausea.

The man gurgled, his throat rattled and choked, and in less than a minute he was dead.

And if that were not enough the grisly team was now advancing on another stricken fellow. Upham could not tear his eyes away. The spectacle was so macabre, so shocking.

This was another leg amputation. Again the dreadful process of holding the man down, hand over his mouth, and the butcher-cum-surgeon sliced around the leg in a jiffy.

It was off, and again the blood came, pulsing out of the hideous stump in great bursts, splashing on to the man next door while one of the orderlies was jumping around trying to avoid being soiled.

And then, as if to cap all other horrors, Upham saw the orderly with something in his hand, and he was trying to jab it on to the bleeding flesh, trying to hold it there and at the same time dodge the spurting blood. And the object he was holding was—a *hot iron*: he was trying to cauterize and seal off the wound with this ghastly relic of surgery a century out of date.

The victim died while they were still working over him.

Charles Upham felt absolutely shattered by these sights. The experience of them was like tearing open some black door and exposing a terrible world beyond, of which he had never known before. How could it be possible? Was he really still alive or was this just the tortured living-on of the mind after death? Was this appalling place really true?

He was aware of the night coming again, and the terror that it brought once more. It was misty in his mind and even the terrible things were like fantasy.

Next morning he awoke. Instantly he felt that something was different. Yes, while he had slept someone had been in and removed part of his bandage. It was lower down, and now high up on his biceps there was a ring drawn with some coloured material like chalk, right round the upper arm. He was feeling bad . . . he didn't bother at first to guess what it meant.

But now in came the orderlies . . . over towards him . . . and now the doctor . . . the kit . . . the saw . . . the thing like a paper-cutter . . . the hot iron.

This was his day . . . his turn.

Quickly they moved him on to a stretcher. They told him—yes, he knew—that the arm had to come off . . . they could not save him otherwise . . . they couldn't devote the time to dressing it. Amputation was all they could offer. Otherwise the gangrene would spread, there would be more infection, and in the end certain death.

He knew now, of course. The chalk mark was the guide line for the surgeon.

Hoping against hope, he asked how they would do it . . . what anaesthetic?

The doctor said casually: 'There isn't any anaesthetic. We haven't got any.'

They would amputate his arm without anaesthetic?

They shrugged, indicated the other suffering men on the cellar floor. They all had to go through with it.

And suddenly he knew—if they did it, it would kill him. In his state of health he could never survive the awful shock of such an operation. He had always hated and dreaded pain . . . why should he be butchered now? Perhaps the others had agreed for fear of being left to die a worse death, of being utterly neglected. Well, he could look after himself better than they.

They prepared him. He protested once; then twice; and again. Until all of a sudden they stopped and looked at him, and realized that he was having the effrontery to refuse their treatment.

Just for a moment the doctor paused in surprise. Then impatiently he pushed Upham off the stretcher, gave him not one further glance, and called sharply for the next case, the next sacrifice. They had given him his chance. He had rejected it—they wiped their hands of him.

But, as he lay on the floor shocked and shaking, Upham knew, with complete certainty, that he had saved his own life. He had been within an inch of giving it away, under the guise of medical treatment. Now he felt he could live, he could get better, he could fight for himself. All he had to do was find someone who would dress his arm decently.

*   *   *   *

The days seemed to pass on and on, and Charles faded in and out of consciousness, too ill to sense the passage of time. Once he became aware that a British doctor was bending over him, a fellow-P.O.W., and that his arm was being dressed expertly.

And then things seemed to become straighter and his mind clearer. He was still in the cellar, but the hot dizzy feeling in his head was subsiding, and the arm no longer felt as if his whole body was tied on to it, with leaden weights attached.

He could soon walk again, shakily at first, enough to move around the cellar and restore some decency to his person, to feel the strength starting to ebb back little by little, and for his mind to begin thinking: get well, the quicker the better; for until health was regained there could be no escape.

He was still in the war, even if he had to fight it behind prison wire. But war, and escape, would have to wait on recovery. It would be senseless breaking off into the African desert without food, with few clothes, a recent leg wound, and a hideously shattered arm that they had just put in plaster of Paris. He must wait.

That he should even think of the future was proof that he was alive again. But he had passed well down the long Valley; he had wandered deep into the Shadow, and he had felt close the enveloping folds of its mantle. His life could never be quite the same after that.

* * * *

The hospital ship leaving Mersa Matruh for Italy did not want prisoners on board with lice in their hair or filth on their clothes. So Charles Upham found himself walking slowly up the gangway with his head shaved clean, feeling faint and sick from a touch of sunstroke on his uncovered pate.

Walking up a gangway completely naked was certainly a new experience. He supposed they would give him fresh clothes on board, or perhaps his old ones would be fumigated and returned.

The Italian girl standing on the deck looked for one moment at the stark New Zealander, adorned only by his identity discs and plaster cast, before turning casually away. Charles's embarrassment was replaced by a sharp feeling of hatred at finding himself subjected to such humiliation.

They took him below. There he would be the only New Zealander. Somehow, already they seemed to regard him as rather a special guest, not to be trifled with, and to be watched carefully.

Some men, like Upham, have that personality that seems to radiate a perpetual challenge. But while that personality deterred them from taking liberties with him, it had the effect of singling him out.

Half-way across the Mediterranean the ship was attacked by British

Hurricanes. Upham did not know if the ship was correctly marked with the insignia to protect it from enemy attack, but he knew the ship was being used for more than hospital purposes. There were a number of Italian soldiers and German officers on board, all combatants, merely being transported to Italy on tours of duty.

As the planes swung away, it was against Upham that the Italians turned their wrath. For a few hectic moments he feared they would pounce on him and cut his throat, so hysterical and violent was their reaction. The Germans on board smoothed out a ticklish situation.

But they, too, looked on Upham as special bait. They taunted him with German victories, revelled in the way he flared up in reply.

'But, Captain Upham,' one English-speaking German said smoothly. 'Surely you realize that all the world's greatest people have German ancestry. Even in your own New Zealand Army have you not a Colonel Dittmer, a Colonel Kippenberger? With those names, would you not agree that they must have come from German stock?'

Upham just looked coldly at him.

'Yes . . . today they would be Colonel von Dittmer and von Kippenberger. And, of course, there is General von Freyberg himself—your commander. Even the discoverer of your country was a German—Abel von Tasman. Ah, Captain Upham, the greatest men in all history were all Germans. It might surprise you to know that the playwright Shakespeare was really Wilhelm von Shakespeare. I can tell you what part of Germany he came from. Does that surprise you?'

'No,' Upham said suddenly, looking up with his eyes glinting. 'No, it doesn't surprise me. But there's another famous man you haven't mentioned. Would you tell me about him?'

'Certainly,' the German officer purred.

Upham drew breath.

'Tell me, then, what part of Germany did this man come from . . . I dare say you'll reckon he was a German too. . . .'

'Very likely,' the officer nodded. 'His name, please?'

'Jesus *von* Christ!' Upham hissed at him.

*   *   *   *

The ship brought them into the port of Reggio, on the southern tip of Italy, right opposite Sicily. He would disembark here, they told him. He would be walking past crowds. Just as a precaution, they would have to handcuff him. It would be rather awkward, of course, with one arm in plaster.

Upham said nothing. He did not mind. As a prisoner he intended to treat his captors roughly. He fully expected to be treated roughly in return.

They gathered around him when the manacles were put on, sitting jovially around a table in the officers' quarters. Despite his truculence and barely concealed contempt for them all, they liked to hear him talk. They knew him now as a V.C. winner, a genuine war hero. It added a little glamour to their own lives to spend time talking with such a notability.

The word came to go. They were all ready. Upham was sitting on one side of the table. A large water jug stood on the table near the opposite side.

With a casual expression Upham rose from the table, his knee out in front. Up went the table suddenly, over went the jug, and the water splashed into the laps of two German officers.

He apologized quickly. After all, a man in handcuffs is inclined to be clumsy. But they had good reason to doubt the sincerity of his apology.

It was time to disembark.

Barefooted, with no more than a shirt and a pair of shorts, still in handcuffs, Upham was directed down the gangway and on to Italian soil.

Here it was a parade. People lined the streets of the town, waiting for their men to leave the ship and march up from the wharves.

First some Italian soldiers emerged. They marched smartly into the town and the crowd cheered them to the echo.

Then came Italian wounded. Abruptly the cheers ceased and, as one, the crowd burst into bitter weeping.

Then cheers again for the Germans.

Then the prisoners.

As if the parade were all for him, Upham was led along the street on his own, walking uncertainly between the lines of citizens.

The hissing and booing grew. Some emerged from the crowd and spat at him as he shambled past, arms crossed in front, looking left and right in contemptuous acceptance of the spectacle they were making of him.

It seemed that the whole town was on the street that day, and all subjected him to abuse as he walked past.

All?

All except one. For as the procession neared its destination Upham saw a little Italian girl run out from the crowd, a child of six or seven perhaps, quite uncomprehending the reason for this demonstration. All she saw was a ragged-looking man stumbling along, ill, barefooted, one wrist fastened to the other, and with one arm in plaster. She ran towards him.

Into the cradle made by his two arms the little girl gently laid a bag of sweet fresh pears. Then shyly she turned and ran back into the crowd.

Perhaps Charles Upham's head rose a little higher as the procession moved on.

*   *   *   *

From Reggio the prisoners travelled north by train. The journey is remembered by Upham only for its discomfort and pain, and the longing for the swaying and lurching to come to an end so that his arm could be rested.

They sat him in a compartment with some German officers, who continued the mild baiting that had been their amusement on board ship. They had food and wine. The food they shared with him, but when he asked for a portion of the wine they brusquely refused. He seethed at the awareness that their good-humour was simulated, merely a cloak for their more natural arrogance.

All around a table again, glasses of wine in front of them, but none for him.

This time it wouldn't appear an accident. The previous incident had been brushed off far too easily.

He chose his moment. Then, in an unmistakable gesture, he suddenly rose from his chair, put his knee under the table, and heaved.

The effect was just as he planned. Into their laps the wine cascaded, over their conceited uniforms it spread its stain, and Upham laughed aloud in rich satisfaction.

It was almost too good to be true that he had pulled the same trick twice!

The rest of the journey was not so polite. Never mind—that round was his.

Into Naples they swung, then on trucks to Caserta Hospital, a short distance out of the city.

On the third floor of a large stone building seven wounded officers found themselves together in one room—Upham with his broken arm, Beau Cottrell with his Achilles tendon, Major Lynch of the 18th, grievously wounded, and four others.

There began then at Caserta the months of waiting and futility that only prisoners of war can truly understand. From the turmoil and stimulation of fighting, suddenly life is switched into a deadening low gear, the thrill is gone, the hope is gone, the end of the war is now in the control of people far, far away. And only prisoners really know what it means, month after month, to be confined by walls or wire.

*   *   *   *

The transition in Upham's life from his intent war-making to the dreariness and clogging tempo of prison camp affected him deeply. For a man of his far-ranging independence, confinement was almost more than he could stand. Not for him the docile acceptance of his lot. Every day as a prisoner was a mental torture, every month a harder and harder fight to retain his self-control against melancholy and boredom.

But for the first long months it was a matter of keeping alive. The only problem was recovery, and that was hard enough. They attended to his arm and managed to save it, but only at the cost of his general health falling perilously low. The Italian doctors did their best with the equipment available, and the attention given the wounded was reasonable and considerate.

But, as the months of 1942 passed, more and more Allied prisoners came flocking in, filling the wards and the passages. Food became shorter, medical attention more hurried and less frequent.

They were grey months of suffering and sickness. Probably only Upham's wiry constitution and implacable determination enabled him to survive. He lived through it. So did Cottrell. But all the other five officers in that room died there.

Charles spent many hours sitting beside Major Lynch, trying to introduce a little cheer into his last days. It was something to be able to move about, not to have to lie abed suffering month after month.

'You know, Beau,' Upham said to Cottrell, 'what a little thing it takes to floor a man. Look at you now—just a little nick through the heel, and you're not worth a tin of fish. You with your one leg, me with one arm—we'll go into partnership after the war, eh, Beau?'

Cottrell said: 'You'd be no good, Charlie, if you thought of coming into partnership with me in law. My God, you'd look awful in a wig and gown.'

'And you'd be no ruddy good, Beau, if you're thinking of coming into partnership with me on a farm. We need two-legged men on the farms. And, Beau . . . do you know what we do to horses that have got the same thing as you've got?' He pointed towards Cottrell's heel.

Beau shook his head. 'All right. What do you do?'

Upham grinned maliciously. 'When that happens to a horse we call it hamstrung. And when a horse is hamstrung it's useless. We shoot the bastard.'

Cottrell aimed a pillow at his head, and the two had a good laugh that lightened the gloom in the ward for a few minutes.

Hour after hour Charles sat alongside Lynch and Cottrell, talking and joking, recalling rather desperately some of his funniest experiences back in the New Zealand mountains, to help keep his friends' minds off their own suffering.

He was too ill himself to give anything more than passing thought to the question of escape. Survival and recovery were all that mattered just yet. His own shaky health was dragged down further by an attack of jaundice, and then he endured weeks of debilitating toothache. While prepared to let them treat his arm, he obstinately refused to accept dental treatment. It was too personal, too close and intimate. He couldn't stand that from people he loathed.

And so the dreary, painful months began to crawl by, death and suffering the chief companions, little left but an indomitable will to overcome the despair of his environment.

*   *   *   *

Upham's health sank very low at Caserta. He might easily have gone the way of his five companions in the room but for a transfer some months later to another hospital in the north of Italy, at Castel san Pietro.

Charles remained at Castel san Pietro about four months before being moved on again in March 1943. They were months of slow recovery. Food was good, medical attention adequate, and all prisoners admired the kindness of the nuns who nursed in the wards.

But, like Caserta, it was overcrowded. Wounded men lay in all the passages. There was no room for any recreation except singing.

Slowly the glimmerings of health began to return. From the lethargy of deep illness Upham's spirits began to stir again. To balance the maddening despair he felt at his own imprisonment, he found that he gained some mental contentment from exerting himself to help the others. Many a night after lights were out, with his room-mates lying silent and depressed in their convalescence, Upham would begin talking—just quietly, talking as if to himself, talking about the ways and the winds of Canterbury, of the snows and swamps in the uplands, of the sheep and the horses standing like pictures on the headlands overlooking the sea, and the rivers running blue with the ice from the far mountain-tops. And the others listened in the darkness, transported to those happy lands of home, and they felt the comfort of nature and friendship. Sometimes a quiet yarn would follow; but often, as he finished, and his last story died away, there would be silence in the room until, after a while, one by one, they would call quietly to each other: 'Good night.'

And some slept then. While others lay awake in the shadows, calmed and refreshed, and their minds would grope to picture her as they last saw her, the shape of her face, her voice, her touch, and they would count the hours back around the world, so as to ask themselves: 'What will she be doing now?'

*   *   *   *

No longer dangerously ill, but still weak and emaciated, Upham now began to display the first glint of rebellion that later dominated his prison life. His mind and body were freed from concentrating on mere survival. He was free to start foraging again.

There was an Italian security officer at Castel san Pietro whom, for lack of a better name, they called Rat-face. Furtive and suspicious, he gradually aroused Upham's contempt and resentment.

Rat-face always carried an evil-looking knife, a most sinister weapon. It seemed to typify his mean personality and, to Upham, it was a symbol he was not prepared to accept. Charles might have been content if Rat-face had carried a revolver. That would have been an accepted weapon of war. But to have a man parading in front of him armed with a *knife* seemed to Charles to be a psychological wrong that needed righting.

He did it by fright.

One morning, as Rat-face moved slyly down the room, the prisoners eyeing him with casual disinterest, Upham made his gesture.

Abruptly he stepped out from his bunk, walked a few paces firmly towards Rat-face, and stood belligerently in front of him, feet astride.

'Give that to me!' he demanded sharply. And with that he reached out and laid hands on the knife.

Rat-face leapt in surprise, clapped his hand over the scabbard, and stepped hurriedly backwards, jerking the knife-handle out of Upham's fingers. He looked up into those frozen blue eyes that were beamed on him like enemy searchlights fastened on a defenceless aircraft.

For several taut seconds the two men stood facing each other. Then Rat-face seemed to shrink, he stepped back another pace, then turned and retreated ignominiously in the face of Upham's silent challenge.

Charles stood and watched him hurry out. Then he looked around and grinned. He felt good. He felt marvellous. He had, for a moment, acquired the moral ascendancy over his captors. That was all he wanted. His spirit was coming back.

Humphrey Hall, an architect from Christchurch, sat back on his bunk and drew breath again. Like all the others in the ward, he had been startled by the suddenness of the incident. He said slowly: 'You nearly started something that time, Charlie. You scared the wits out of little Rat-face.'

The others laughed shortly in agreement. But it was a somewhat uneasy laugh. It died away quickly.

It is always a tense and gripping moment when, after months of silence and stillness, any man, or any animal, suddenly shows a fang.

14

Escape at the River

LEAVING Beau Cottrell still incapacitated at Castel san Pietro, Charles was transferred to a normal P.O.W. camp in March 1943. Here at Modena (not far from Bologna) he found himself again amongst friends—Neil McPhail, Dick and Wally Ormond, Tiny Armour, Tom Bromley, Wynne Mason, Bill Allan, Doc Beattie, and others.

Charles has never forgotten the kindness that greeted him at Modena. The other P.O.W.s there had little enough for their own comfort, but when they saw Upham come in, obviously still weak, they immediately made everything stretch a little further so as to provide for his well-being. He came in wearing only a pair of thin Italian trousers and a shirt. It was only a matter of seconds before Dick Ormond forced him to accept a heavy, warm, polo-neck sweater—a garment which Charles kept to the end of his war-days, and which probably saved him from dying of cold more than once.

Someone else had a spare pair of boots, and each man contributed a little from his own meagre supply of tobacco. Charles has declared that never could anyone have met such kindness from those who were themselves ill-equipped to give anything away but fellowship.

Modena was a new camp, well constructed, and with good food. Some of the camp appointments reached quite a level of splendour, with marble generously lavished on washrooms and lavatories. It housed about 240 New Zealand officers and 800 or so South Africans—and it was here that Charles developed some of the friendships with the South Africans that he still treasures. There was Neville Holmes, a South African lawyer who later became a Supreme Court judge, and Sir de Villiers Graaff, one of that country's personalities and leader of a political party.

Charles arrived at Modena still suffering from his wounds and illnesses, but fit enough now to take part in regular P.O.W. camp life. He was quiet to the point of moodiness at times, scheming and thinking, preferring a serious talk or argument with a close friend rather than the greater jollification of cards or singing.

Charles loved arguing. He would willingly argue over any subject whatever, and the longer the argument lasted, the more dogmatic he became, the more intent that others should agree with his point of view. Yet if Charles knew that the other man was an expert on his subject he accepted the other's view almost too willingly, quite humble in his respect.

Few knew him better than Neil McPhail, and there were few whom Charles liked better.

They were sitting together peeling potatoes.

Upham wound up the long argument by saying: '. . . the Huns caused the war, they began it, and they'll start another war unless we wipe all their industry off the face of the earth. No armistice terms, just destroy the whole ruddy lot. There's never been a good German yet.'

'Oh, I don't know, Charlie,' McPhail said. 'Blame Hitler and the Nazis if you like. And blame the German people for not stopping him when they had the chance. But there must be good Germans, just like there are bad New Zealanders.'

Charles's eyes suddenly flashed. 'Good Germans? There are *no* good Germans. There never has been a good Hun.'

'Oh, come off, Charlie. I don't hold any brief for the ruddy Huns, but there have been good ones.'

'Doing what?'

'Well . . . in the arts, for example. Take music . . .'

'Music! Music!' and with an oath Upham threw down the potato knife he had in his hand, jumped to his feet, and stalked away.

He refused to speak to Neil McPhail again for a whole week.

But that was part of Upham's make-up—an implacable hatred of the enemy, coupled with a refusal to make any concessions that would weaken his single-minded attitude.

It was part of that same attitude that made him refuse to learn Italian or German, which so many others found comparatively easy to do. He knew it would help him if he were to escape, but he could not demean himself to do so. Likewise, he persistently refused to look at any enemy newspapers, or to give more than a contemptuous glance at enemy notices or orders that appeared in English.

In other words, he refused to merge himself mentally into the life in which he was physically confined.

But with John Batty he spent hours and days discussing high-country and low-country farming methods, and with his friends was always ready for a serious yarn—not about camp life, or the Germans, or the Italians, but about New Zealand and home, and things that were British—things that were all far away. He wanted to keep them in the forefront of his mind, to show that he did not accept, and never would accept, the fact that he was no longer a free agent.

Charles's attitude was so completely unyielding that any slight brush with the guards was likely to flame suddenly into a serious incident. This naturally was the source of tension and worry to many of his friends. They were equally intent on escaping if ever opportunity offered. They were equally anxious to stop the enemy obtaining any psychological advantage over them. But there were ways and ways of going about it.

Charles was so continually arrogant to the Italians and Germans that trouble seemed to be just round the corner, day after day. His friends became afraid for Charles's own safety, concerned that one day he would go too far in his baiting. More than once they intervened to save an unpleasant incident from breaking out into a grave one.

It was like that on the night of Tom Bromley's birthday. It had become a custom that a certain amount of vino would be saved up for birthday celebrations. As the night drew on, the others faded from the party one by one, leaving Bromley and Charles alone at the finish. But these two were tipsily determined not to go to bed.

As always happens at such parties, the others first suggested that Tom and Charles should break it up. It had been a good party. Charlie was merrier than the rest, but surely he had had enough. From polite suggestion, they turned to asking, then to pleading, then to threatening.

'I won't go to bed till Tom goes,' Charles declared thickly.

'And I won't go to bed till Charlie does—good old Charlie.' So said Bromley.

And nothing would make them decide who should go first.

So amid the clamour of their arguing, and the weary shouting of their friends, it was not surprising that the captain of the guard should decide to look in and see what the row was all about. It might be a diversion to cover an escape. He would count the bodies.

Inside the hut the first man his eye met was Upham. Here was a prisoner still fully dressed. The Captain naturally turned his attention to him. Unhappy decision!

As the innocent and conscientious Captain stared suspiciously at the boisterous New Zealander, he became aware that the man was advancing on him, an intent look on his face.

The restraint and self-control of all the long months of confinement were dissolving in the warmth of the vino. Straight in front of Upham was the symbol of the enemy.

Like a man unleashing a savage dog, Upham launched into an abusive tirade at the unhappy Captain. He swore at him, shouted at him, let his feelings run raw and wild in a truculent display of simple hate and temper.

As men turned over in their bunks and peered at the two figures in the gloom of the darkened hut, they gained different impressions of what happened next. There certainly was confusion, with other P.O.W.s jumping out of bed and hurrying to Charles's side. They simply had to save him from getting in too deep.

But in the rush there are some who say that Charles finally leapt on the startled Captain, seized him by the throat, and began to shake him savagely. Others didn't see this happen. Questioned after the war, Charles cagily said: 'I might have.'

Whatever did happen it is, at any rate, common ground that his hut-mates leapt into action, dragged Charles reluctantly away from his victim, and then poured soothing words over the head of the affrighted Captain. The episode had gone too far already, and they feared its consequences.

Only two things saved Upham. One was the immediate intervention of his friends. The other was the solemn assurance given the Camp Commandant that Upham was so drunk that he knew not what he was doing and mistook the captain of the guard for his mate Tom Bromley, with whom he was having an argument.

For the first of many times Upham went to the 'boob'.

*   *   *   *

With health returning, Upham began to look for freedom. His subsequent escape attempts were mostly opportunist affairs, but on each occasion there is evidence that he had swiftly weighed up the risks and the chances. When he had been in action a feature of his leadership had been the rapid balancing of risks against the value of the objective. He brought the same kind of reasoning to his escape attempts.

Charles thought that escape from the punishment cells at Modena would be easier than escape from the compound or the barracks. So by some carefully phrased insolence he obtained another short gaol sentence and cheerfully went off to the boob.

It was a simple plan. If he could get out on to the roof of the cell-block he would have fewer obstacles to surmount before getting free. And they'd never expect an escape from the security cells—that sort of thing isn't done. But the cells had one weakness—they had plaster-board ceilings.

He had no tools. All he had in the cell was his bed.

Upending the bed was hard enough, for his arm was still withered

In typically casual clothes, Upham says goodbye to Molly as he leaves for Greece

Amanda, Caroline, and Virginia

'I'd always be jealous of my friends on farms'

and weak. But he got it there at last, standing it up vertically at a spot which would be screened from view if someone opened the door and casually glanced inside.

He waited till he judged the guards were out of hearing. Then, with a physical effort that almost broke him and gave him agonies in his arm, he lifted the bed bodily upwards and crashed its end against the ceiling.

His strength wouldn't have allowed him to do it more than three or four times, for the strain seemed prodigious; but on the second lift the plaster cracked, and a large slab fell away.... One more heave ... and a hole big enough to squeeze through gaped in the ceiling.

He propped up the bed like a ladder. He doubted even now if he would have the ability to climb up.

But, with the fervour of escape coursing through him now, extra strength seemed to come. Before he was fully conscious of it, he seemed to have his hands, then his knees, at the rim of the hole, and he was dragging himself through.

Inside the ceiling now. One glance inside the cell, of course, and he was doomed. From now on he would have to work like a demon. It was only a matter of wrenching off a few tiles, then he'd be out on the roof, with the whole world at his feet.

He grabbed at a tile, shook it, felt around it, wondered why it wouldn't shift. He tried another. Not a budge there either. Quickly he shifted position, attacked the tiles at another spot, until with a dawning exasperation he realized that every tile was tightly wired down in place. Not a single one seemed to be lying free, which would give him a gap to use for tearing out the others.

If only he had a hammer, a screw-driver, a nail-file even—anything at all. But his fingers alone were not up to a task like this—not in the time available.

It was only after he had twisted and picked away with his fingers, with little success, that he heard the sounds from below. He heard his cell door opened, heard the uproar when they saw his bed upended, and the hole in the ceiling.

They caught him there, crouching under the roof. But it took them quite a time to find him in the shadows.

*   *   *   *

As 1943 advanced there was not so much enthusiasm for escape schemes. The war had at last turned in favour of the Allies. From a low point in August 1942, when the Axis forces were deep into Egypt, were

N

pressing on Stalingrad, and had much of the Russian oil-fields in their hands, the tide had changed.

In the Pacific the Americans had come ashore on the Solomons and were taking the first land offensive against the enemy there. By December, Montgomery's 8th Army was sweeping across North Africa, and the first great amphibious campaign of the war saw landings in Algeria and Morocco with the Americans now, at last, involved in the land fighting.

By May 1943 the war in Africa was over and the whole continent of Europe was now the target for the next Allied assault. The great German war machine, which three years before had seemed so invincible, was on the defensive, suffering its appalling losses at the hands of the Russians, enduring destruction at home from the bombs that the British and Americans rained from the skies.

Then in July came the invasion of Sicily. Mussolini resigned that month, his Fascists were broken up, and in a few weeks the armistice with Italy was signed.

To meet the likelihood of an armistice the British War Office had sent an instruction to almost every P.O.W. camp in Italy. All personnel, it said, were 'to stay put when war ends'; they were to organize themselves into military units and await orders; arms and assistance would be flown in; officers were to be prepared to take command of nearby other-ranks' camps.

That was the order that every Senior British Officer in P.O.W. camps received. No order cancelling or amending it ever arrived—nor was ever given. The failure to amend that order was one of the war's most obtuse blunders, with grim results that were all too quickly glossed over. Those who disobeyed and broke away into the Italian country-side mostly reached safety.

In Modena, where almost all New Zealand officer–P.O.W.s were held, preparations had been well made. There were plans for taking over a nearby airfield with all its aircraft. The machine-guns guarding the camp were to be reversed, so as to protect the prisoners from the ire of retreating Germans.

Then to Colonel Shuttleworth, the Senior British Officer, the Italian Commandant added confirmation of what Shuttleworth had already been ordered. It was best, the Commandant said, for the prisoners to remain where they were. The Germans were 'pulling out of Italy', and a British force had already landed near Genoa and was heading eastwards.

Shuttleworth passed on this information to his fellow-officers at a parade. He told them the orders he had received.

But by 2 p.m. on 9th September Shuttleworth feared that he had been betrayed. He called the camp together, told them that the situation was so uncertain that any who wished to go could go—but they would have to move quickly.

At 2.30 p.m. German troops swept into the camp and took over.

Upham was in the camp hospital as these fateful days were unfolding. He was still wasted and gaunt, and was running a high temperature, as the news of the armistice swept the camp. Sinus trouble had been plaguing him, bringing such severe headaches that he had blacked out twice in the last few days. On the second occasion he was taken off to hospital. But he was not going to witness these events from a hospital bed, so, as rumour after rumour flooded in on the inmates of Modena, he found his way out of hospital and back to his friends.

Charles Upham, Johnny Sullivan, one or two others—they gathered together to debate the latest news.

They argued it out and in the end agreed it was their duty to obey the orders that had been given. They would stay in the camp. Some others were already on their way out, haversacks of clothes and food rapidly packed. But how would those men get on when the relief troops arrived—would they be heroes then or would they be on the mat for wilful flouting of orders that had been prepared for their salvation?

No; the proper course was to stay.

Upham was weak and shaky. He was glad to return to the hospital. He was still there when the arrival of the Germans showed how Shuttleworth had been deceived.

With the Italians drifting away, and the Germans moving swiftly to regain control over the prisoners of Modena, Charles spent the hours in hospital fretting at his weakness and roaming the buildings on the look-out for escape openings.

It mightn't be so hard to escape from the hospital. Probably the patients would not be moved on by the Germans until they were fit enough to travel. Perhaps they wouldn't be guarded so closely. Yes—he would stand a better chance of escape if he stayed in hospital. He mightn't be fit enough for a few days—but after that he might sham, then make a break while they still thought his illness made him immobile.

But something was radically wrong with that idea, and it took a little time before Upham recognized what it was. It was a matter of conscience.

The hospitals—the Red Cross—they had been good to him, he pointed out to a friend. Wouldn't it be an abuse of the Red Cross if he used its freedom to aid him in an escape? If a man did that, would hospital and Red Cross privileges for other prisoners be tightened up, perhaps withdrawn?

To Upham the answer seemed clear.

So he left the hospital again, this time in pyjamas, carrying his clothes, and walked back into the compound. He knew the first convoys for Germany would soon be leaving. Once back in the compound, away from the hospital, he could carry out his break, and there would be no reprisals on the people who had shown consideration towards him.

One of his friends of 20th days, Evan Wilson, saw him come back inside. He knew Upham was still a sick man.

'What are you coming in here for, Charlie? You'd be better to stay with the sick.'

Upham replied: 'I'm going to make a break for it, Evan; but I won't escape from the Red Cross. That's why I'm here.'

Charles had his plans ready. He knew of an enlarged drain where he could hide. Others had similar ideas. Hiding-places were being rapidly constructed in ceilings, under floors, in short tunnels, in angles of buildings, all by men who reasoned that they could hide up quietly for a few days while the Germans took over and removed the prisoners; then they would steal out and break off into the fields.

Upham found the M.O. beside him.

'Don't do it, Charlie. You're not well enough. You'd never survive two or three nights in the open. Chaps in good condition can face up to it, but you just couldn't make it.'

Upham looked at him soberly. 'I'm ready to take a chance. What show have I really got, Doc? Go on—tell me straight.'

The M.O. told him straight.

'You have no show at all, Charlie. None whatever. The condition you're in—you're a dead man if you go. That's certain.'

Upham accepted his verdict.

*   *   *   *

On 12th September 1943 the Germans started shipping out the Allied prisoners of Modena. Many were taken to the local railway station, where they entrained for Germany. Others travelled the first stage of the journey, from Modena to Mantua, by motor-truck.

Charles Upham was amongst those sent by road.

German S.S. troops guarded the convoy. The prisoners travelled in open Army trucks, one S.S. man driving, another armed guard sitting beside him. There were no guards in the back of the trucks with the prisoners. But immediately behind every truckload of P.O.W.s came a truck manned by armed guards, who could cover both the prisoners in front and those on the truck immediately behind. So the convoy was spaced—one P.O.W. truck, one S.S. guard-truck, and so on.

On each guard-truck a machine-gun was mounted, able to fire instantly in case of trouble either to the front or behind. The S.S. guards were all heavily armed.

Out of Modena the convoy swung, turning north towards the Reich, first stop Mantua. Between the two cities lay the River Po.

Charles recognized that once they reached Germany prospects of a successful escape were very poor. The further north they travelled, the more slender became his chances. If he could seize a chance while they were still in Italy he felt well enough now to risk days and nights in the open, dodging the Germans, gradually working his way south.

But in a convoy like this it would be madness to try it, except under the most favourable circumstances. The trucks were following one another so closely that any man leaping to the ground would come under fire in a matter of seconds. And with all the fire-power the S.S. were carrying a run for it was just not 'on'.

But he decided to keep his eye on the road and the surrounding countryside. Something might turn up. An opportunity might suddenly develop, and as suddenly disappear. Any decision would have to be a quick one. And every further mile they went put him that much further from success.

He learnt with some respect that none of the other officers in his truck thought the journey offered any escape prospects. The guards were too close, too alert, too heavily armed. This was just not the time or place.

Nor was it any use making a break while the daylight lasted. It would need to be getting dark—not so dark that he couldn't see the road and the cover that lay in the fields alongside, but dark enough to avoid being a sitting shot for the S.S.

The problem: if he decided to make a break, should he choose the first opportunity where the cover looked good, and take the risk of daylight; or should he wait for twilight and perhaps find then that there was no cover?

There could be no answer to that problem. He would just have to wait and see if any chances turned up and make a decision on the spot. Something would *have* to happen—once he allowed himself to be taken across the border he was lost.

His restless eyes peered from side to side as the afternoon hours advanced, but the trucks churned remorselessly on, almost bumper to bumper. Once or twice his pulses stirred as the convoy approached a wood, but the S.S. seemed to sense the danger, the trucks closed right up, and the man behind the machine-gun looked far too attentive. No hope.

By sundown he realized how hopeless it was. The others were quite right—a closely guarded convoy like this gave a man no chance at all. He had better resign himself to it.

*   *   *   *

It was coming dusk when they reached the River Po, and the convoy began the slow crossing of the river on a pontoon bridge from the southern to the northern shore. Upham looked ahead with dull interest. On the northern shore the road, after leaving the pontoons, crept up an embankment about thirty feet high, then ran along the top. Beyond that the bank probably fell away again, protecting the fields like a dyke.

Almost like an abstract theory, the idea gathered in his mind. They were half-way across the bridge then. When they reached the other side and the truck started climbing up the slope what would happen at the top? Coming off the pontoon bridge perhaps the S.S. truck might fall behind. So—if a man jumped from the truck when it reached the top of the embankment, and leapt down into the fields beyond, he would be shielded from the guard-truck behind for a few seconds—until it reached the top also—a few seconds before the S.S. men could fire.

It was hardly more than a casual thought, wandering into his mind like a wisp. But, as he followed the idea out to its end, it began to blossom, and the risks of it, the chances of it, started to surge through him. It all turned on that blind spot—when the S.S. men were below the lip of the embankment and the prisoners' truck was on the top. Jump off—and the S.S. might not even see him. Hardly likely, but at any rate they would have to get to the top before they could fire after him.

But would there be cover in the fields? Would there be a field at all? Would it be swamp? Would the guard-truck be too close?

But this could be *it*. He had to be ready in case.

Quickly he nudged his way to the rear of the truck, saying nothing, getting into position in case the chance came. Here again was the old feeling—the tight-gripping hollowness that comes just before action, that makes a man conscious of every sound, every whisper, every movement, magnified. But now it was rushing on fast.

And his truck was off the bridge now, grinding up the slope of the embankment.

Yes! It was the time, the chance! For Upham saw, in a moment of savage satisfaction, that in crossing the pontoons the convoy had become strung out. The nearest S.S. truck was lagging behind. It was only just coming off the bridge.

On to the top, speed dead slow. The guard-truck was churning up the slope behind them.

He could see beyond the embankment now. First there was a low bank, about three feet high, rising up from the road. But beyond that there was a long thirty-foot slope down to the fields.

Long lines of vines down there. Poor cover. Some trees about 150 yards away. He would have to make it to there. It was too far. They'd be firing at him before he'd gone half the distance. He wished it were darker.

But there might not be a better opportunity. Better to take the risk now, when he still had a chance, than later on when there'd be no chance at all.

In a flash he made the decision. He chose the very spot, the very instant.

He grasped the tail-board, braced himself for the effort, then flung himself over. He hit the ground hard, went crashing on to his face, and felt the sudden sharp distress of being 'winded'. He groped to his feet, staggered to the three-foot bank at the side, climbed up it, then seemed to pause an instant on the very summit of the embankment.

It had all happened before anyone realized.

And now he literally threw himself forward, lost his footing, went sprawling, rolling over and over down the slope. His withered arm gave him an awful twinge.

Near the foot of the bank he scrambled to his feet, set off running towards the trees as fast as he could. The going was flat, but he had to run down the lane between the vines.

He seemed to have gone only a few yards before the bullets came. The S.S. men, well-trained marksmen, were into action in seconds. Leaping from their guard-truck, they lined the top of the bank, had a clear view of Upham as he raced across the fields below them. With sub-machine-guns and rifles the fusillade started, fire pouring towards the hapless man as he sprinted for cover. He felt the bullets around him, whipping past his ears, plucking into the earth at his feet. And he ducked and he dodged, praying that he might make it to the olive trees. Had he ever run so fast, and felt so weak?

Upham rarely experienced fear in the days when he had faced enemy fire. Fear had become submerged in greater emotions. But now, as he ran from the bullets, he felt more scared than ever in his life, knowing that he was the hunted, not the hunter, that he couldn't hit back, that any moment . . .

The convoy had halted. In truck after truck the New Zealand and South African officers watched and feared, wondering who it was who had attempted the impossible, stimulated by the drama of it all, steeling themselves against the inevitable result of such a torrent of fire poured after one fugitive.

Gasping and lurching, Charles covered the first hundred yards, knees like jelly, incredulous that he had got so far without being shot down. It had been too close—the spot was all right, the light not bad, but that guard-truck had closed up rather too quickly.

There was a grove of olive trees and undergrowth ahead. If he could reach it, hide there till dark, they might miss him. The guards couldn't let the convoy remain stationary for long in the fading light. Others might make a break. Anyway, he was finished—he couldn't run much further.

He dodged again and again. They hadn't hit him yet. They never could, these Huns.

And in a sudden moment he found himself crashing to the ground. Something had hit him, tripped him up, sent him sprawling headlong.

But there was no shock, no pain.

In an instant he realized it. He had been hit all right—but on the heel of his boot. In a flash it had tumbled him into the dust.

He crawled into the grove, dragged himself out of sight, lay there helpless and panting.

There were shouted orders in German. While some remained on the embankment covering the fields, about ten S.S. men climbed down the slope, spread out carefully into extended order and began moving steadily to the spot where Upham had last been seen.

It was rapidly getting darker.

They moved down through the vines, arms at the ready, while the convoy waited. And the word spread from truck to truck, like a silent, sympathetic flame: '*It's Charlie Upham.*'

Some said: 'They'll finish him this time.'

Charles heard the searchers coming closer. He lay dead still.

Then he couldn't believe it—they were passing him. They must think he had gone further on.

He raised himself cautiously on hands and knees, looking at the backs of the S.S. men as they began probing at the undergrowth, working further and further away from him.

Grant him another quarter-hour and they'd never find him in the darkness. He might win out yet. He watched their backs as they picked their way methodically through the trees.

But one S.S. man had lagged behind the others, unseen by Upham. He caught sight of the dim shape crouching in the leaves, sprang at the prisoner with a shout of triumph, and delivered a mighty kick. It struck home, sent Upham pitching on to his face.

Then he covered him with his rifle while the rest of the guards came racing back.

They led Upham back to the trucks, surrounded and tightly held.

As the group came into earshot of the waiting prisoners, they heard his voice, cursing loudly, working out his disappointment in a verbal barrage.

But Upham's onslaught was not all. The Feldwebel in charge of the guard ordered the S.S. man who had recaptured Upham to stand before him. Then, in full view and hearing of the P.O.W.s—several of whom understood German—he gave the successful soldier a vicious dressing-down.

The escaper should have been shot immediately, he stormed. He should never have been merely recaptured and returned to the convoy. By refraining from shooting the escaper he had encouraged all the other prisoners to attempt it. He was entitled to shoot fugitives in the act of escape. There was no excuse for not having done it that night.

They loaded Charles on to a truck again, but this time into the Guard Commander's truck, where he would travel with S.S. men all around him. They still found it prudent, however, to bind a length of wire clumsily round his wrists.

But, just before they separated him from his friends, Humphrey Hall managed a word with him. 'We thought you'd bought it that time, Charlie,' he said. 'You're lucky to be alive.'

'Lucky?' Upham flashed back in reply, his temper still flaming. 'Lucky? Look what the bastards have done to my boot!'

And he pointed angrily to where the heel of his boot had been neatly shot away.

*   *   *   *

The journey towards Germany continued.

First night the convoy lay up in the Mussolini Stadium at Mantua. From here they were put aboard trains next morning and headed towards the Brenner Pass. Then on through Austria.

The discomfort and privations of travelling in crowded cattle-trucks, forty men in each, were beyond words. Some men have since made light of similar experiences, but Charles Upham, even with his adaptability, still describes this journey as 'awful'. In the whole history of humanity the twentieth century has seemed to set a new low mark in the treatment of men as animals.

Five days in the cattle-trucks saw them finally right across Austria into Silesia. There, near Breslau, they were left at Lamsdorf, one of the largest P.O.W. camps in Germany, known as Stalag VIIIB. This was a sprawling, ill-disciplined camp, holding over 30,000, many of them rationed out to working-camps in the district. It was an unlovely place, and one of the worst controlled.

They spent a week at Lamsdorf before travelling again, this time far to the west. Again the journey was made in cattle-trucks, a period of four days' acute misery, until finally they were disgorged at camps in the vicinity of Strasbourg, close to the French border. Many of them, including Upham, were held at Stalag VC at Offenburg.

A fortnight later they were on the move again, this time finally to Weinsberg, Oflag VA, about seventy miles to the north-east.

15

Wire-break at Weinsberg

WEINSBERG held about 140 New Zealand officers, as well as many hundreds of South African, Australian, and British prisoners. It was to be Upham's home for nearly a year.

There were old friends again in the hut Charles occupied. Johnny Quilter, Tiny Armour the lawyer, Humphrey Hall with his architecture, Dick Ormond, Gordon Washbourn, Wally Ormond, Neville Holmes, Johnny Sullivan—all of them had something to contribute to making camp life bearable.

With Neville Holmes, the South African lawyer, Upham became on close terms. They shared the restlessness that never let them desist from thinking of escape. Neville's legal logic was a complement to Charles's intuitive kind of judgment, and the pair found a deep satisfaction in the sharing of ideas to which each contributed so differently.

Years later Neville Holmes wrote from his position as a Supreme Court Judge in Pietermaritzburg:

'Captain Upham had many friends among the South Africans. It was a privilege to enjoy his friendship. He was not a parade-ground soldier, but his exploits in action were legion. In appearance he was slight, with a magnificent head, and he was astonishingly wiry and strong. He was "Charlie" to everyone, and he hated sham, and was no respecter of rank without merit. I never knew a more generous nature. For example, it was always a great day for a P.O.W. when a clothing parcel arrived from home. But when this happened to Charlie he would empty the contents on the table, pick out one or two items he needed urgently, then call out: "Anyone need a shirt? Who wants socks? Anyone short of blades?" Small wonder that he had the respect and affection of every man in the camp. He was very well read (he had even read the Bible right through) and his general knowledge was amazing. Above all he loved to talk about farming, and one of his favourite cronies in this respect was Lieutenant Sir de Villiers Graaff. Charles was cast in an heroic mould, but withal he retained the warm human touch. . . .'

He had many an agreeable argument about farming with John Riddiford, whose family have farmed many New Zealand acres for several generations. Upham was a South Islander, Riddiford a Northerner. Charles advocated South Island Corriedale sheep, Riddiford argued for his Romneys, with which his thousands of acres were handsomely stocked.

One day when the mail arrived Charles seemed to be unusually eager to hand it around. After flicking through the envelopes he loudly announced: 'Another one for you, John. Been torn about a bit. No postmark.'

Riddiford gratefully opened his extra letter. It appeared to be from home, signed by his farm manager. Riddiford thought the writing wasn't as familiar as it ought to be—but there was the signature.

He read the letter, and his jaw dropped.

> . . . and, Mr. Riddiford, I decided to sell all your Romneys. I only got fifteen bob a head for them. I have replaced them with Corriedales at 35s. each . . . and I'm afraid I've had to shoot all the old dogs, including your favourite Spot. . . .

Into the blank horror that was rushing through Riddiford's mind came a sudden doubt. He looked up, then glanced quickly again at the strange writing on the terrible letter.

'Charlie, you——!——!——! . . .' and he sprang in loud pursuit of the practical joker.

Shrieking in mock terror, Charles fled from the room.

*   *   *   *

'Come on, Humphrey, another two laps.'

Humphrey Hall shook his head. 'It's going to rain in a minute, Charlie. Let's go in.'

'Rain? Not on your life. Come along.'

'Oh, all right.'

So they continued their walk around the compound.

And, as Humphrey had predicted, the rain began to fall, gently at first.

Upham did not increase his pace.

'Come on, Charlie. We don't want to get wet. Get a move on.'

'We won't get wet. It's not going to rain.'

'It's raining now, you clot. Come on in.'

The gentle rain started to fall a little harder.

'I suppose you reckon it's not raining?' Hall said sarcastically, feeling the drips starting to go down his neck.

'*It is not raining,*' Upham said cheerfully.

'For God's sake, Charlie. Well, if it's not raining, what's making you wet?'

Neil McPhail shouted to them from the door of the hut. 'What are you getting wet for, you two? Come on in.'

Upham tramped past the hut door, continued on walking. From sheer curiosity, Humphrey kept up with him.

'I call this rain, Charlie. I call this *wet rain*. I say that it is raining. Don't you?'

'All right,' Upham snapped irritably, the water pouring off his shoulders. 'All right, all right. It . . . is . . . raining.'

'Good. And I say it is raining *very hard*. It is what I call wet rain.'

'Wet rain? It is *not* wet rain. It is *dry rain*.' And Upham glared at Hall in a way which defied him to argue any longer.

'Dry rain? Oh, my godfather! Well, if this is dry rain, Charlie, it's wet enough for me, and I'm going in.' He dived for the hut.

Upham shouted after him. 'You idiot, you don't even know what *dry rain* is.'

'I know I don't,' Humphrey shouted back.

When Charles entered the hut a few minutes later Neil McPhail saw that he was quite annoyed.

'Dry rain is it, Charlie?' he baited.

Upham snorted. 'You fellows have never seen dry rain before. That's dry rain out there, I tell you. *Dry rain.*'

For several days Charles refused to speak to Humphrey. Of course the hut gave him little chance to forget the silly incident. Charles had to suffer being called 'Dry-rain Charlie' for quite a long time.

* * * *

In community activities Upham took his part. Though by nature a lone ranger, and one who preferred the company of one or two men to that of a crowd, he did his share.

In sport there was basketball and some baseball, in both of which he was an aggressive, militant sort of player, some would say 'over-enthusiastic' at times. He gave all he had at the time.

In between spasms of enthusiasm and heartiness he occasionally

dropped into periods of acute moroseness. Like a caged lion he paraded
the camp, frustrated and depressed, his hatred of the enemy completely
stultified by the physical confinement.

There were days when he refused to get up from his bed, lay there
hour after hour with the blankets pulled right over his head, like a
wounded beast. It was useless interrupting him—he would either snap
back a curt reply or just burrow deeper into his darkness and melancholy.

Prison for him was a mental torture to be endured over and above
the physical fact of confinement. When he was feeling well he maintained his self-respect by hating and baiting the guards and working on
escape schemes. But if he was off-colour the misery inside him closed
around and he went to earth, locked away from everyone else.

*   *   *   *

'It's under the gym,' they whispered. 'Johnny Royce has got it
worked out. While we dig we'll have to get a bit of an orchestra going—
you know, practising and all that; have a few stooges around.'

'You and I keep together, Charlie,' Neville said. 'The break-out will
be in pairs.'

The tunnel started.

The orchestra scraped away, hiding the sounds of excavation
beneath.

And, like all tunnel jobs, hiding the spoil was the most difficult task.

Upham and Holmes worked on it together, taking their turn with the
others who were included in the 'break'.

Plans began to be made for the big night. They would hold a concert
in the gym, right on top of the tunnel, and have the band playing flat
out, community singing, lusty choruses, all hiding the inevitable noises
accompanying the final burst. Invite the Camp Commandant and the
guards—they might thin out round the wire.

Then . . .

'I'm sorry, we've had it, boys,' Johnny Royce told them dolefully.
'The game's up. They've found the hole.'

A careless tunnel-digger had left a mud-covered singlet lying in the
gym. Hauptman Knapp, the Security Officer, had spotted it, and
guessed its significance immediately.

But next morning their spirits soared again. There had been rumours
and there had been graphic stories told by men who had seen it from
other camps. But now, this morning, they saw it themselves for the very
first time.

It was a slow drone on the horizon at first, gradually louder and louder, way up in the sky; closer and closer it came; and the sirens wailed, and then the air seemed to throb as the noise pervaded everything.

Like schoolboys welcoming home the conquering team, they rushed out into the open, shouting and cheering, heads craned into the skies trying to pick up the planes.

There was one plane, then another, then another, then a dozen, twenty, fifty, and men grew hoarse with excitement and wonder as hundred upon hundreds of bombers sailed majestically over them into the heart of Germany.

It was the most exciting and uplifting experience these P.O.W.s had ever known.

During the day that followed orders were issued that all men would return to their huts during an Allied air-raid. There was silence now from the German propaganda machine, which had so stridently proclaimed that no enemy aircraft would ever cross the Rhine in daylight.

Then, early next morning, as if to drive home the lesson of the day before, over they came again—snarling steadily into the Reich, so many that men could not keep count. Five or six hundred of them, and right over Weinsberg.

It was cheering and laughing again.

'Go on, you beauties. Go on! Go on!'

And men danced and slapped one another's backs. For here was might and power, the like of which no one had seen before.

But now the men were being rushed back into their barracks. Reluctantly they obeyed, feeling consciously superior to the guards who herded them in.

All were pushed inside, except one.

It would, of course, be Charles Upham who stayed outside.

He remained standing in the open, cheering the planes, until a section of guards, with fixed bayonets, came over towards him at the double.

Condescending to go inside, he turned at the door and shouted to the German officer: 'No planes across the Rhine, eh? What do you think those are—ruddy ducks?'

And he waved his pipe at the bombers cruising through the upper air.

Next there were orders about pamphlets dropped by Allied planes. Prisoners were required to retire to their barracks during the passing of enemy planes; but in addition any man picking up a pamphlet dropped from the sky would be instantly shot.

Orders like that were made to be defied by men who constantly believed in challenging the authority of the enemy.

Down the pamphlets fluttered over Weinsberg a few days later. Into the huts the P.O.W.s were rushed, while the guards paraded the open ground to pick up any pamphlets that fell inside the camp.

Upham spotted one floating down near his hut. Poised in the doorway, he waited for the right moment. Then he rushed out right past two of the goons, plucked a pamphlet out of the air before it even reached the ground and doubled back towards the hut at top speed.

With shouts and clicking of rifle-bolts, the two guards gave chase.

Charles bolted in through the door, thrust the pamphlet into the hands of the first man he saw inside, then dived for his bunk.

The guards burst in.

Upham was lying in bed, blankets up to his chin, snoring gently.

*   *   *   *

'Captain Oopham—I want to ask you some questions,' Hauptmann Knapp said.

'UPham, not OOPham,' Charles explained.

'Yes, Captain Oopham. Now, I have a report that you and another New Zealand prisoner have been detected making measurements near the fence. And a map has been found beside your bed. Your explanation, please—that is, if you have one.'

Upham looked serious.

'Yes, I suppose I had better explain, Hauptmann Knapp. I confess we were making measurements. And seeing that you've found our map I suppose the game's up. There's no use trying to hide it from you. You'll find all the measurements on the map. I'm very sorry about it.'

Knapp rubbed his hands. 'Ah ha, Captain Oopham. You are being sensible at last. You have been a difficult prisoner. But now you are being reasonable. But you will realize this is very serious, very serious. Now, let me look at the map.'

The sergeant beside him smoothed out the map, drawn carefully in ink, with many signs, directions, and measurements.

A minute went by while Upham tried to conceal his feelings.

Then Knapp suddenly jumped to his feet. 'Out! Out!' he shouted. 'Take him out!'

And Upham, chuckling, was unceremoniously removed and taken back to the barracks.

Along with Ian Reid and several others, Charles got a lot of fun out of standing by the wire, taking useless measurements in a furtive manner. It always worked. The guards would rush off in a great state to report.

And the maps. Many happy hours could be filled in concocting the most ridiculous false maps. They always got a bite, too, Maps showing the lay-out of Christ's College, or an imaginary desert island, with hidden treasure, always set the Germans running.

* * * *

'Tom Bromley says it's only twenty feet from his hut to the wire. It'll have to be deep, because I reckon they've got underground mikes.'

'What about the spoil? Where'll we put it?'

'Try distributing it around first. Then, if we're in a hurry, put it up in the roof. It won't be a long tunnel, so there won't be too much spoil.'

'All right. Count me in. When do we start digging?'

'Tonight. . . .'

They tried scattering the clay about the camp, carrying it around in bags slung inside their trousers. But this was a dangerous method. Weinsberg had a lot of black coal dust, and clay showed up on the black surface like a painted sign.

It was a slow method too. So they soon decided to stow it all in the ceiling—Humphrey Hall, Bill Allan, Neville Holmes, Charlie Upham, John Riddiford, to name but a few of those who worked on it.

Out went the tunnel, snaking underground towards the fence. In came the spoil and, with ever-increasing difficulty, was spread over the ceiling in the hut.

As more and more came in, so the ceiling sagged down and down. It became a question of which would happen first—the tunnel breaking out, the ceiling breaking down, or the goons breaking up the whole thing.

It seems that the microphones behind the walls detected this one. A friendly goon said: 'Walls have ears. . . .'

* * * *

With the failure of these two tunnel schemes it was obvious that something better planned and better constructed would be necessary. Experience gained from the other tunnels would be valuable, but this time two important points had to be covered: first, it was simply not good enough having a tunnel break ground just outside the wire. The ground was too open, and the heart-break would be too severe if the

o

hole were detected at the very end, when all the work had been finished. Second, a better place for hiding the spoil had to be found.

A group got together on it. There were some New Zealanders, some South Africans led by 'Div' Graaff and Neville Holmes, and a number of British Army officers. They soon solved the first problem. Rather than bring the tunnel up through open ground, they decided to surface it inside a storehouse that stood outside the wire. It would need a careful survey to determine exactly when the tunnel should become vertical, so as to come up right beneath the floorboards of the storehouse, but, with a surveyor and a Senior Wrangler in the group, no trouble was expected on this account.

The second problem did not permit of any clever solution. There were just no satisfactory ways of hiding soil. It was no use trying the ceilings again. That was old-hat. Instead, they decided that wardrobes in the hut be emptied, then soil packed tight into them.

So the digging began, and this became a splendid tunnel. Stooges were well organized to warn of approaching guards; the Senior Wrangler used logarithms and other devices to determine exactly how far the tunnel had to go before driving up to the surface; and into the large wooden wardrobes in the huts the soil was compressed.

The day came when the tunnel was due to surface. Little trouble with this was expected, as the surveyor and the Senior Wrangler had made their calculations with deliberate care. But, just to be sure, the tunnellers were to stop about a foot beneath the surface and carefully probe up with a long thin stick.

'She'll be all right,' the Senior Wrangler said smugly. 'We won't see the stick. It'll be rapping under the floorboards of the shed by now.'

Then, with something approaching panic, the escapers, watching casually from inside the wire, saw the end of the probe break up through the ground and wave about in mid-air—six feet short of the storehouse!

There were frantic signs and messages. With great relief the probe was retracted before being seen by the guards, and the tunnellers were set to work burrowing a further six feet outwards.

They did it, surfaced safely inside the shed. Now all was ready.

The break would be next night.

Then one of those chances intervened.

On the morning of the great day a German workman arrived in the escape hut to mend the fireplace—a job that had been standing idle for months. One of the wardrobes was in his way. Putting his shoulder to it, he expected to ease it quietly along a foot or two. But it wouldn't budge. No wonder—it held about a ton of soil. He tried again.

'Give you a hand?' the conspirators offered genially, with a remarkable show of friendliness and co-operation.

With many willing words they eased the puzzled workman out of the
way and laid gentle hands on the wardrobe. It must look as if it's
moving easily. Don't make it look difficult. Just giving him a hand.
Many hands make light work.

With happy smiles they pressed against the wardrobe; then a little
more strongly; then with every ounce they possessed. But it was as
immovable as the Rock of Gibraltar. They nearly died trying to shift
that wardrobe.

Very puzzled indeed, the workman wandered off.

Hauptmann Knapp arrived within the hour and opened the wardrobe.

It had been a beautiful tunnel.

Undismayed, ten of the conspirators, Holmes and Upham prominent among them, set to work on another. This time it would be a
different approach. Not for them this time the meticulous care, the long
weeks of toil and cunning. No—this would be a crash project. Dump the
soil wherever they could—and the best available place was in the
lavatory cubicles. That wouldn't escape detection for long—but maybe
long enough to enable the hole to be rushed through.

They began work like beavers.

It needed only a suspicious guard to open the closed door of the
lavatory in the course of a casual inspection—and that is exactly what
happened.

*   *   *   *

Appell! Roll-call!

The prisoners stood in line, five deep, and the goons went down the
front line, counting the numbers—five, ten, fifteen, twenty, etc.

Upham was at his rebellious best on *Appell.* He loathed the com-
pulsion of it and he showed, by every means he could other than downright disobedience, that he accepted nothing. If to bait and infuriate
them was the only way he could continue the war, then he would do it.

No smoking on *Appell!* The orders were clear and strictly enforced.

Upham stood in the front rank, looking calmly ahead, and puffed
at his long curved pipe.

The guard sergeant stopped in front of him, pointed at the pipe, and
rapped out an order. Upham knew what he meant.

Leaning slightly forward, he inhaled, then removed the pipe slowly
from his mouth so as to comply with the order. Then he breathed out,

long and slow, and the smoke wreathed and circled about the face of the sergeant.

The guard captain strode up. He snapped an order at Upham to produce his identity disc.

Charles knew what was being said. He stood still, made no move.

The order came again. Upham slowly shook his head, pretending not to understand.

Then the order was given to the ranking British officer standing nearby.

'He orders you to show your meat-ticket, Charlie.'

'I know he does,' Upham replied sharply. 'And tell him if he wants to see it to come and get the bloody thing himself.'

*　　　*　　　*　　　*

It was Christmas Eve 1943. Weinsberg was enveloped in snow, and it was still snowing. Some of the Germans were celebrating the day well, drinking the wood alcohol issued to them for their cigarette-lighters.

Upham was in despair over these tunnels. All the tunnel schemes had failed, and none of the men had any new ideas that the Jerries weren't wise to already. The trouble with tunnels—there was so much organization, so much evidence to be concealed, the marks of the clay seemed to show up everywhere. Couldn't conceal the stuff. . . .

And he was watching the snow falling outside while his mind turned over the problem of concealment. Concealment and camouflage—the old lessons he used to teach the boys. Up in Syria, he recalled, where some of the div had to work above the snowline, they issued them with white uniforms. Ski-troops, they called them, didn't they? Good camouflage that—hardly credit the Army for thinking it up, would you? Probably an Austrian idea in the first place, or the Ruskies perhaps. White clothing in the snow. Damned good camouflage—you wouldn't spot a sniper at ten yards if it was a bit dark.

And clear as crystal the idea swam into his mind. How simple—why hadn't anyone else thought of it? Christmas Eve. . . . The way the Jerries were tearing into the plonk there wouldn't be many of them sober by midnight. Sentimental about things like Christmas, they'd have a good sing-song and booze-up tonight. And the guards—the ones in the towers, those who patrolled outside the wire, the pairs who prowled around inside the compound—all they'd be thinking of would be the end of their watch, stamping their feet to keep warm, shaking the snow off their shoulders, keeping under cover if they could. They'd be thinking: no prisoner would be crazy enough to try to escape tonight, in a blinding snowstorm, with almost a gale beating the snow in under the doorways and against the windows. And the dogs would be frozen stiff, too.

It was tailor-made, Upham thought. The Krauts who went off duty about midnight would be relieved by those who'd been drinking flat out all evening. They'd be half pickled; and the last thing they'd want to do would be to tramp around like eager Boy Scouts on a hell of a night like this.

And if he made it—there'd be a fair number away on leave . . . not so many to chase after him in the morning.

Aitken of the 19th Battalion had made a saw out of a watch-spring and one day he had sawed through the bars on one of the hut windows. Now was the time to make that pay off.

It was after midnight, still snowing hard, when Charles pulled the bars aside, wriggled his way through, and dropped softly into the thick snow outside. He told no one he was going. He went like a shadow, and in a second the snow outside had swallowed him up.

But he couldn't take any risks. The searchlights on the towers were constantly playing backwards and forwards over the compound, searching along the walls of the huts, running their beams around the wire. They were not so effective in the snow, but he still had to contend with them . . . and the picquets . . . and perhaps the dogs.

He went across on his knees, worming his way through the slush. He watched out for the searchlights, froze like a statue when they swung near him.

But he was safe so far. For he had reversed his clothing. He had his white underwear on top of everything else (just like the ski-troops) and he knew that only a very sharp-eyed sentry would pick him out. He had merged into the snow.

Here was the trip-wire. Now the double-apron fence. Through it, and he was at the foot of the main wire. Now just climb over.

He crouched low on his haunches, listening for the patrols and the sentries. Just as he had guessed: not a sound of them—they'd be under cover somewhere, sheltering from the cold and the snow. It was pretty thick at present. Suited him perfectly.

Alongside a post he rose to his feet, began to climb the wire. It was easy. Up and up he went. He was almost contemptuous at the simplicity of it—just climb over the wire in the middle of the night. Odds all in his favour—the combination of Christmas Eve boozeroo, the white ground, the snowstorm—and he was almost at the top now, a triumphant feeling starting to well up in him. Then . . .

Crack!! The rifle-shot came from right beneath his feet. Starting convulsively, he lost his footing, clutched wildly with his hands, missed, and in a flash was falling backwards off the fence. Down he crashed into the snow, inside the compound, waiting every second for the *coup de grâce*. He lay there rigid, unable to see a thing.

The seconds passed. Nothing happened. Looking round, Upham could see only a few feet through the white gloom. He could see no one, but the shot had seemed to be right under him.

Perhaps the sentry had been half asleep or half drunk, fired at the blur on top of the fence, then convinced himself that it must have been a ghost. Upham's instant disappearance from the top of the wire, with hardly a sound as he fell into the soft snow beneath, may have convinced the German that it was imagination, after all.

He was soaked through. He was wearing every stitch of clothing he possessed, and he couldn't live outside in the European winter in wet clothes. He daren't attack the fence again. Next time the German would know he hadn't been mistaken.

So he crawled cautiously through the snow, back to the hut, along to the window, shivering violently. He made good his ground to safety inside without any alarm being sounded.

It had been a good scheme, he reckoned afterwards. Might easily have pulled it off. But that wretched sentry must have been standing silently in the snow, only a few feet from where he tried to climb the wire. Five yards further away and he might have made it.

*   *   *   *

'Nev,' Charles said to 'Judge' Holmes many weeks later as they strolled around the compound. 'This tunnelling business is a dud. The Jerries are up to all the tricks now. I reckon we have to think up a different line.'

'All right, Charlie, but let's look at it. There are only three ways of getting out: first—through the main gate; second—a tunnel; third—over the wire. Well, "Div" tried it through the gate but didn't get far. No one can work his trick again. And there'll have to be something pretty new in the way of tunnels to have any show.'

'That's what I mean, Nev. The only practicable thing is—over the wire.'

'But how, Charlie? I know you almost made it on Christmas Eve—but there were special circumstances that night. There's no snow now, summer's coming on. You can't try that one again.'

'I know, Nev. But I still reckon the wire's the thing.'

'All right; then which way? Cut the wire or climb over the top?

Whatever way you try you've got this against you—get out of the hut first—and I suppose we can do that if Aitken's still got his saw—but outside there are the damned dogs. You've got to beat them to the wire. Then the lights, the goons, and the guns. Really, I don't think it's on. . . .'

Charles said: 'I can poison the ruddy dogs. And I reckon I know where I can get a pair of wire-cutters.'

'Right-oh, Charlie, I'm with you. Let's talk about it.'

So they worked on that and it wasn't long before they had the wire-cutters.

They agreed there was a chance. If they waited for the night of an air-raid, when the floodlights were switched off, they might get through the wire, then strike out for France or Switzerland.

First, more bars on the hut windows had to be filed through. Under the noses of the guards they managed this one day on the pretence of washing the hut windows.

Charles tried many schemes for poisoning the Alsatian dogs that roamed the camp at night. When you live alone in the back-country you get to know about dogs, he declared. But none of his poisoning plans seemed to make any noticeable increase in the death-rate of the dogs.

Then, in company with Neville, he made a number of night-time reconnaissances round the wire, having several narrow escapes from the beasts, and causing a good deal of jitteriness amongst the guards.

When their turn came they decided they would have to risk the dogs. . . .

They made their preparations.

Then one night the air-raid sirens wailed again. Holmes waited beside the gear, checking that both of them had all they required. Charles waited at the window, watching the perimeter lights.

The lights blacked out.

He walked quickly along the hut.

'They're off, Judge,' he said laconically.

'Then so are we, Charlie,' Holmes replied, bending down and picking up his gear.

Without another word they moved to the window, lifted out the severed bars, quickly squirmed through, and dropped to the ground outside.

They moved out of the deep shadow of the hut, bending over almost double, treading on tip-toe, making across the open to the point in the wire where they had decided to make their break.

They reached the trip-wire, stepped over it carefully.

Then there was the double-apron fence. They dropped on their stomachs and wriggled through beneath it.

Now just the main wire ahead—first the inner fence, then tangled wire beyond, then the outer fence. Then freedom.

No sign yet of any dogs.

They came to the inner fence. They lay on their backs while Holmes took firm hold of the bottom wire with his two hands. Upham got out his cutters. It was pitch dark. They had to feel for everything. But so far so good. Luck was with them. Thank God the dogs hadn't found them yet.

Upham squeezed the cutters.

The wire parted with a 'ping' that seemed to resound all over the camp.

'Oh, hell, that'll wake 'em up,' Charles breathed. He thought of the man on the tower, barely thirty yards away. Surely he must have heard it.

They lay dead still for a full minute, frozen into position, waiting to hear the sound of an alarm. But still their luck held.

Then Holmes whispered: 'O.K., Charlie?' and he reached up cautiously for the next strand, took hold of it, while Upham lifted the cutters.

As he groped in the darkness, Charles had a momentary feeling that something was going wrong with their scheme. It was the way that first 'ping' had resounded so clearly. Everything else had been so silent.

With an air-raid alert on, normally there would be the sounds of ack-ack guns in the distance and often the great drone of the bombers cruising overhead. There would be noise.

It wasn't usual for everything to be so quiet. Could even be a false alarm—in which case the faster he and Nev worked, the better it would be.

He closed his fingers around the handle, whispered a word to Neville to hold the wire steady, and prepared to squeeze the cutters again. . . .

Then in a blinding instant all the camp lights flashed on, the flood-light on the tower drenched them in its beam, and the 'All clear' siren wailed through the night.

Everything was visible—the huts, the wire, the two escapers—all silhouetted in brilliant clarity.

With a gasp, both men dropped on to their faces, pressing themselves into the ground. There was just a chance the men in the towers would not be looking their way at that vital moment.

They lay there motionless, keeping their faces and hands covered, knowing that one false move might be their last.

Holmes whispered: 'We're for it now, Charlie. We can't get through with all the lights on. They'll see us here any moment.'

'I know. I know. We've had it. We'll have to try to get back. What do you reckon—go separately or keep close together?'

'Separately, Charlie. . . . I'll follow about five yards behind you . . . but for God's sake keep flat on your stomach . . . we might make it if we go slowly.'

'O.K., Nev. I'll make for that nearest shadow—by the corner of the hut.'

They shrank away from the fence, clawing their way over the ground on their faces, making every movement slow and deliberate, freezing into stone whenever the big lights swept near them.

The temptation to jump up and run blindly for the hut became almost irresistible. But they crept on like snails, knowing that was their best way of survival.

They reached the shadow of the hut at last, edged their way along to the window with the bars sawn through, and climbed swiftly in the moment the next searchlight went past. . . .

* * * *

There would be just a chance they could repeat the scheme during the next air-raid, but Hauptmann Knapp put a stop to that. For next morning, to their chagrin, they watched Knapp snoop suspiciously round the wire, saw him find the cut strand, and watched him go swiftly into action.

Knapp knew how to deal with prisoners who had wire-cutters. There would be things he could do with the dogs, with the lights, with alarm wires, with patrols outside, with special searches of the huts. The wire-cutting men wouldn't put it across him. Knapp gave them only one chance. He probably wondered if that devil 'Oopham' was one of them.

Meanwhile Upham sat back and brooded. He was sure it could be done over the wire. The two of them had come pretty close to it. But at night there were the dogs, the lights, the noise. That's when they expected a man to try to break. Funny if a man tried to go through the wire in daylight, wouldn't it? They'd never expect that.

And, as the thought wandered into his mind, something gripped him. A wire-break in *daylight*! What could be more totally unexpected? Of course it was hopeless, ridiculous. The guards would see a man at the wire, cut him down before he was through the first couple of strands.

But what about climbing over the top?

He thought more about it.

First there was the trip-wire. The prisoners were not allowed over that. Next you came to the double apron, which would take a little time to clamber over, or underneath. And then you came to the main fence.

There were two main fences, really, with a gap in between them. Each was of barbed wire, about ten feet high. In between them was this gap, filled with concertina and dannert wire.

It all presented a fair maze to get over—but it wasn't impossible. The stuff lying in the gap was the trouble. Perhaps he might swing from the top of one fence to the other.

But the time! Surely it would be impossible to go across in less than a minute. And there weren't ten seconds when every stretch of the wire was not under close and direct surveillance.

Still—what a thought! Dare say nobody had ever thought of climbing the wire in broad daylight. Just not done.

He chuckled. Might try it some day—when he couldn't stick the damned place a minute longer.

'John,' he called out suddenly. 'You're on the Escape Committee. Anybody ever got over the wire in daylight?'

John Riddiford looked surprised. 'In daylight, old boy? Come off it. Nobody's that crazy. No one can do it even at night . . . or perhaps you didn't hear about those two chaps last night? . . .'

Upham threw a sock at him. Then they turned to yarning about Corriedales and Romneys again.

But a funny idea lurked at the back of his mind.

*   *   *   *

It was a fortnight later, a fortnight in which Charles Upham had become more sour and depressed than ever. He couldn't stand it much longer—just the hopeless waiting and waiting. He couldn't wait any more.

They'd landed in Normandy all right. But it was going slowly. There was no sign of the Jerries packing up. They were as tough as ever. And he was not so sure about this bombing. Chaps came in who said how Berlin was being smashed up—they'd passed through in trains —and Mannheim, and Hamburg, and Essen, and Frankfurt. But it seemed to make the Jerries fight harder.

He couldn't stand it. He had to do something. He just couldn't stand being an animal in a cage any longer. Sometimes he wondered if he was going mad. Other chaps didn't seem to care. They were prepared to sit it out, wait till the end of the war. But when would that be?

There were no escape schemes on foot now. Not worth while, they said, now that the Allies had landed in Europe. War would be over soon, they claimed. Who said so?

It was Sunday. Summer. Summer in the Black Forest. There were couples out in the fields beyond the camp. The camp was lazy and sleeping. The chaps in the compound were just idling around.

He'd been nearly a year in Weinsberg. If he had to stick it out any longer he'd crack up. He knew it. He felt the crisis coming on.

Upham wandered around the compound on his own, smoking his pipe, restless and miserable. He looked again and again at the guards slowly walking their beats, at the man up in the tower with his machine-gun. He had looked at them ten thousand times, and hated them more each time. They represented the enemy. He hated the enemy.

Just where he was looking the wire took a right-angled turn. There were always three guards patrolling outside the wire along this sector. It meant that every inch of the fence was always under the eye of at least one guard. In addition there was always the man up in the tower. He could see everything. In fact he could see rather more than he ought to today. He was having fun watching the couples out in the fields. But one glance and he could see the whole of the wire.

One man always in the tower . . . three men always patrolling the wire . . . Upham had studied them countless times, wondering if there could be any possible chance. . . .

He watched them with lack-lustre eyes as he walked aimlessly around the compound, his spirits almost at zero. Let those guards give him just one decent chance—he wouldn't even care if they shot him. . . .

And in one sudden instant he froze, and his breath caught. He stood dead still. It was like a film that stops abruptly and everyone is turned to stone.

Something inside him was ringing and ringing, like a sharp, shrill bell.

He watched the guards. He watched them walk up and down, once, twice, three times. And he began counting the seconds.

And it was churning inside him now, something clear and desperate.

Steady. Steady. Count the time again. Watch how they did it. Was it the same every time? Yes, yes, it was! And the man in the tower was watching the boys and girls.

And instead of the first amazement there was a savage exultant feeling coming over him. A chance! A chance! This could be the moment, the impossible, hopeless chance that came only once in a blue moon.

For his hungry eyes had seen what no one else appeared to have noticed. There were not *three* guards patrolling the wire today. *There were only two.*

Only two guards instead of three. When they marched outwards they left a blind spot behind them—they paced slowly away from each other, then turned.

He counted again deliberately.

Forty-five seconds!

There was a space of forty-five seconds in which the angle of fence was not being watched! Except by the man in the tower.

Forty-five seconds to get through the wire! Once they turned again they would see him. And the man in the tower with the machine-gun could see him the whole time.

Out through the wire were German washing-huts. Hide there till dark.

No use rushing it, clambering over the wire in a hurry. They'd hear him. No—a steady, careful climb, hand over hand, then a jump from the top of one fence across to the top of the other, leap down to the ground, and fly for the huts. He could do it in forty-five seconds if luck was with him all the way.

The daylight break! The escape they had all scoffed at as impossible. Well, it was not! It *could* be done. Split-second timing. But over the wire in broad daylight! They'd think he'd gone round the bend.

He moved back calmly to the hut, unhurried, but his heart beating fiercely inside. He got out his escape gear, all in a little haversack.

When he was ready he went out and looked for 'Judge' Holmes.

Holmes was lounging in the sun, doing nothing. He saw Upham approaching, carrying his haversack.

Upham spoke to him and his voice was a little thick. 'Judge, I'm going out over the wire. Get the boys to make a bit of a show, will you—down there under the tower. Keep the goons looking down. A fight, or anything you like—you know. Start when you see me at the trip.'

Holmes saw the look on Upham's face. He didn't argue. Lately he knew that Charles had been feeling desperate. It was no use trying to stop him when he was in a mood like that.

He said quietly: 'How on earth are you going to do it?'

Upham explained shortly.

Holmes nodded rather sadly. He said: 'I'll fix the diversion. You can leave that to me. And . . . good luck, old boy.' Then he got up abruptly and moved away, so Charles couldn't see the look on his face.

Holmes spoke quietly to half a dozen friends. One by one they sauntered casually to the place Charles had indicated, close under the tower.

Upham waited in the doorway of the hut until they were all ready. Then he moved out across the compound, slowly and inconspicuously,

and stood languidly beside the trip-wire. He looked out to the main
fence, deciding exactly where he would climb.

Then he gave Holmes the signal.

The men under the tower started to argue. One man shouted. Another
shouted back at him. Suddenly one lashed out at the other, and they
rushed together, fell wrestling to the ground.

The onlookers gathered around, some calling encouragement. The
man in the tower heard the commotion, looked down and watched the
fight with interest.

Upham had his eye on the guards, waited till they passed each other
and marched outwards. Then he quietly stepped over the trip-wire,
advanced across the forbidden ground to the low apron fence.

He was up and over it in a few seconds.

And now he was at the main wire. He seized the strands, began
climbing steadily. It was easy. In no time he was at the top.

All around there were dozens now watching. Others were catching
sight of him for the first time and were staring in amazement. A wire-
break in broad daylight! What maniac was trying that!

Some who recognized his small wiry figure called out softly to those
near: '*It's Charlie Upham*,' and there were some who remembered the
same words, passed from mouth to mouth, when he had run from the
trucks alongside the River Po. There was a sudden aching sympathy for
a man who would dare such fearful odds.

But there were some who said: 'He must be mad.' They waited for
the volley of fire any moment, waited to see his body crumple up and fall
from the wire to the ground, like a sack of old clothes. But those who
said that hadn't counted the guards today.

The fight became more furious and several others had joined in,
while Upham paused for a second at the very top of the fence.

Now, with studied care, he lifted one leg across, and he was astride
it. He was in full view of the goon on the tower if he were only to look.
But a real mêlée had developed below, and that was more interesting.

Upham swung his other leg over, measured the distance across to
the outer fence. It was a fair leap, but it was his only chance. Down
between the two fences was a maze of tangled barbed wire. He couldn't
climb down there and up the other side. No, he had to jump. If he could
make it to the other fence it would be just a swing over the top, then a
leap to the ground, and a wild sprint for the huts. With any luck they
wouldn't see him at all.

He climbed down one strand, paused, then crouched for the spring.
About thirty seconds gone!

Then, as he gathered himself together . . . *snap!* A staple flew out of the nearest post and the wire Upham was standing on went suddenly slack. Desperately he hurled himself out, lunging for the other side. But the broken staple had spoilt his leap.

He fell short, came crashing down into the rolls of barbed wire lying between the two fences. The moment that staple pulled, he knew he was lost.

He heaved and wrenched at the wire, swearing and cursing, tearing his hands and his clothes. If he could free himself, dive at the other fence, climb over it even under fire, there would be a chance—just run for it over the fields, with the odds against him.

But the more he strained, the tighter the grip of the barbs.

He was aware now that the sentries were patrolling back towards him. There was still the faintest hope that they might not notice him lying amongst the wire—they might possibly just walk past.

But now, suddenly, he was aware of a face—a German face, eyes bulging—staring at him from outside the wire. A man with a working party, just going past, and he had caught sight of Upham, and his jaw had dropped in startled amazement.

And then the workman's voice was raised. He was shouting. The guards looked round. They all saw Upham. They were running. The alarm was on. Whistles were shrilling. Rifles unslung, bolts clicking, the pelting of racing feet.

Meanwhile some of the diversion party were dashing to the spot. They'd seen that Charlie's jump had failed. Any moment now and the shots would blast the summer air. Charles Upham, hero and gentleman to them all, would get the treatment that was allowed. A prisoner may be shot in the act of escape. They surged to the wire, calling and waving, hoping to stop the guards from shooting.

Others stood transfixed, staring at the spot, waiting for the inevitable. That any man could attempt such a thing . . . the sheer bravery of it . . . the desperation . . . the terrible sadness of it.

There was pandemonium as the guards dashed to the scene.

The first guard arrived with his rifle at the ready, finger on trigger. Simultaneously, Charles whipped out the compass he had so laboriously made, tried to throw it back inside the compound. His hand caught, the compass dropped to his feet.

So he kicked at it, and it scudded along the ground inside the wire. Peter Maxwell was there, one of the first to reach the scene, bent down quickly and picked it up.

The guard's rifle swung towards Maxwell and he shouted. There was an instant when it appeared certain he would shoot Maxwell, who had turned to run, but the rifle pointing at him held him fast.

Then Upham suddenly called: 'Hey!'

Diverted, the guard swung back on Charles. More prisoners were on the spot, shouting at the guard, warning and threatening him not to fire.

The man hesitated. Upham was lying absolutely still. And in that hesitation the moment of killing was lost.

But now a corporal of the guard was on the scene. He was angry. He feared the consequences of a prisoner having almost outwitted his patrols. He had drawn his pistol and looked dangerous.

He shouted in German. He declared he was going to 'finish off' the prisoner. He would shoot him there and then.

The P.O.W.s tried to dissuade him. Keep him talking till his temper cooled.

He was standing by the wire, pistol raised, jaw set. It might be any moment.

Then Upham, in almost exaggerated slow motion, made a cautious move. So far he had been lying motionless, knowing that any move would assuredly result in a bullet.

But now, as the corporal aimed his pistol, Upham moved one hand carefully to his pocket and he drew out—the others strained to see—he drew out a *cigarette*.

Then he took out his matches, struck one and, doing everything with studied slowness, lit the cigarette.

An English major watching the drama didn't dare look away, but breathed to his companion: 'My God, what nerve!'

The corporal looked on, pistol still ready, but hesitant now, undecided what to do. The sight of the cigarette being lit had thwarted him. It shouldn't happen that way. He knew he couldn't shoot now. There was something about the demeanour of the man caught in the wire that deterred him.

The Senior British Officer was there, pushing his way to the front. 'Are you all right, Charlie?' he called.

Upham growled: 'Yes.'

'What are you going to do?'

'Nothing. They can damned well come and get me. And I refuse to be shot by a bloody corporal. Tell 'em to bring an officer.'

'Judge' Holmes whispered to one of the New Zealanders: 'Did you hear that? Charlie's dictating who he's going to let shoot him.'

There was a stalemate. The P.O.W.s still crowded close to the wire, the guards trying to clear them back. The Germans were still talking loudly and gesticulating.

At last the man arrived—Hauptmann Knapp himself, his podgy little figure rolling from side to side as he bustled along.

He took in the scene swiftly, gave sharp orders to the other prisoners to move back. They obeyed.

For a few seconds he watched Upham lying in the wire, puffing unconcernedly at his cigarette. Then: 'Captain Oopham, what are you doing there?'

No reply.

Louder: 'Captain Oopham, what are you *trying* to do there?'

Again silence.

'Captain Oopham, are you all right?'

Upham puffed a cloud of smoke into the air.

Hauptmann Knapp appeared to sigh. He unleashed something from his shoulder, stepped closer to the wire, aimed it at Charles. It was a camera.

He took three photographs.

He looked very satisfied, very pleased indeed. At last, he thought, here was concrete evidence about this dangerous prisoner. Photos of the man caught in the act of escaping.

Then he called: 'You can come out now, Captain Oopham.'

Again Charles ignored him, went on smoking.

There was quite a long pause. Then Knapp finally leant through the wire and said, quite softly: 'You are a very, very brave man, Captain Oopham. Now please come out.'

The Senior British Officer intervened, and it was only when he finally ordered Charles to pick his way back out of the wire that Upham agreed to do so.

He was promptly led away to the cells.

Something new was added this Sunday afternoon to the legend of Charles Hazlitt Upham.

*   *   *   *

Colonel de Beer, a South African, was the Senior British Officer at Weinsberg at this time. Knowing the record Charles Upham already had with the Germans, and having seen the performance at the wire, he felt very anxious about Upham's safety. He feared that the Germans might seize this opportunity of disposing of a very recalcitrant prisoner —and if they explained that Upham made another bid to escape from the cells there would be no one to deny it. Twice now German guards had refrained from shooting Upham in the act of escape. Any guard who now took the law into his own hands and finished off Upham while in custody would probably receive an official rebuke but unofficial congratulations.

So almost immediately after Upham had been taken away, de Beer applied for an interview with the Camp Commandant.

He was promptly escorted in.

He announced that his visit concerned the New Zealand prisoner Captain Upham, now in the cells. The Commandant looked smug.

Colonel de Beer came straight to the point. 'All I want to say is this —this man Upham is *the ace soldier of the British Empire*. If anything happens to him I will see that you are held personally responsible after the war. That's all.'

The warning was well timed. News later reaching the New Zealanders confirmed that the question of shooting Upham was indeed mentioned the morning after his arrest.

The guard corporal was brought before the Commandant. He faced a tirade for not having shot the New Zealand officer the moment he saw him in the wire. Why was he not shot? Why was it not done immediately and then there could have been no complaint?

But the corporal, indeed all the guard, knew about Upham. With Hauptmann Knapp himself, they shared an admiration for the New Zealander, a reluctant respect that stemmed from Upham's complete refusal to submit, and his never-flagging antagonism.

Many Germans are single-minded people. Those in Weinsberg recognized in Upham a similar quality and they admired him for it.

The Commandant railed and stormed at the corporal. Until the officer in charge of the guard, stung by the criticism, finally burst out: 'Well, Herr Oberst, the prisoner is in his cell, and you have your pistol.'

Such an insolence might well have driven the Commandant to precipitate action, had it not been for de Beer's timely threat.

As it was, Upham received the customary sentence of thirty days' solitary.

*   *   *   *

It was his morning exercise time—half an hour marching in a circle around the guard-house parade ground. They gave him thirty minutes of that in the morning, another thirty minutes in the evening.

The sentry stood in one spot, rifle under his armpit, and Charles was required to walk around him in a circle.

On a parapet above was a man with a machine-gun. His job was to cover Upham with the gun every pace he took. As the prisoner marched around the circuit beneath, the barrel of the machine-gun followed him like a shadow.

The Germans were taking no chances this time. The goon standing in the centre was routine. But the special machine-gunner overlooking

P

the parade ground, whose job it was to keep Upham in his sights every
second of the time, represented the measure of Hauptmann Knapp's
respect.

From the prison compound the other P.O.W.s could see it, and
they marvelled at the spectacle—one machine-gun allocated to cover
one solitary man, traversing steadily backwards and forwards as the
prisoner went about his exercise.

Charles paced his circuit patiently. They had taken his boots away
and given him wooden clogs, which were awkward to clump about in.
Pity the wire-break hadn't come off! He would have been in France by
now. There wasn't much chance of escaping from this place, even
though it was outside the main wire. The goon with the rifle was too
close, the goon with the machine-gun too dangerous—though he
reckoned a man continually traversing a machine-gun would not be
able to fire accurately very quickly.

The goon with the rifle looked a fairly old codger—an old 'blood
pressure', unfit for the front line. If he could shoot an elephant at ten
paces he would probably have been on the Russian front.

Then Charles suddenly noticed, with a feeling of amused contempt,
that the old boy's rifle was not cocked. He looked belligerent enough,
watching Charles intently with his hand along the trigger-guard and the
rifle under his armpit. But to fire he would have to open the breech,
then close it, before being able to shoot. Silly old codger.

Upham hardly thought of escape, but he was as determined as ever
to harass the Germans.

The circuit went on and on, Upham's head down, round and round
in his own footsteps, the goon patiently turning and watching him.

Then, without warning, Charles suddenly jumped round, faced the
way he had come, and set off walking rapidly in the reverse direction.
That was all—he just turned round quickly.

But the goon! Charles nearly burst out laughing as he saw the guard
leap in startled surprise, fumble stupidly with the bolt, open and close
it, then look at Upham again, his eyes wide in sudden apprehension. It
was as good as a play.

But the steady circuit resumed, and slowly the guard's anxiety faded.

Next exercise time Upham did the same thing again—and once
more the ludicrous display of startled fear on the part of the goon.

Upham thought this was good fun and well worth the money. If the
goon carried his rifle cocked then he wouldn't dare try it—the fool might
fire it off by accident. But there must have been some orders about
carrying round cocked rifles.

Then another idea drifted into his mind.

On one side of the small parade ground stood a barrack-room occupied by the guard. It had a door opening out on to the parade ground. There was another door on its far side. Out beyond that there was a wire fence dividing the guard-house from the main road down to the village.

He thought about it.

Why not, anyhow? He hadn't much to lose. The risks—the goon with the uncocked rifle; the goon with the machine-gun. The first couldn't fire instantly. The other would probably fire inaccurately. The main trouble would be his wretched clogs.

The next exercise time came around. A good time too. Over in the camp there was an *Appell*. Everyone was paraded. There would be lots of guards on duty there.

Yes—he would try the sudden jump round again. By now the old boy wouldn't get excited about it—he was almost getting used to it.

He began the circuit.

Round and round—everything exactly the same as before—round and round, head down, everything the same. . . .

But imperceptibly Upham began widening the circle, just faintly, doing it so gradually that the goon became used to the distance separating him from Upham.

Round and round, a little bit wider, a couple of circles like that, then a fraction wider again—and he checked to make sure that the rifle was not cocked again.

Wider . . . a little wider.

And the circuit was now taking him close to the door of the barrack-room. He kept going steadily, everything the same as usual.

He passed the door of the barracks, plodded on around the circuit, gathering breath, digging his toes into the clogs to give him a better grip.

He came round to a point opposite the door again . . . moved past it.

Then like a flash he leapt round, sprang into action, and dived straight for the door beside him.

The goon had hesitated when he saw the turn—just the same silly jump the New Zealander had done before. But by the time he woke up to the realization that here indeed was something real, the quarry was out of sight, in through the barracks door, racing across the room inside.

Upham dashed straight for the far door, was through it and outside again, running towards the fence and the main road beyond.

He knew the machine-gunner could see him, would have the gun trained on him in a matter of seconds. He was entirely in the open. But it was one of the fastest things he had ever done. Surprise was on his side.

Only the fence to climb. It was of netting, about six feet high, but the mesh was too small for him to climb up the wires. But there was a sloping stay-post . . . he ran to it . . . up the face of the post, over the top, dropping to the ground beyond. Now on to the road.

Best plan—run straight down the road until he could break off into cover. But first—put some distance between himself and the camp.

He sprinted down the road, the clogs thudding awkwardly on the bitumen.

Back in the camp the whistles shrilled again, the shouting, rushing, the panic—and on *Appell* the prisoners of Weinsberg knew that something serious was on once more and it would be that man Upham again.

But it was not to be.

Charles had hardly covered fifty yards down the road before he ran straight into a group of German guards returning to camp. He darted to one side, but they were at him in a moment, surrounding him, pawing at him while he cursed and struggled.

They led him back to the cells, unrepentant and still aggressive.

The whole affair had taken less than a minute.

Why hadn't the machine-gunner fired? How had Upham managed to get as far as he did?

The way it was between guards and prisoners it wasn't long before the man on the parapet told his story to one of the New Zealanders.

'I saw it all happen,' he claimed. 'I could have shot him down any time after he ran out of the barracks. But I could see the guards down the road and Captain Upham was running straight into them. I knew they would catch him.'

Then he went on to admit that another reason he withheld his fire was out of sheer admiration for such a bold but hopeless attempt.

Hauptmann Knapp mounted a *second* machine-gun on the parapet overlooking the parade ground.

*   *   *   *

Upham was allowed back amongst his friends before he was taken from Weinsberg.

He had his last breakfast with them.

'Judge' Holmes says: 'I think the whole camp was sorry he was leaving. I remember the morning he left. His immediate friends gave him items of food for his journey—and at this time food was as precious as uranium. I cooked him a tin of hot porridge. Charlie was touched, but all he permitted himself to say was: "You old beggar." '

Then they took him away.

'This time, Captain Oopham, it is the end of the road for you. You are being transferred to another camp—to Oflag IV C.'

'IV C? That's a Straf-lager isn't it? A punishment camp?'

'Oh no, I would not call it that. IV C—it is just a camp you cannot escape from. There are some very interesting prisoners there, what we call the bad prisoners. No escape. Oflag IV C is in Saxony—at a little place called ... now let me see ... ah yes, a little place called ... Colditz.'

Colditz!

16

Twelve Hours

THE German Commandant now had a deep anxiety that Charles Upham might still escape, despite all precautions; and the transfer to Colditz would provide the prisoner with opportunities he dared not let him seize. So it was the measure of the Germans' respect that, as the train settled down for the journey eastwards, Charles found himself alongside not merely one guard, not even two, but no less than three stalwart custodians.

One was a sergeant. He was content with a pistol. The other two were one-stripers, one of them armed with a pistol and sub-machine-gun, the other with a pistol and rifle. Quite enough fire-power to keep him subdued, Upham thought.

But they were quite agreeable company. Past the age for active service, they were still useful for the immense guarding and occupation duties Germany had to perform. They were not of the arrogant Nazi type, not like the Gestapo men who came through the train. On the contrary, Charles found them considerate and helpful, provided he co-operated. But he soon knew they were afraid. They were afraid of him physically, and not for a moment did they relax their concentration on his every movement. But, more than that, he could see they were literally terrified at the possibility of his escaping. They acted as if their lives would depend on it—and perhaps they would.

The journey took over three days. One of them would get out at the stations and bring in the food for all of them to share. One would sleep while the other two watched the prisoner. Never did they allow him the slightest rope.

It was a tedious, yet interesting, journey. The train would halt for hours on end, held up by the effects of Allied bombing on station yards or bridges ahead; or it would alternately race and crawl, go on to sidings, reverse into loop lines; and all along the route Upham saw the devastation to industry and transport that the war was now bringing to Germany.

The train was chock-full. Among the passengers were German civilians moving east to escape from the battles drawing near their homes; there were wounded German soldiers; and threading through them hour after hour were the Military Police and the Gestapo.

The M.P.s were looking for deserters, and every man in uniform was closely examined. They were tough, heavily armed, and they looked well fed. In contrast, the German soldiers and civilians appeared thin and miserable.

Upham had heard from other prisoners about the Gestapo. He now saw them in action. Every passenger was scrutinized carefully, all papers examined slowly and suspiciously. Upham found he was the only one not having to fumble with his wallet every few miles. The Gestapo, too, looked affluent and over-healthy, like fat stock, and their uniforms were smart and new.

*   *   *   *

It was on the second night, as they clattered further and further eastwards, that Upham realized his time was running out. These three goons were intelligent enough to prevent his escaping unless he took some unprecedented risk. They were so afraid of anything happening that they would obviously take great risks themselves to stop him, for fear of the punishment they could expect if their captive made a successful break.

He knew he had to try somehow, somewhere. But the hours dragged past to the tune of the clacking wheels and nothing happened to give him hope. Hour upon hour he sat and brooded, and it grew in his mind that each minute saw him further and further away from freedom.

It was in the deadest hours of the night, about three o'clock in the morning, when Upham decided the time had come. This was not an occasion when opportunity would be presented to him. It was too late for that. His only chance lay in taking the kind of risk he had always shunned—stepping into danger without being able to assess the chances of success.

He said he wanted to visit the lavatory. One of them—'Blue-Nose', Upham had dubbed him—came along with him, saw him into the little cubicle, and stood guard outside. They had allowed him that amount of privacy, even though a desperate man could perhaps effect an escape through the tiny window. But there was no risk, they must have thought, of a man hurling himself from an express train travelling at top speed. For that reason they allowed him to visit the toilet only when the train was travelling fast.

But that was the very risk Charles decided he now had to take.

He tried the window. No, of course they wouldn't leave it so that anyone could just push it open. It was well nailed up. Well, that meant he would have to smash the glass.

He broke the glass quietly, peered uncertainly through the gap into the black night outside. The window was so small he didn't think he could possibly get through it. No chance whatever with his heavy coat on, and with the small pack of belongings that he rarely took off his shoulders.

He looked out again. It was pitch dark. The train was roaring through the night. He could see absolutely nothing. For all he knew they might be travelling alongside a river, along a mountainside, on top of an embankment. Many men, he knew, who had jumped from trains had simply thrown themselves to instant death as they were dashed against rocks, posts, or in one or two cases straight over the edge of precipices. And at this speed . . . it was the sort of risk he would never dream of taking—the dangers were so great, and he could not judge the chances of success.

But now time was short. For once he had to risk everything.

Swiftly he peeled off his pack and his coat, wrapped one around the other, then stretched out, and threw the bundle out of the window.

Now to follow himself.

He began to edge himself through. The window was still too small for a comfortable exit, and he feared he would stick half-way.

He hesitated as he lay twisted in the window space, peering into the night, hoping to pick up the nature of the ground alongside the train, but it was all just one rushing blur.

It was madness, he thought. And for a moment an inner voice seemed to be calling: 'Go back, go back!' And he would have tried to squeeze back inside again were it not for the thought of his coat and pack lying on the railway track down the line. He felt really scared.

Then sharply came a rattling of the door-handle and Blue-Nose was calling: '*Aus! Aus!*'

That was enough.

In a moment of sudden resolve he pushed harder, balanced for a moment, and then was gone. . . .

The incredible feeling of hurling himself out into space . . . the dread of it . . . the sharp clutch of fear as he knew he was on the way . . . the roar of the wheels as his last thought. . . .

Something seemed to whip at his feet and then, in an instant, a tremendous crashing impact of his whole body . . . his head blazed . . . and he knew no more.

*   *   *   *

Slowly his brain came awake . . . ever so slowly, it seemed, and with every moment the splitting pain in his head grew worse. He was lying huddled up on the ground, and for a while he had no idea where he was or how he had come there. It was a half-world from which he was reluctant to fight clear. Every moment of fighting seemed such an agony.

Then suddenly he was sharply awake. He knew everything—the train . . . the window . . . the jump . . . the black night . . . the shattering impact.

He was lying across railway sleepers. But they couldn't be the ones his train had run on. No—he could see now—there was a double railway track. When he leapt he had hurled himself out on to a parallel line. He must have hit his head against the rails, or the wooden sleepers perhaps.

Which meant the train must have gone *that* way. He got to his knees, peered through the darkness in the direction where his train had disappeared. There was not a sound up there, not a sight of anything. So far, so good. The train had gone on. They mightn't have missed him yet. How long had he been unconscious, he wondered.

But there was no time to lose. Old Blue-Nose, whom he last saw standing outside the lavatory, would be breaking in the door before long, staring in horror at the open window, rushing back to his fellow-guards, stopping the train, alerting all the search forces. They would have patrols out in no time.

He had to be under cover before daylight.

Every bone aching, he dragged himself to his feet, blessing his luck to find that he had no injuries apart from his appalling head. Urgency lending him wings, he began immediately trudging down the railway track, heading westwards away from the train that had been taking him to Colditz.

He had one thought: get further west, then find cover for the day.

He tramped steadily on. What real chance did he have, he wondered. Couldn't speak German, no false papers, no German money, no maps—he had a very thin show, he knew. Still—might meet up with some foreign workers. And if not—well, he'd give the Huns a good run.

He had been walking more than a mile down the line before he came upon his coat and pack. They were intact, but he shuddered again as he tried to work out how fast that train must have been travelling.

It was bitterly cold, and he was grateful to snuggle into the coat again, and to feel the reassuring pressure of the little pack over his shoulders.

He hardly noticed the darkness beginning to fade. On and on he stumped, mile after mile, following the line until daylight would enable him to see the lie of the land. He had to be careful of another train coming along, but he would have plenty of time to get down out of sight.

The dawn was coming quickly—he could see a clear quarter-mile now. Nothing suitable on either side of the line; just cultivated fields. Hopeless breaking off into that kind of country. Better stick to the railway as long as he could.

Lighter now, and he glanced behind. . . .

He stopped.

He turned deliberately full round and narrowed his eyes. Was that someone way back along the line? Could it be someone walking along the tracks, following his own footsteps, perhaps half a mile back there?

Yes, it was someone, all right. Might be a farmer or a workman taking a short cut to work. Nothing to worry about that—he could out-distance him if necessary. But could it be possible they were after him already, that it was someone's job to walk back down the line?

He turned sharply round and began walking again, clapping on the pace. A strange man seen walking the railways tracks would excite suspicion in this kind of country. And every young German was trained as a junior Nazi scout, on the look-out for escaped P.O.W.s. He needed cover pretty soon.

Then he breathed again. Not far ahead, off to the south of the line, lay a wood. He would move off there, get deep into a thicket for the day, reconnoitre just before dark, then travel again during the night.

He hurried along now, keen to reach the haven of the trees. It was still very early, very unlikely for anyone to be about. Make the last few hundred yards at top speed, duck off to the side, and he would be safe for the day.

He decided where he would leave the tracks. He was right alongside the wood now, but it didn't please him so much. For it was a plantation, not a natural wood, and the trees grew in straight rows. You could see right down the lanes between them. But that couldn't be helped. He had no choice.

He paused as he prepared to strike off away from the line . . . looked back again. . . .

There, curse it, was that same figure, way back along the lines, but perhaps even a little closer. That fellow must have been really tramping to have made up ground like that. But he was still a long way off.

Upham stared hard . . . and he had a haunting feeling that the man up there was Blue-Nose. Absurd, he sharply rebuked himself. Turning away, he quickly ran off the lines, into the shade of the trees, and moved rapidly down one of the lanes. He would get right into the centre.

The sight of that figure far up the line made him uneasy. Surely they wouldn't waste time sending a man along the railway on *foot*. And surely the train must have gone several miles before they discovered his escape. No—he was getting too suspicious; the simplest explanation was that it was a workman hurrying to a nearby farm. The places where they would be watching for him would be railway yards, picture theatres, isolated barns or hay-ricks, and in the ditches alongside the main roads. They wouldn't expect him to walk along the railway, as plain as a wooden duck moving across a shooting gallery.

Still, the thought of it made him restless. He would see what this plantation was like. He would reconnoitre around it, decide where to make for after nightfall. He would have to lie up under cover all day.

He tramped through to the far end of the wood, peered cautiously out over the countryside beyond. He would have to make south, or south-east perhaps. Maybe his best hope lay in going east towards the Russians. Next night he would go across country, pick up some food, make the journey in bounds.

He told himself again that he didn't really have a show, with no maps and no gear. But it was a grand feeling to be at large, to have called the tune again, to know that he had licked them. This freedom was a heady feeling, nice to the taste.

Deep in the centre of the wood he found himself a deep thicket. It was broad daylight now and no time to be lost in making himself inconspicuous. Pressing in under the branches, he burrowed a hole midst the leaves, curled up gratefully, and closed his eyes.

Upham was always able to sleep in conditions of discomfort. It was a knack he had acquired from his early days, and whether it was the back of a jolting truck, or a stony hole in the ground with the rain beating in, he had but to drop his head, close off the mind, and the privations of the body never intruded on his will to sleep.

*   *   *   *

The greatest mystery of the body—the subconscious mind—is a better watch-dog than the most eager sentry. Upham knew, as he struggled into wakefulness, that his mind was warning him.

He awoke stiff and sore, but his mind immediately alert and cautious. From the way the shadows lay he judged it was late afternoon. He must have slept about eight hours. That was just what he wanted. He would be out on the edge of the wood by nightfall, ready to move into the open as soon as it was dark.

But there was something wrong—he felt it.

Carefully he rose to his knees, then crawled to the edge of the thicket. Parting the branches with elaborate stealth he peered out.

There was no one near him. Everything looked just the same.

It would pay to have another reconnaissance around the wood. He crawled out into the open, stretched himself up on his feet.

Then he looked up the lane towards the railway.

In an instant he dropped back to the ground. Too late, he wondered? Had he been seen? Who was it up there? Searchers? But how could they have chosen this wood to search?

For the figure of a man was standing there, right at the end of the lane, looking straight down towards Upham.

And, even as Upham stared at him, the figure began to move, with slow, cautious steps, like a man who is waiting for something to happen in front of him. And he was coming, slowly but steadily, straight down this very lane.

Upham watched him in cold tension. Should he crawl back into the thicket, hope to lie there unobserved? Then as he passed he would see if it was a searcher or just a local wood-cutter or farm boy making his slow way home. But the deliberate, methodical approach of the man worried him. . . .

And then, like a flash, he knew . . . for coming out of the trees on each side of the man were three others, and they all had rifles.

Quick . . . into another lane . . . he couldn't stay there within feet of the men as they passed. They would be peering into every thicket. They must be here looking for him. Four armed men stalking through the wood—what other reason could there be?

He squirmed his way past the nearest tree, into the next lane, then began jogging silently away from the spot, at right angles to the lane down which the searchers were advancing.

He paused when he saw the light increasing ahead and he knew he was approaching the edge of the wood on that side. He drew himself in close beside a tree, looking back to see if he could pick up the other men as they passed down the lane.

Then again, with a feeling of urgency, the warning bell seemed to be ringing inside him. Almost by instinct Upham turned round, looking out towards the edge of the plantation.

Right on the edge there, rifle in hand, stood a figure, peering uncertainly in Upham's direction. The outline of the man was familiar, the way he held the rifle, that cant of his head.

It was Blue-Nose!

Blue-Nose himself, whom he had left in the train, now patrolling through this very wood, looking for his precious prisoner; Blue-Nose, whose whole future probably depended on Upham's recapture.

That meant five men. Blue-Nose and four others. And Blue-Nose was now starting off slowly, pacing down the lane towards Upham, towards the centre of the wood.

The searchers were going through the wood at right angles to one another. That was grim enough but, given luck, he might dodge them, keeping in the sector away from them. The trouble was— these lanes enabled each man to see from one end of the wood to the other.

Upham planned it out rapidly, moving like a shadow as his brain ticked over. He had never felt so alert, so much now dependent on his wits.

Deliberately he began running at an oblique angle, to take him away from the two paths that the searchers were following. He ran through the trees as fast as he dared, trying hard to make no sound . . . on and on, until at last he reckoned that he had crossed almost from one side to the other. Somewhere on the way he must have crossed behind the first party of men, but he had not sighted them.

Now he was panting with the running, trying to think what plan they would follow. They would divide the wood off into squares. He would have to keep moving either ahead of them or, better still, behind them. Move into a square they had just left. It wouldn't be impossible with only five men to beat.

His mind was still dwelling on 'five men' before the signal lights abruptly changed. For now there, far down the lane in which he was standing, there was *another man*—another searcher, carrying a rifle at the ready, moving confidently, looking right and left as he strode down the lane.

Upham darted out of sight, peered back towards the railway end of the wood. And there . . . oh my godfather! . . . there was another . . . and another!

Eight of them now!

He ran quickly now, deep towards the centre again . . . paused . . .

pressed himself up against a tree while he got his wind back. Up this lane? Yes—but up at the end of it there was the next man—only a hundred yards away.

Upham slid round into the next lane—looked up it, caught his breath in desperation. There was a man coming down this one too. Chancing being seen, he dashed across the space, into the shadow of the tree, looked up the next lane.

There was a soldier moving down there, too.

No time for planning now—just jump where the whip cracked, and he had to chance it again to leap across this lane in the hope that there would be clear territory ahead.

The shout from somewhere out to the side of him was like a battle-cry. He wasn't surprised to hear it. It had to happen pretty soon.

Like a hare he darted away from it, doubling back across the lanes, and as he ran the shout seemed to be taken up around the wood, like voices echoing back from a dozen mountainsides. He found himself wondering—how many of them altogether?

And he ran this way—and there was one man running towards him . . . he veered off sharply . . . but there was another down there . . . again and again he swerved away . . . but it seemed everywhere they were coming at him . . . he tried in all directions, but they were always there, some running, some moving steadily . . . all with rifles.

At last as he stood at bay he could watch them coming. From where he was he could see down several lanes, and there was a rifleman advancing down every one . . . coming in on him fast.

Run here . . . but again they were in front of him. It dawned on him ominously—there was a cordon around the whole wood. They had surrounded him while he slept. Now they had spotted him, they were moving in steadily, in a circle, narrowing him down.

He could see most of them now—there must be a whole platoon of infantry on the job.

He had only once chance—if it were a single ring closing in on him he might dash straight through it—like the night at Minqar Qaim. There was nothing else left.

He began running again, straight towards the ring of searchers. Perhaps it would surprise them.

Sixty yards . . . fifty . . . thirty . . . and he saw the look on the face of the man he was racing towards. Then . . .

Crack!! The rifle-shot echoed through the wood like cannon-fire. *Crack! Crack!* And all around him now the shots were coming, and he felt the dry 'phew . . . w . . . w' as the bullets plucked the air close by his ear.

The man in front of him was firing too—point-blank range. They seemed to be all running in on him.

And he knew the game was over.

He knew when the lure of escape no longer blinded him to the prospect of certain death. His time had run out . . . he knew it . . . and it was no use any more.

The next few bullets would strike him down, but he threw in his hand before the inevitable end.

Hands raised in surrender? No—not for him. That was too humiliating a gesture.

When he knew it was all over he stopped running abruptly, then deliberately sat down on the ground, watched them as they paused uncertainly.

They must suspect him, for they came crowding in to a range of about a chain; but there they stopped, covering him with their weapons, while the shouting and calling continued.

Fully two minutes passed, while Upham remained sitting on the ground in simulated indifference, before they finally moved in cautiously. In they came. Yes—there must have been an entire platoon.

They searched him meticulously. They told him later that if they had found any German food on him he would have been executed for 'pillage'.

But now—here was old Blue-Nose. The old codger would probably slap him over the head with his pistol-butt.

But that was strange. Old Blue-Nose was coming up with his face wreathed in smiles, and he put his hand on Upham's shoulder as if he were greeting a long-lost friend. He almost drooled at his delight in recapturing the fugitive, and grinned and bantered away at Upham in the highest good humour.

In contrast to the rough reception Upham expected, he had never found himself so popular. Blue-Nose was full of concern for his welfare, and fussed around him like an over-indulgent nanny. Charles found himself grinning at the experience, but the truth was obvious enough: this was one of the greatest days in the old boy's life—the day his prize prisoner was recaptured.

Charles was led out of the wood in a spirit of camaraderie and effusive goodwill. Blue-Nose explained that it was he himself who walked back down the line—it was he whom Upham must have seen a long way back—for Blue-Nose correctly judged how the fugitive would behave. He trailed him along the line, not anxious to catch up too soon, and saw him disappear into the wood. Then he phoned for help and the local military commander provided a force to surround the plantation.

Upham was at liberty for just twelve hours. It was well worth it.

*   *   *   *

In another train the journey to Colditz continued. But now there had to be more care still. The guards couldn't risk a second escape. So for the remainder of the journey Upham sat handcuffed to one of them.

The guards tried now to take Upham with them when they got out at stations to obtain food. But the restaurant people brusquely refused to have the prisoner inside or to serve him with any food at all.

What, then, to do with him?

So they hit on the convenient idea of handcuffing Upham to a post on the platform, in a position where they could keep an eye on him while they bought their miserable black bread and soup at the restaurant counter.

Upham never expected concessions from the enemy, nor did he give any. After the war he once said that he would never have tolerated the same conduct from a German prisoner that he himself showed towards his German guards. He felt ashamed of some of it, he said, for he thought afterwards that his contempt and antagonism only made things more awkward for his mates. But the war was always such a personal thing to him that he had to go on fighting by the only means available.

So, not giving or asking any mercies, he accepted stoically the in-dignity of being manacled to the iron stanchion on the station platform, where the crowds gazed upon him in curiosity and resentment. He felt like a bear in a circus, tied up for the audience to gape at and torment.

For he suffered both. There were those who merely gaped. There were some who reviled him in language he fortunately did not under-stand, but he guessed their meaning. And there were some who came and spat on him.

Until at last a group of young Luftwaffe toughs strolled by. They stopped and stared. Then one of them, a petty little brute with a pasty face, after making sure that Upham was securely tied, came up bravely and lashed out with his foot. The kick caught Upham on the side of the knee. It hurt.

That seemed good fun for these young worthies. One after another they stepped in and contemptuously added their kicks to the assaults of the first comrade. Upham could do nothing but endure their violence with a black heart, while they vented their cruelty and hatred on him until they tired of their sport.

The kicking and roughing-up he suffered on that station platform remained one of Upham's most vivid war-time memories. Even over the mellowing years he has found it hard to forgive. So often a person forms his opinion of a whole nation from the actions of a degraded few; and in modern times so often the leaders of a nation set the pattern for those few.

Bruised and humiliated, Upham was led back to his seat in the train.

17

Colditz Castle

THEY marched in past the sentry at the gate, then over a bridge across the moat; beyond that an archway with another gate and sentry; then through yet another gate, up a sloping cobbled walk, and finally into a courtyard entirely surrounded by high buildings.

He had arrived in Colditz.

The Germans called it '*Sonderlager*'—Special Camp. To it they sent the most desperate and troublesome of all war prisoners, not for punishment, but because Colditz was reputed to be escape-proof.

The story has been told elsewhere how the ingenuity of a number of Allied prisoners destroyed the reputation of Colditz's invincibility. They beat it, they beat the walls, the precipices, the mass of sentries, the Gestapo inspectors, the German officers who came to know everything that could be known about escape technique and stratagems. And, despite all these, the escapes, fabulous and well-nigh incredible, continued.

Built and rebuilt, altered and added to over four centuries, Colditz was enough to make the bravest quail. Its great walls—seven feet thick in places—its gloom, the five-storeyed buildings rearing up around the tiny courtyard, its rigid discipline—all bore heavily on the aggressive spirits of those confined there.

Some men broke under its strain and became mental cases. Others fought against the torpor and awful depression that the place bred in them. Few were released from it without some deep mark left on their personalities.

Men of lesser resource might have withstood Colditz with equanimity. But those sent there were the most arrogant and daring, the ones who refused to accept being prisoners, the persistent escapers. To their free-roving spirits Colditz was a more dreadful ordeal. Little wonder that schemes of the greatest bravery and skill were hatched beneath its ramparts.

When Upham arrived in the late summer of 1944 the years were taking their toll of the occupants. Sickness had increased, the mental balance of many of them was insecure. And, as the winter of 1944–5 drew on, the pressure of war on Germany made conditions for the prisoners doubly austere.

Just before Upham's arrival the prisoners had realized there was a traitor amongst them. Information obtained by the Germans could have come only from the mouth of a man who knew the prisoners' secrets. So the senior Allied officers decided that every new arrival should receive a private screening from his fellow-prisoners.

Martin Gilliat—then acting as Adjutant of the British prisoners and later to be an official in the household of the Queen Mother—heard of the new arrival. He went to Fred Moody, a New Zealand medical officer in the fortress.

'Fred, I'm told another New Zealander was brought in last night. Name of Upham. See if you can check on him, will you?'

Moody was interested in this new arrival, particularly as no combatant officer from the New Zealand Division had yet been sent to Colditz. There had been a dentist, a doctor or two, one or two orderlies, and some others—but hardly more than six or seven all told. As it turned out, Charles Upham remained the only combatant officer from the New Zealand forces ever sent to the Castle.

The new man was having a shower. Moody stood in the courtyard, edged along till he was within earshot of the grilled window of the shower-room.

'What d'yer know, Kiwi?' he called out softly in unmistakable New Zealand accents.

A pause. Then: 'Who are you?' came the cautious reply.

Moody told him, gave him some identification.

Upham whispered: 'What the hell is this place? Looks bloody awful to me.'

Moody gave him more information, meantime keeping an eye on the sentry in the courtyard.

'Do you want any food?' he asked.

'No.'

Then they talked guardedly, Upham still cautious about Moody's identity, Moody asking questions to satisfy himself about Upham.

And when at last they had satisfied each other the voice came out through the grill, wary but eager: 'Any chance of getting out of here, Doc?'

'Not much,' Moody whispered back. 'But I'll tell you about things when they bring you out.'

Then the sentry moved him on.

Moody went before the prisoners' Security Committee a few

minutes later. He told them what he knew. 'I know it's Upham,' he said.
'He comes from Christchurch. Father's a barrister. Went to Christ's
College. I heard of him at O.C.T.U., and I was on Crete when he got his
V.C. I remember the boys in the 23rd at Maleme talking about Upham
of the 20th tearing the Huns to bits.'

The Chairman said: 'The V.C. doesn't count. He's just a man called
Charles Upham until you can vouch for him. Is he all right?'

Moody told them more about Upham, his family, and his war
record, finally satisfying the Committee that the prisoner was one who
could be trusted.

In a few hours Moody helped Upham to settle in, took him to the
Canadian mess—the group that shared one eating table—and introduced him around.

Once again Upham asked: 'Now tell me, Fred, what's the story
about escaping?'

The doctor answered: 'No hope at all. The Huns have sewn up just
about everything now, and there's not much escape activity—not like
there used to be. If we stick out the winter, looks as if it might be all
over. Most fellows think escaping isn't worth the candle now. Whatever
you try here it's a death or glory business. You can get killed falling off
the roof, or down the cliff, and the goons will shoot you without hesitation if you're caught. But if you've got any ideas you have to register
them with the Escape Committee. Dick Howe's in charge—and he's got
to give you the O.K.'

It did not take Upham long to realize that Colditz had reached the
stage where it was almost completely escape-proof—granting that
desperation might still drive a prisoner into attempting a break in the
face of great odds. Mike Sinclair, an unquenchable escaper, had just
made his final bid from Colditz, reckless and doomed to failure, and
had been shot dead just over the wire. The impersonations, the tunnels,
the long ropes, the drains—all had been tried before, some successfully;
but now the loopholes were sealed and men who fretted for liberty paced
the narrow confines of Colditz in frustrated despair.

Upham, moreover, was not well enough to attempt any escape that
involved climbing. His arm was stiff and painful, ruling out any
prospect of climbing the steep gables and ridges of Colditz's jagged
roofs.

*   *   *   *

As the Allies gradually pounded back the failing Germans, the winter
came grimly over the Castle. It was, so the longest residents said, the

toughest winter of them all. Gone now was the fervour for escape; gone, too, the resilience and energy that men possessed in their first months of captivity. Life was gaunt, grey, deeply depressing. Men had to fight with their very souls to remain balanced and undismayed.

Upham could not escape from Colditz. He knew it. If any reasonable avenues for escape were left, the brilliance of Dick Howe and his helpers would have discovered and exploited them.

Charles was rather a solitary figure. He made few friends, kept largely to himself, and gave no sign that he was, and had been, a man of dynamic action. The misery of Colditz seemed to dampen the active side of his character; he was often dour, morose, and unresponsive. The finality and efficiency of his confinement weighed heavily on him. Only now and then did his fiery spirit emerge.

Somehow his legend seemed to come with him, and questions were asked him about the deeds that had made him famous. But he was like a clam. Dick Howe later said: 'He was quite the most modest person, and during the time I knew him at Colditz it was impossible to extract any information on his deeds during the war.'

Mickey Hargreaves (a New Zealander in one of those mysterious British parachuting units) and Fred Moody became Upham's closest friends, and the only ones in whom he confided. They tried to draw him out sometimes, to set him talking about the old days on the battlefields of Crete or North Africa. They found then, as many have found since, that Charles would quickly talk about the exploits of his old platoon and his company, about the deeds of Bob May, Dave Kirk, and the others; but once his own name was introduced into the conversation he would frown and look uncomfortable, taking the first opportunity of changing the subject.

Pressed about his own part, he would growl: 'Thousands of others did the same. . . .' And once when Moody talked about fear, and questioned him about it, Upham spoke as if he didn't understand, finally blurting out: 'I got so bloody angry with them nothing else seemed to matter.'

Colonel W. Tod, D.S.O., O.B.E., M.C., was the Senior British Officer at this time. He found Charles to be very quiet and reserved. 'From time to time he and I walked round the depressing little cobbled yard but as far as I remember our conversation was usually about sheep farming and the merits of different breeds of sheep-dogs. Conditions at Colditz were somewhat trying and sometimes people were apt to lose their sense of proportion, but Charles Upham always remained level-headed and sensible. He was the type of man one instinctively likes.'

Dick Howe undertook the task of teaching Charles how to cook.

Now this was rather different from cooking in a shepherd's hut on the slopes of the New Zealand Alps, or with a section in the Western Desert. Cooking at Colditz was a fine art. As Howe puts it—one had to start with practically no ingredients.

Dick Howe gave Charles a lesson in making soup—tasty soup, that is, of superior quality. First the two of them ransacked the swill-tubs—the scrapings from the kitchen. What they wanted were peelings, because here and there some of the vegetable would still adhere to the skins. These minute prizes were carefully gathered together and fried with a little fat. Then unlimited quantities of water were added, depending on the number who were to partake of the meal. Any odd scraps available would of course be added by way of seasoning. Result—tasty soup.

'Having mastered this árt,' writes Howe, 'Charlie went from strength to strength until he became a very accomplished chef, which under those conditions was most important.'

But among the hungry grey faces of prisoners enduring the last winter in Colditz, Upham made no special mark. They recognized his restrained hatred, the intolerable burden of close confinement which he suffered just like them, the deep longing for freedom, the determination that nothing in the end would defeat him. But if any picture of Upham remains clearly in their eyes it is only of a tough solitary man plodding round and round that dreary courtyard, head sunk, brow furrowed—still the caged lion, but now with the heart being crushed.

Nevertheless, while towards his fellow-prisoners he was a mixture of warmth and dourness, towards the Germans he never varied. Never did he compromise. His attitude remained one of constant antagonism and contempt.

Counting the prisoners was a procedure that infuriated Upham. It probably infuriated the Germans too, having regard to the number of times the roll-call was faked or given a false impression of correctness. Refinements of the roll-call technique even included rigging it so that, while it was in fact correct, it gave the impression of being wrong.

The British contingent would stand casually in their ranks, reading or chatting, while Hauptmann Pupcke made the count. Pupcke was one of the more tolerant Germans and was not disliked by the prisoners, but he was an awfully poor counter.

'This damned counting business makes me bloody angry,' Charles said on a dozen occasions. 'And here's old muck-up Jack coming,' as Pupcke entered the courtyard to begin the business of counting.

Pupcke liked everything lined up nicely. He gave orders that no one should smoke on *Appell*.

Upham stood in the front rank, waiting to be counted, smoking his pipe.

Pupcke stopped in front of him, pointed at the pipe, and barked. He seemed to take a long time to say what might have been said in a few words. All he was doing was ordering Upham to remove the pipe.

Upham looked at him steadily, took the pipe out, and said: 'Oh, go shoot yourself.' Then he replaced the pipe.

Hauptmann Pupcke looked quickly at the interpreter. 'What did he say?' he asked in German.

Fred Moody, standing alongside, nudged Charlie. 'Don't cause any trouble, Charlie. No point in it today.'

Pupcke faced Upham again, rapped out in English: 'Stand to attention!'

Upham took no notice, went on smoking, looking blandly ahead.

Then Pupcke stormed at him, all to no effect. He tried persuading, then ordering, then shouting.

And then, tolerant German that he was, he suddenly stopped, smiled, and said magnanimously: 'Perhaps there's something wrong with him.' He took no further notice of Upham and resumed his counting.

It was a near thing on another occasion. Again Charles was in the front rank, reading, this time with a cigarette in his mouth.

The Security Officer, Hauptmann Eggers, was doing the count. He walked slowly down the line, counting methodically; then came to Upham.

In a high-pitched voice he shouted at Upham to take the cigarette out.

No one expected Charles to obey. Nor did he. He stood still, looking up from his book in a bored way, still smoking.

For a moment the two men eyed each other.

Slowly Eggers raised his open hand, drew it back, then slashed Upham violently across the face, sending the cigarette flying.

Nothing would then have saved Eggers' life had it not been for the violent intervention of Upham's friends.

His face 'like a bayonet charge' (says Dick Howe), Upham threw himself at Eggers.

Almost as quickly, his friends on each side grabbed him. Livid with rage, Upham struggled furiously with them, obsessed with nothing else but getting at Eggers to avenge the insult he had suffered. Eggers backed away hurriedly.

With difficulty they restrained him, and Hauptmann Eggers was quick to dismiss the parade.

It was an incident that could have had a more serious ending.

There occurred also at Colditz a flare-up with a German officer that Upham now describes as his 'nearest thing'. The Germans had had a fright and, fearing an escape, had sounded the *Appell* siren just on midnight. This was not uncommon.

Stumbling and cursing, the prisoners gathered their coats about them and filed out for the count.

A number of men were called on to show their identity discs. They did so—all except Upham. When asked for his he threw it on the ground in front of the inspecting officer.

He was ordered to pick it up. He took no notice. Again and again the orders were given. Upham said once: 'Pick it up yourself,' then kept a defiant silence. Having taken his stand, he was not going to shift.

The German officer finally gave up speaking, drew his revolver, and cocked it, then advanced on Upham and pressed the muzzle against his stomach. 'Pick it up!' he ordered for the last time.

Upham was always an expert at judging a risk, knowing how far he could risk himself or his men without incurring too great a danger. This time he knew where he stood. He could tell it in the manner of the officer standing before him.

For a long twenty seconds he stood there, eyes blazing. Then, defeated in the face of death, he relaxed, bent down, and picked up the disc, handed it over.

He made it appear, however, as if he were conferring a favour.

Those alongside agreed that Upham could never have been closer to it than in those tense moments.

*   *   *   *

Sometimes there was fun, even with the Germans. And when these prisoners of Colditz had fun it was hilarity unlimited. It had to be.

Appell! And this day the prisoners knew that Pupcke was the Orderly Officer of the day, and that he would accordingly be making the inspection and doing the count. There would be nothing drastic.

They filed down into the courtyard in bored disinterest, shuffled into their ranks, and waited for Pupcke to appear. Punctual and punctilious, it wasn't like him to be late. But no sign of him. The German N.C.O.s gazed vacantly on the parade and stood around uncomfortably.

Where on earth was Pupcke?

Ah! At last, there he came, entering the courtyard almost at the double, looking red-faced and bustled. It seemed clear that the good

Pupcke had been away from the Castle, had just made it back to the fortress in time for the parade.

With no time to collect himself, Pupcke advanced to the front rank and began his task. It was his habit to lean close to the front-rank men. . . .

He passed down two or three of the files . . . then paused, because the first man had begun giggling. Seeing nothing to giggle about, Pupcke continued the inspection. But as he went steadily on, so steadily did the giggling turn into chortles, one man after another . . . and the further he went, the less they could restrain themselves. They began to laugh, gradually louder and louder, and by the time the startled Hauptmann had reached the end of the line the noise was swelling into uproar.

'Three cheers for old Pupcke!' someone shrieked, beside himself with mirth, and the prisoners cheered hilariously, applause growing wilder and wilder, the men letting their feelings burst out in a positive furore of helpless laughter.

It seemed so uproariously incongruous for the precise, rigid Germans—these inhuman guardians of Colditz—these automatons who possessed few, if any, human weaknesses.

But there, dear old Pupcke, he went blissfully down the line, more and more puzzled, with his breath stinking of liquor, and around his mouth a generous plastering of rich red lipstick, implanted on him in broad tell-tale imprints.

Their delight—their hilarious surprise—was at finding out so ridiculously that Germans were human too.

*   *   *   *

Winter dragged on, and 1945 came round. There were concerts and plays in the camp theatre; there was the stimulation of hearing the B.B.C. broadcasts from the secret radio in the attics. The war on land was advancing into fortress Germany.

There was the interest of seeing Colditz being used for hostages. Inside its walls were assembled a number of prisoners closely related to prominent people in the Allied war effort—Giles Romilly, who was Winston Churchill's nephew; Captain the Master of Elphinstone, a nephew of Queen Elizabeth, the Queen Mother; Lieutenant Lord Lascelles, nephew of King George VI; some prominent French and Polish generals; and Lieutenant John Winant, son of the United States Ambassador to Britain. It was obvious why they were being held. Their lives and safety were to be traded by the Nazis at the time of reckoning.

Three Americans also entered Colditz, captured from an unsuccessful parachute mission into Hungary. One of them, Colonel Duke, had been advertising manager for the American magazine *Time* and became one of Upham's close friends.

As the final months drew on, agonizingly slowly, escape seemed futile. The end would come, of course, but by now men had lost ambition, and many had lost hope. Escaping was not receiving encouragement from the camp's senior officers, because the Germans let it be known that they would no longer treat escaped prisoners under the terms of the Geneva Convention, and would shoot them upon recapture. The mood of the Nazi leaders was so dangerous that this threat might well have been carried out. Unnecessary risks with the beaten Germans were no longer wise.

Nevertheless, Charles Upham and Peter Winton made some explorations. They revived interest in the old drains, one of the earliest of schemes, thinking that a few innovations might see them pay off again. But time was on their side now. Closer and close came the war.

*   *   *   *

On Tuesday, 10th April 1945, the war on land came within earshot of Colditz. Used to the crump of bombs falling on Leipzig, twenty-five miles away, now the prisoners could distinguish the unmistakable sound of shell-bursts in the distance. There were few *Appells*. Colonel Tod began spending a good deal of time in conference with the Commandant. Just as freedom was approaching, he sensed that the safety of his fellow-prisoners was now at its most critical stage. One false move by the German Commandant, or one tactical error on his own part, could mean bloodshed in the Castle. The inmates of Colditz were not people to be trifled with at this late hour.

From the village the news drifted up that an S.S. division had moved into the area and promptly murdered the remnants of a Jewish working gang quartered there. In their last straits what would the fanatical Nazis do with the desperadoes of Colditz?

The prisoners recognized the gravity of their position, Upham amongst them. He had few illusions about the lengths to which the Nazis might go. It was perhaps unlikely that the prisoners would be slaughtered outright. But the Germans might order them to be shifted. What would the prisoners do then? Refuse? And if so with what consequences?

Upham became very thoughtful over these last few days. Finally Fred Moody asked him point-blank: 'What'll you do, Charlie?'

Upham clenched his fists and replied solemnly: 'I'll never let them shift me from here, Fred. If it comes to that I'll try and fight my way out.'

Next day, Wednesday, the noise of battle drew nearer.

Thursday. Earthworks and defences were being hastily constructed in the village below and orders came for the hostages to be removed from the fortress to the final mountain redoubt in Austria. Here now were the last bitter writhings.

Friday; then Saturday. And all that day the shells whined and screamed over the Castle, and a few slammed into it. Tod told the prisoners that the German High Command had ordered that they be evacuated further east, out of reach of the approaching Allies. He gave the Commandant the answer: 'We refuse; we will resist, by force if necessary, any attempt to shift us. Responsibility for bloodshed will be on the head of the German authorities, particularly the Camp Commandant.'

By nightfall that day the Commandant had yielded to the inevitable and arranged terms of surrender with Colonel Tod. It was only a matter of hours now.

Sunday the 15th. By 11 a.m. American tanks were seen in the streets of the village, infantry moving in their wake and clearing the houses. It was only half an hour later when four Americans of a reconnaissance section walked through the castle gates. Inside they found the senior British officers ready for them and the Germans lined up in formal surrender.

They went down from Colditz into the village—tramping up and down the streets, looking into the shops. Some walked in and un-ashamedly took the cameras and the binoculars they wanted. Upham felt he couldn't do that. He saw some eating utensils in a hardware shop that lay unattended. They represented normalcy to him. He walked in, helped himself to a plate, knife, fork, and spoon, then walked out. He saw others with the cameras and the watches. Then he headed for the headquarters of the American unit who had captured the town. He knew exactly what he wanted to do.

'Why not?' the sergeant asked in reply. 'Plenty of it. Help yourself.' And he helped Upham select the goods he had come for.

Upham changed into the American combat uniform, fitted on the boots and the U.S. helmet. Then the arms—the Tommy-gun, the revolver, two grenades, compass. . . .

He prepared to go into action with the Americans.

For four days Charles stayed with the U.S. forces in the Colditz area, clothed and equipped as one of them, waiting for the call forward.

So far as he was concerned, the war was not over. He was intent on fighting it to the last.

But the inexorable pressure of higher orders finally caught him up. 'Under no circumstances are released P.O.W.s to be permitted to join active service units, unofficially or otherwise. P.O.W.s are to be evacuated without exception.' He couldn't beat that order, so reluctantly he left his Americans and was soon part of the great movement back towards England.

18

Telegram in the Studio

FROM Europe the flood of released prisoners streamed towards England, among them 9000 New Zealanders. Then, armed with a free rail pass, and with twenty-eight days' leave, they roamed every corner of Britain.

Charles Upham waited impatiently for his own 'processing' to be completed. Molly was in England, and when reunions are close time never passes more slowly. Fretting, but at last freed, he rushed to find out where she was.

The clerk seemed to be awfully slow in looking up the records. 'Miss McTamney, sir? Actually she's not here. She's not in England at present.'

'What?' almost shrieked Charles. 'Then where is she?'

'In Germany, sir.'

'In Germany!!' Charles nearly collapsed.

Yes, she was in Germany, working with the Red Cross Auxiliary not far behind the lines.

Leaping for pen and paper, Charles dashed off an urgent appeal. 'Come out of there,' he demanded. 'It's dangerous.'

He grabbed another sheet of paper, dashed off an application for permission to return to Germany. Even Charles appreciated the twist of it. Here he was, just freed from Germany after spending nearly three years trying to escape from it, now appealing to go back.

But Molly worked things her way, and the week-end saw her winging back to England and to the meeting both had been waiting for so long.

There she was at last—the Molly of so many quiet sentimental talks with Beau Cottrell in Italy, with 'Judge' Holmes at Weinsberg, with Dr. Fred at Colditz. He had never seen her before in her war uniform.

And for her—there at last was the man whose letters and postcards had been so homely and placid that she sometimes wondered if he were the same man the newspapers wrote about.

There was just that one week-end when they saw each other. Molly had to fly back to Germany, but their plans were made before she left.

While she was away, and Charles waited again for her return, he was meeting all the old faces again—his friends from Crete whom he had left bitterly on the beach at Sfakia, those who had never returned from Belhamed while he sulked as an L.O.B., and the mass of others who had been scooped up in the man-made disaster on Ruweisat Ridge.

And there, at last, was old Leggy; Leggy the incorrigible, as bright and chirpy as ever. And who other than Leggy would have turned P.O.W. life into that of a country gentleman, waited on hand and foot by a family in Poland who protected and fed him? Charles and Leggy-boy walked through London arm in arm.

Then a letter arrived with a coat of arms on the envelope. It read:

'. . . The King will hold an Investiture at Buckingham Palace on Friday the 11th May 1945 at which your attendance is requested. . . .'

Charles was allowed to take two guests. He took Molly and his sister, Mrs. G. H. Holmes-Siedle, who lived in Hampshire.

King George VI pinned the V.C. on Upham's tunic—as if to per-petuate the temporary investiture in the desert that seemed so long ago.

There were many being decorated and the King had time for only a few words with each.

'Well, Captain Upham,' His Majesty said, 'I believe this is not your only award. I'm told you've just received a Mention in Despatches for your attempts to escape. Congratulations for that, too. Tell me, though, what have you been doing since you arrived in London?'

'Mostly eating, sir,' the lean ex-Colditz veteran replied.

They came away from the Palace and walked through St. James's Park. There was plenty to talk about. Relaxed and cheerful now, Charles was chatting freely when a stern voice stopped him.

A brigadier stood disapprovingly above him, one of the very old school.

'Don't you Colonials salute your senior officers any longer?' he demanded pompously.

Charles looked startled. He hadn't even noticed the old boy approaching. Then his rancour rose. The old bag—fancy making a point of it when a man was walking with his sister and fiancée, the war over, and using the incorrect and offensive expression—'you Colonials'.

Restraining his temper he said quietly: 'I'm sorry, sir, I didn't mean to be disrespectful. I didn't see you approaching. I would have saluted if I'd seen you, of course.' Then his impish malice came through. 'But actually I've just come from the Palace, sir, yarning with the King, *and he didn't seem to be fussy about saluting.*'

The Brigadier swelled and seemed about to burst. Then suddenly he noticed the crimson ribbon on Upham's chest.

His eyes popped. Then he clicked to attention, swung his arm in salute, turned about, and marched stiffly away.

Charles threw him one as he went.

* * * *

'Application declined.'

Oh well, perhaps it's all for the best, Charles philosophized as he read the reply. He had felt so strongly about it at the time.

On his way out from Germany Upham stopped at a transit camp near Weimar, and had gone with a party to inspect the nearby concentration camp of Buchenwald, where countless atrocities had been perpetrated by the Nazis. This experience quickened his resolve, for he had been toying with the idea of joining some unit after the war for the purpose of tracking down these Nazi criminals. One or two he had met in the camps he wanted to see brought to justice.

So, as he arrived in England, one of his first moves was to enter his name for the Occupation Force—for police duties, he asked. That would be the quickest way to have some of those old scores settled.

But no—there was a rule against ex-P.O.W.s being accepted, and his application was 'declined'.

* * * *

On 20th June 1945 Charles and Molly were married quietly at Barton-on-Sea, Hampshire. There were few people present, for Charles wanted nothing but quietness and solitude.

They honeymooned on the Isle of Wight, in the New Forest, and in Scotland. Friends provided them with cars. Then back to a flat in London, where at last Charles began to feel the freedom from the great military maw, and he was able to sink gratefully into the total privacy and seclusion of his own home.

* * * *

The ships were sailing for New Zealand. Charles was posted to one of them. The shipping clerk told him: 'Sorry, sir, but wives aren't allowed. Have to wait for normal civilian transport.'

Upham was never one to throw his weight about or seek the intervention of any of his superior officers. He accepted without demur what the clerk told him.

For Molly it was cruel to have to part so soon. But now only time separated them. Perhaps a boat for civilian passengers wouldn't be too long.

Charles did not feel aggrieved, only disappointed, to find there were a number of civilian wives on board his ship. Perhaps the shipping clerk had told them something different. Perhaps their husbands had used influence.

Molly stayed on in the London flat, a welcome figure at the New Zealand Fernleaf Club (where the division forgathered) and a close friend of Lady Freyberg, who throughout the war had worked actively behind the lines in helping the men of the New Zealand Division.

The two were having tea together at the club one day. 'And how's Charles?' Lady Freyberg asked conversationally.

'All right, I should hope,' Molly replied. 'I suppose he's somewhere off Africa now.'

Lady Freyberg looked startled and put her tea-cup down. 'You don't mean to say they've sent him off without you?'

Molly told her the story.

The wheels turned, the cables flew, and in no time orders came through that Molly was to have a seat on an aircraft made available to her immediately.

But Molly, like Charles, did not like to gain any advantage from his renown. If it was good enough for her to be flown out, why not all the other wives? No, she would be glad to have an early sea passage—but wouldn't take advantage of the offered air trip.

So on 2nd September 1945 Charles stepped ashore at Lyttelton, New Zealand, to face alone the wave of public acclaim that was to sweep over him in the weeks that followed.

*   *   *   *

Only relatives were admitted to the railway platform as the troop-train steamed in. There were his father and mother—and no words can ever describe the first moment of reunion with loved ones. Unrecognized by the rest of the crowd, Charles was quickly passed through, and within minutes was on his way home; quietly, without fuss—that is how he wanted it.

Back into the old living-room at 32 Gloucester Street that he had last seen in December 1939—nearly six years before. For the last time he swung his kit-bag off his shoulder, tumbled it on to the floor.

One waits so long for homecoming. Then when it comes it seems to arrive so quickly.

Tea, chatter, the feel of the old sofa, the way one can completely slouch only when one's family are present; all of them feeling for a subject of conversation with just a little discomfort. It would take some time for them to know him again.

He remembered. Some presents. He jumped up, opened his kit-bag quickly, and rummaged inside it.

'For you,' he said to his mother, producing a scarf. She scolded him for bringing so magnificent a scarf, with European embroidery on it that few people in New Zealand would ever see.

Then a meerschaum pipe for his father, presents for the others.

'Not forgetting this,' he joked, producing a denture they had had to give him when he came back to England.

And then his hand touched something else in the kit-bag. He drew it out.

'Something else for you, Mother,' he said almost diffidently. Perhaps only in the bosom of his own family could he feel the spark of pride that he sternly rejected everywhere else.

Mrs. Upham opened the little box, looked at the Victoria Cross lying inside.

*　　　*　　　*　　　*

The Press soon cornered him. Would he give an interview on the exploits that won him the Cross? He declined. What about impressions of prison life? He agreed to that, and local dailies gave him two columns. 'Wherever New Zealanders were imprisoned in Germany or Italy,' he said, 'they invariably got the enemy down by a mixture of ridicule and defiance.'

It was lovely meeting his old pre-war friends, though he had to endure their congratulations. They were so proud of him, but he felt their pride was misplaced. 'Congratulate the boys of the division,' he said. 'Not me.'

Allen Shand had known Charles since his mustering days. They spent some happy hours together, for, with Allen, Charles seemed able to relax more freely. It suited him to talk about farms and animals. ('He always had the deepest love for animals,' Shand said.)

A few days after Upham's return he was walking in Cathedral

R

Square with Allen when they stopped to speak to a little old lady whom
Shand knew. He introduced Charles to her.

But she was obviously rather deaf and had trouble in hearing the
name.

'And have you been overseas?' she asked sweetly, smiling pleasantly
at Charles.

Shand bent his head closer. 'Yes, he has,' he said clearly. 'He got
back only three days ago.'

The little old lady's eyes lit up. 'Oh, how lovely,' she said. 'Then you
must have come home on the same ship as *that wonderful Captain
Upham.*'

Shand guided Charles away tactfully.

But a more difficult occasion now forced itself on him. He was to be
tendered a civic reception by the city of Christchurch.

Held on 10th September 1945, Charles awaited this ceremony with
distress and embarrassment. And when the speakers paid their tributes
to him, telling of his great deeds that were matched only by his great
modesty, Charles sat on the platform with his eyes on the floor, feeling
miserable.

When he finally rose to speak he was greeted by a storm of applause.
Unnerved, he fumbled for his opening words, began with the shakiness
of the veriest amateur. The crowd felt prouder of him than ever.
Everyone loves a nervous hero.

'I should like to point out again,' he continued, 'that this honour is
really due to the division as a whole. I am only one unit in the division.
There were thousands of better soldiers than I was.' (There was some
happy disbelieving laughter at this remark.) 'In the Army, as you all
know, everything is cut and dried—already planned by someone else—
and carried out by the people underneath. The only way to get things
done was by taking risks, and those who took the risks were those who
did not come back. . . .' Then he proceeded to appeal for help to the
less fortunate, to those who had lost the 'men who had taken the risks
and died'.

'If we are going to make all this worth while,' he concluded, 'we
have got to get rid of want and misery in other parts of the world. Before
this war the world's riches were pretty badly distributed, and although
they changed hands considerably during the war' (more laughter) 'they
seemed to do so in big lumps.'

For a speech from a man who hated speaking, it struck just the right
note. He walked out, tremendously relieved it was all over, to the sound
of sustained cheering and clapping.

*   *   *   *

There was no man whom Upham respected more than Professor Eric Hudson, Principal of Lincoln College, where Charles had taken his farming and valuation courses. So when Hudson came to him and said that the College wanted to commission Archibald F. Nicoll to paint a portrait of their former student, Charles could do little but agree.

Almost simultaneously the old boys of Christ's College arranged a similar commission with Nicoll—so the two portraits were begun.

It fell to the lot of Charles's mother to make him report for the sittings. Charles fumed and evaded and did everything he could to escape—but his own inflexibility of purpose had been inherited. Mrs. Upham got him to the studio by hook or by crook. Nicoll worked patiently on. Professor Hudson did not dare tell Upham that Nicoll had estimated the sittings would extend over six weeks.

Resigned to it, but ready to be short-tempered if he got the chance, Charles took his place in the studio on Wednesday, 26th September 1945. Nicoll started the day's work.

After a while a telegram boy was admitted to the studio. 'Telegram for Captain Upham,' he said, and he was directed across to the chair.

Charles thanked him, ran his finger through the envelope, and drew out the telegram. It was from Wellington—from the Hon. F. Jones, the Minister of Defence, he was surprised to see.

'Head still a moment, please, Charles,' Nicoll pleaded.

Charles kept his head still, holding the telegram out in front so he could read it. It was not long. He read it slowly twice.

With no change of expression he carefully folded it up again, re-placed it in the envelope, put it in his pocket.

Perhaps his shoulders drooped a little, or his eyes dropped to the ground, for Nicoll said again: 'Hold it, Charles, just a few minutes longer.'

Charles resumed his pose, held it stoically.

The studio was silent again as they worked on.

19

Desert Echo

FAR back in July 1942, after the division had broken through the German ring at Minqar Qaim, Jim Burrows had gone along to Kip one evening to talk about Charles Upham.

'Kip,' Burrows had said, 'Charlie's got to have *another* V.C. . . . For Minqar Qaim. . . .'

So all the necessary evidence was collected, all the reports made out. They went through to General Inglis. He decided what recommendation he would make, what award was fitting for Upham's conduct in the desert at Minqar Qaim.

But then came the business of Ruweisat Ridge, the triumph of the infantry, the shambles of their capture. And, as Upham went into captivity, the tales were told again and again of how he had acted in those dramatic hours. It had been Upham on Crete, Upham at Minqar Qaim, now Upham at Ruweisat. What could be done about a man like that?

'Another V.C.? Not likely. Not many officers get the V.C. Certainly not a second one.'

'But they're recommending him for a V.C. for Minqar Qaim—and he deserves it.'

'Then what about Ruweisat? He ought to get one for that.'

'He can't have *three* V.C.s, old man, can he?'

What was to be done? Here were the reports on Minqar Qaim; here were the reports on Ruweisat. Upham figured in them both. Each report seemed to support the claim that the Commonwealth's highest awards would be appropriate for *each* of the two occasions.

But as the dust settled over the African battlefields, those in authority decided that the exploits of Charles Upham should be rewritten, no longer in separate reports, but in combined form. General Inglis prepared a new comprehensive report, complete with its sworn statements and proofs. It went through to London.

But Upham was now sunk into the deep heart of the enemy prison system. Was it appropriate that a very remarkable award should be

made to a man *in absentia*? On went the war, more urgent files covered
the stories of desert gallantry, and the years of conflict slowly passed.

Then war in Europe ended and the prisoners flowed back to England.
General Inglis would never forget the epics of Minqar Qaim and
Ruweisat. He had commanded the division at those times, seen its
victories, seen them snatched away by the failure of others whom he
could not control. He saw no reason why mere passage of time should
gloss over the courage of former days.

He went to Freyberg. 'Upham's back,' he said. 'He's sick, pretty
worn out, but he'll be all right in time. He's got a Mention in Despatches
for his escape attempts. But what about that award for him? It's lying
in War Office—never been looked at since Alamein.'

'I'll see about it,' Freyberg promised. And forthwith he did. He
went to the Army Council, the files were disinterred, and the recom-
mendations studied again in the cooler light of history. It was decided
that a draft citation should be submitted to Buckingham Palace, to be
studied by the King himself.

The papers finally reached King George VI.

This is what he read:

'From Jun 27 to Jul 15 1942 Capt Upham performed five acts
of conspicuous gallantry. He was with his company during all the
fighting that took place during this period, though he was wounded
on three different occasions—on the night Jun 27/28; on the night
Jul 14/15 and again on the afternoon Jul 15. On the first two
occasions he rejoined his Company as soon as his wounds were
dressed and after the third occasion, when he could no longer walk,
he was taken prisoner of war. He showed fine leadership at all times
and under his command his Company earned a remarkable reputation in attack. Capt Upham's complete indifference to danger and
his personal bravery has become a byword in the whole of the
N.Z.E.F.

Jun 27th: During the afternoon, when the Germans attacked the
N.Z. positions at Minqar Qaim, the enemy made several attempts
to clear a path for their tanks through our minefield. One forward
section post of Capt Upham's Coy was occupying an important
position on the edge of the minefield, and it was very heavily shelled
and machine-gunned. Capt Upham walked forward over the ground
that had no cover of any sort and which was swept by enemy fire,
stayed with this section for a short period and came away only when
he had assured himself that it could carry on and hold its ground.

Night Jun 27/28: During the night when the N.Z. Div broke

through the Germans at Minqar Qaim, Capt Upham led his men in
inspiring fashion and his Coy overcame several enemy posts. The
attack took place in very bright moonlight and at one stage a truck
full of German soldiers was seen moving slowly through the soft
sand. Capt Upham and a Corporal ran forward together, and in
spite of heavy Tommy-gun fire from the Germans they reached the
side of the truck and with hand grenades wiped out the entire truck
load and left the truck in flames. Not one German left the burning
vehicle. Capt Upham was slightly wounded in both arms from the
explosions of his own grenades. He did not report to get his wounds
treated until the following night when the Div was back in new
positions, and he then rejoined his Coy.

Night Jul 14/15: During the attack on El Ruweisat Ridge Capt
Upham's Coy was part of the reserve battalion which, during the
six miles advance, was about two miles behind the leading battalions.
Wireless communications had broken down and Capt Upham was
instructed to send forward an officer in a "jeep" to contact the
forward battalions and bring back information. He went himself
instead and after being fired on by an enemy post procured a
Spandau gun and set it up in the car. He had several further en-
counters with enemy posts but by operating the gun himself while
the driver of the "jeep" drove through anything in their path, he
contacted the forward troops and brought back the necessary
information.

Just before dawn, when the reserve battalions and the anti-tank
guns were almost on to their objective, very heavy fire was encountered from a strongly defended enemy locality. There were four
machine-gun posts and about five tanks. Capt Upham's Coy was
the leading Coy and he quickly directed the attack on the two
nearest M.G.s, which were using tracer bullets. He personally led
the attack on one post which was silenced and the enemy bayoneted.
During the attack Capt Upham was shot in the elbow by a machine-
gun bullet and his arm broken. He stayed with his men until the
objective was captured and until positions were consolidated. He
then reported to the R.A.P. and then, with his arm in splints, went
back to his Coy and stayed with it all day under the most trying conditions of heavy enemy artillery and mortar fire. The enemy made a
strong counter-attack late in the afternoon, and Capt Upham was
again wounded by mortar fire. He was no longer able to walk.

Capt Upham was taken prisoner of war on 15 Jul 42.'

*   *   *   *

Freyberg had by now returned to the division in Italy. Kippenberger was the highest ranking New Zealand officer in England.

One day he was walking in the Strand when an Army despatch rider braked to the kerb alongside him. Would he telephone his head-quarters immediately?

The message from H.Q. was brief: the King wished to see Major-General Kippenberger urgently.

It was not long before the General was in His Majesty's study. They had a sherry together.[1]

The King turned the subject to Captain C. H. Upham. He remembered Upham's investiture only a few weeks before. Then, indicating the papers lying on his desk, he said: 'I've spent an hour going through these new papers about Upham. I suppose you know—he has been recommended for a Bar to the Victoria Cross.'

Kippenberger nodded.

The King continued: 'It has very rarely been done, you know, General. Only twice before in nearly ninety years.'

His Majesty studied the papers again for a minute. Then, looking up, he said firmly: 'It would be very unusual indeed. But tell me, Kippenberger, what do you think of Upham yourself? *Does he deserve it?*'

Kippenberger replied slowly: 'In my respectful opinion, sir, Upham won the V.C. several times over.'

The King looked at him thoughtfully for a few moments.

Then he said: 'Well, thanks very much, General. Now . . . how are your arrangements going for getting your men home to New Zealand?'

Archibald Nicoll worked away silently. Charles sat in wooden stillness, prepared to co-operate only because it would see the un-pleasant duty out of the way all the sooner. Sun streaked in through the skylight, the traffic noises of Christchurch coming as a subdued murmur from a distance.

Nicoll spoke. 'You know, Charles, these two portraits are going to be different. You've got a different expression now from when I sketched the first one.'

'What do you mean—different?'

'Well, your expression for the first portrait was more direct, more self-confident. That's how I've shown it. But today, I've really just observed, you're looking different. You're looking more withdrawn, not

---

[1] The conversation that follows is as reported to the author by the late General Kippenberger.

so confident, a bit cynical, if you don't mind my saying so. That's how I have to paint you, you know—just as I see you.'

Upham grunted. So he looked different already, did he?

They worked on again quietly. Just an occasional word, a little lift of the head perhaps, a slight change in position.

Then almost before they knew it the man was in the room.

'I'm from the *Star-Sun*,' he said briskly. 'Heard I'd find you here. I understand you've had a telegram this morning, Captain Upham. We've had a flash about it. Could you confirm the news?'

Upham stared at him coldly.

Nicoll paused. 'What on earth is this all about? Was there some bad news in that telegram, Charles? You didn't say anything. I naturally thought . . .'

Then Upham began arguing defensively with the reporter, a feeling of dismay growing on him second by second. Somehow he knew what he was in for. It was not exciting. It was frightening and depressing, making him feel that he would be a fool in the eyes of his friends. He wanted then and there to jump up and run, to run and run where they'd never find him. Because it was all a mistake. He was no different from the others. Why make him the one to be singled out and pointed at?

Then, as the reporter pressed him further, he despairingly handed over the telegram. It was no use arguing, he supposed.

The newsman read it eagerly, then handed it on to Nicoll.

The telegram from the Minister of Defence, sent from Parliament Buildings, Wellington, read:

'I have learned with very great pleasure that you have been awarded a Bar to the Victoria Cross for most conspicuous bravery and devotion to duty in action. . . . The Prime Minister desires me to convey to you on behalf of the New Zealand Government his heartiest congratulations.'

Archibald Nicoll looked up at Charles, his mouth open and his eyes wide. 'And this is the wire you got this morning, Charles? And you just stuffed it in your pocket and said nothing? Goodness gracious me!'

The reporter from the *Star-Sun* went into action. He talked, and he questioned, and Nicoll resumed painting, and Charles continued sitting, fighting a losing battle.

That night the paper said:

'Captain Upham, whose present role of artist's model does not sit altogether comfortably upon him, said that he had no idea of what particular incident might have prompted the recommendation for this new award. He was wounded in the El Ruweisat engagement and, as he put it, "things were a bit hazy". Captain Upham does not accept the view that he is now a figure of almost unique fame. "I never did anything out of the ordinary, I can tell you that," he protested at the suggestion that the whole Empire would be talking about him today. . . .'

*   *   *   *

In the hours that followed, the news that a New Zealand officer had won the Victoria Cross a second time swept the newspapers of the Commonwealth. The award of the Cross is reserved for valour of the highest order, and the comparative handful of men who receive it are for ever singled out from their fellows.

But for one man to win it *twice*—here indeed the unattainable, the impossible, had occurred. In an instant it placed Upham beyond the understanding of most men.

Streamer headlines all over the British world hailed the news:

'HIS VOICE WAS HEARD ABOVE THE BATTLE'

'FIRST DOUBLE V.C. OF THE WAR FOR AN INCORRIGIBLE HATER'

'NEW ZEALAND HERO'

As if a torrent had suddenly been unleashed, a flood of admiring publicity suddenly descended on the reluctant figure of Charles Upham in Christchurch, New Zealand.

To his family the news came bewilderingly. Charles had been such a poor correspondent about his own experiences. One of his sisters, Mrs. Agatha Wynn-Williams, was busy bathing her baby at the family home in Gloucester Street when the newspapers first rang. Charles's mother answered the phone. There was a conversation. Then Mrs. Upham walked into the bathroom. The baby was being lifted out, the water being gently shaken off.

'They've just given Charles *another* V.C.,' Mrs. Upham said simply.

Mrs. Wynn-Williams let out a startled 'What?' and dropped the baby into the bath.

In the streets of Christchurch that day Charles's father found himself beset. A well-known local figure, he could make no headway along the footpaths on his way to lunch. He tried crossing the street. Cars stopped beside him and hands were outstretched towards him. It was difficult to reach the other side. There were more waiting for him there.

In London the reporters besieged Molly. 'He used to get awfully annoyed when I spoke of his experiences,' she told them. 'He did not even hint that he had done anything special in the desert.'

His sister in England, Mrs. Holmes-Siedle, wondered how Charles would bear up. 'He is so modest . . . he finds public admiration tremendously embarrassing.'

Towards evening, as the flood of telegrams and cables began to cover the Uphams' drawing-room, and the phone beat a never-ending clangour, Charles looked around for a place of retreat. There were reporters in the front hall, people waiting at the door, and so-called friends demanding to speak to him on the telephone. He darted into the bathroom, locked the door, and looked despairingly out of the window.

Mrs. Upham gracefully shepherded the invaders out of the front door, then seized a moment when the phone was not ringing. She rang Allen Shand.

'Allen—do you think you could come over? There are newspaper reporters at the doors and Charles has gone and locked himself in the bathroom. His language is terrible. I think you might be able to help.'

But Charles didn't wait. Finding a way out, he slipped unobtrusively to a friend's flat, let himself in like a fugitive from justice.

'Peter,' he beseeched, 'what's all this bloody rot about this Bar? What's it mean?'

'Oh, come off, Charlie. It simply means they've awarded you another V.C. That's all.'

'But what on earth for? Are you sure that's what it is?'

Upham looked appealingly at his friend, hoping against hope that Peter was wrong, that his own understanding of it was wrong. Perhaps the explanation would come out later—something like merely a confirmation of his first V.C., but surely not *another* V.C. He clutched at any straw, however remote, in the hope that some great mistake was being made.

'Read the paper yet, Charlie? They've printed the citation. It's for Minqar Qaim and Ruweisat.'

Upham read the write-up in the evening paper, the eulogies, the wave of acclaim that was welling up. He gripped the paper in despair.

'What's the matter, Charlie?' Peter queried. 'You can't do anything about it now. You've got another gong, and you might as well get used to it. Everyone except you would be mighty proud.'

Upham shook his head as if bewildered. 'It's wrong, Peter, it's wrong. They shouldn't give it to me. What about all the others? We all did exactly the same things. Why pick on me? It just makes me a bloody fool.'

Peter looked at him wonderingly. What a mixture of a man! Tough, intelligent, incredibly determined and brave, an absolute man's man—yet there were times when Charles seemed a child.

Upham sneaked home that night hoping not to be seen. But outside the house there was gathered a group of boys from Christ's College, his old school. They stood outside the gate, sang the school song, and did a haka, while Charles and his mother stood on the front porch, both fighting against the emotion of such a scene, the one filled with a fierce warm pride for a famous son, the other literally afraid of the fame that he now knew was his lot.

There were cheers and songs. And Charles walked down to the gate, and looked in the eyes of boys who now occupied his old desk and his old bed, eyes that shone now with open hero-worship. To wish them all good luck was about all he could manage.

Meantime at the Christchurch Officers' Club they were talking about the wonderful news. They knew the effect it would have on Charles's life.

'What can we do for him? Old Charles will need help. This sort of publicity will just about put him out on his feet. He loathes it so much.'

One of them said: 'Best thing I can think of is to pull any strings we've got to get Molly back as soon as possible. That would help.'

London papers whose dead-lines missed the announcement made up for it in their next editions.

'FIRST COMBATANT TO WIN V.C. TWICE'
News Chronicle

'AT THE BOTTOM OF O.C.T.U. CLASS—BUT HE'S NOW A DOUBLE V.C.'
Daily Sketch

'DOUBLE V.C. FOUGHT ON TILL HE COULD NOT MOVE'

'WON FIRST V.C. AS LIVE SKELETON'

and alongside a happy photo of Molly:

'SHE'S THE WIFE OF A DOUBLE V.C.'

There had been two others in history who had won the Cross twice. Arthur Martin-Leake, of the Medical Corps, won his Cross in the Boer War for saving wounded at Vlakfontein on 8th February 1902, and gained his Bar on the Western Front in 1914.

Noel Chevasse, another medical officer, performed the double during the Great War of 1914–18, again for saving wounded men under fire.

Theirs were great deeds. But never had a combatant soldier won two Crosses. That after nearly ninety years the feat should be performed by an inconspicuous man from the Dominions, one who impressed his instructors so little, made the event more remarkable.

Charles hated the publicity that followed. Everywhere he moved there were groups gathering around him, staring, asking for autographs, mobbing him like a film-star. Men whom he had never seen buttonholed him in the street and claimed acquaintanceship. It became quickly fashionable for a returned man to explain how well he had known Charlie Upham on active service overseas.

When he arrived at supper-time at a smoke concert given to welcome home a draft of 650 men from England the hall rose and cheered. Charles acknowledged the acclamation, and all the other tributes, with polite modesty. Inside, his heart craved to be relieved of it all.

The local Christchurch paper mirrored the feelings of many when its leader said:

> 'Captain Upham's outstanding characteristic, apart from the determined courage and soldierly skill which earned his decorations, is the extraordinary modesty with which he wears them. . . . That he should wish to give the credit for his exploits to the men who served with and under him is typical. . . . Those who were privileged to hear his reply to the citizens' welcome in the Civic Theatre will remember not so much what he said as the manner of his saying it. He is no public speaker in the accepted sense of the term, but the sincerity of his utterances touched his audience to profound admiration for the qualities of heart and mind that they unconsciously revealed. . . .'

It would be tedious to record the hundreds of congratulatory messages that descended on the Upham home in Gloucester Street. They came from young and old, soldiers and civilians, locally and from overseas, from other V.C. winners, one of whom wrote: 'Those of us who knew you and your conduct overseas are not surprised. In fact we had expected it.'

From men of his old platoon and company the letters arrived. Charles feared their judgment more than the others', because they knew him. There were messages from the Indian Army, from Returned Servicemen's Associations, from Governors-General, Prime Ministers, Archbishops, and Mayors.

From England came a message from two ex-Colditz pals: 'Many congrats. If you ever want two good stooges send for us.'

And: 'Hope Knapp reads English papers.'

One sweet letter that Charles enjoyed came from some little children in an infant school. 'Teacher told us about you. . . .' they wrote neatly.

Charles set himself the task of answering every one by hand, spurning the temptation of having a standard 'thank-you' letter typed above his signature. It was a formidable task. But he made it a point of duty, as he has ever since, to answer personally, and as quickly as possible, every letter he received.

To some he knew well he wrote shortly. He knew they would understand. Ian Reid, friend of Weinsberg days, received: 'Dear Ian. Thanks for your note. Lot of bloody nonsense. Yours, Charles.'

Then there came honours from one after another society and organization—life memberships, special functions, eulogies. . . . And when the Lincoln College Old Boys' Association amended its constitution so as to provide for Upham to become its one and only life member the speaker said: 'His brilliant leadership was exerted whether he was wounded or whole, well or ill, exhausted or rested, and he set an entirely new standard for those who would win the words "For Valour".' Laudatory words indeed, but were they any more than the truth?

From the Prime Minister himself came an offer to fly Upham to England for the investiture of the Bar.

'I'm sure you understand,' Charles's parents said to reporters, 'that Charles is really tired and over-wrought with all this publicity.' ('Withering publicity', the paper described it.) So, almost like a pair of cloak-and-dagger agents, Charles and his mother stole off to an inaccessible seaside haven at Diamond Harbour, not far from Christchurch, but where there were no roads, telephone, or mail delivery.

For a fortnight Charles sank gratefully into the seclusion he longed for, free from the turmoil and the adulation, free to think of his own future and the life to which he would soon have to introduce Molly. He knew it must be farming. He could do a job as a farmer. He wanted nothing else than the sense of owning his own acres, far away and isolated, roaming for miles in the open air that no one else challenged. That would be real freedom, he thought. His own farm. . . .

Others, too, began thinking that Charles Upham should have his own farm—and what more fitting than that his fellow-citizens should give him one?

By now Charles was a public figure whose every word was listened to. Unused to public speaking, he found himself in positions where he was disclosing more and more the philosophies that had so long been private to him. Now, when he expressed his views, people listened.

It was just so on 11th October. That day the Government tendered a complimentary State Luncheon to all the New Zealand winners of the V.C. They gathered in the capital city, Wellington, at 1 p.m., Parliament itself specially adjourning to mark the occasion.

Deputizing for Prime Minister Fraser, who was ill, Mr. Walter Nash spoke feelingly of the debt due to our servicemen, and the special regard the country had for its greatest heroes. Then after a toast proposed by him, and seconded by the then Leader of the Opposition, Sidney Holland, Upham was called on to reply on behalf of the other V.C. winners present.

Speaking with his usual sincerity, Charles began by saying that the only circumstance that had brought him to the function was that he was the representative of 100,000 others whose exploits were as fitting of the reward as his. 'Those exploits were only made possible through the sacrifice of others,' he said. 'In my case there were many others who did more than I did, but many were killed or wounded.' He continued on to extol the virtues of the ordinary fighting New Zealand soldier. Then he concluded in a manner which, from its simplicity and earnestness, moved every one of his listeners. 'One thing I want to ask . . . when these men come back people who are in a position to do so should show their thanks in a practical way. There will be among them men who are maimed, still suffering from wounds, ill, or mentally ill. They'll need homes, furniture, and jobs. Please show them your practical help and your greatest patience.'

Charles returned to Christchurch after the luncheon to find that a committee was being formed. Its object—to present a farm to their famous, favourite son.

*   *   *   *

Ever since the Bar had been announced groups of people in Christchurch had been discussing some suitable form of public recognition for Upham's distinction. Such an honour as he had brought to his home town should not be merely accepted and unmarked. Even the Government had thrown out feelers for a 'National Gift'.

Those who knew Charles best were aware that his heart was set on becoming a farmer. He could become one all right. It was only a matter of how large a mortgage he could afford to shoulder. Those closest to him knew that he had little, if any, savings, and that his only cash resources would be Army back-pay. And, while his father was prominent in the legal profession, there was a limit to the financial assistance Charles could expect from that direction, for New Zealand lawyers, while highly respected in the community, rarely acquire great wealth.

On 17th October 1945 the Mayor of Christchurch called a large public meeting. One speaker said: 'My committee believes that if Mr. Upham were financially independent his influence for good in the community would be given wider scope.' He referred to Charles's exploits, predicting: 'School children of the future will read in history books of his deeds of valour.'

The meeting was of one mind. This was a fine cause. Here was a way of showing the community's admiration and thanks for one man's war service. The war had revealed a man of greatness. Let him now be freed from the burden of onerous financial commitments—surely he had earned such a position?

They decided to launch a public appeal for £10,000, to be subscribed by the people of Canterbury. With that money they would buy the farm of Upham's choice and install him on it.

The appeal was immediately opened to the public and as quickly adopted by the proud people of Canterbury. It was practical, realistic, a very concrete way of doing something of permanent value. The funds rolled in, reaped by the enthusiasm of the scheme's sponsors, aided gladly by the Press, local bodies, and other public organizations.

Over his head Charles saw it all happening, aware that something had started that he couldn't stop. In front of him loomed the wonderful prospect of a farm that he could call his own, debt-free, a gift from people who had not been called on to suffer and endure as he had done —a home for his bride.

Worried and uncomfortable, Charles thought it out from every angle. Of course it was a wonderful opportunity. The people of Canterbury might well resent it if he just brusquely refused.

But to Bill Allan, a friend of Weinsberg days, he confided his fears. 'What would be the good, Bill, of having a farm, and every second person going past saying "I put a hundred pounds into that place"? I'd never feel it was really mine.'

'How could I accept it?' he said to his mother. 'I'm alive and well. Think of the wives of those who haven't come back. I don't need the money; they do.'

Mrs. Upham thought the same, but she asked Charles what he thought would happen if he accepted the gift.

'I'd lose all my friends,' he replied surprisingly.

Charles waited for a time when he knew he would be alone for an hour. Then he got out pencil and paper, began to compose a letter. He knew it would be one of the hardest letters he would ever have to write. He laboured slowly over every word, intent on making sure that the letter expressed his feelings exactly.

When he was at last satisfied with his draft he wrote it out carefully in ink, sealed it up, and arranged for it to be delivered.

It was addressed to the Mayor of Christchurch, Mr. E. H. Andrews.

'As you can imagine' (it began) 'I am having great difficulty in composing this letter which I want you to read and pass on to the other gentlemen of the committee which met in this city and decided on behalf of the Canterbury Province to present me with a gift of money to purchase a farm.

I am deeply conscious of the honour intended to be bestowed upon me and I shall always carry with me the knowledge in my heart that the people of Canterbury wished to pay me such a wonderful tribute.

The military honours bestowed upon me are the property of the men of my unit as well as myself, and were obtained at considerable cost of the blood of this country. . . .'

In Christchurch the newspapers carried Charles's letter, handed on to them immediately by the mayor. The rest of it read:

'. . . Under no circumstances could I consent to any material gain for myself for any services that I, in conjunction with 100,000 more, rendered to the Empire in her hour of peril, and I most humbly request that you will understand my position in having to decline the Province's most generously intended gift.

This, as you all know only too well, was a war for survival; and if we had not had wholehearted support from all members of the Empire we would not have attained victory over our enemies. It would be unworthy of the occasion for any member of the Empire to have benefited in any way through having carried out his or her duty during the last six years.

Some of us have been fated to play a more glamorous role than others. Many serving overseas have not returned; others have returned unable to live a full life, condemned to disability and sickness, while I am little the worse for my experiences.

Could I suggest, sir, that the fund which you all so generously proposed to give me be used to alleviate genuine distress among the children of those men who gave their all for us, and to help brighten the lives of those men who because of some war disability are unable to lead a full life in the community.

Trusting, sir, that you will not think me ungracious and that you will convey my wishes in this matter to your fellow committeemen,

I am,

Yours sincerely,

Charles Upham.'

The publication of this letter roused the people of New Zealand to an admiration and respect for Upham's personal character that had previously been reserved for his deeds on the field of battle. Now they saw that his personal qualities matched his heroic record.

Naturally leader-writers in the Press seized on such a display. One wrote:

'. . . No one will read without sincere emotion the words that have come straight from the heart of this very great young New Zealander. . . . Independence and sincerity of spirit shine through his gracious refusal of a gift which lesser men would have found it difficult to reject. . . . His thoughts are still with those who lost their lives. . . . It may be hoped that his wishes will become the wishes of the people of Canterbury and that they will respond even more generously than they intended to the raising of the Charles Upham Fund to widen opportunities for the children of the fallen. It is a conception worthy of the man.'

Canterbury did indeed respond to the new appeal and to the new object of Upham's choice. Over £10,000 was soon subscribed, while meantime the committee discussed ideas for carrying out the spirit of the gifts and the purposes Charles had in mind.

Finally the announcement was made. The money would go to a Charles Upham Scholarship Fund, to be held and administered by a group of trustees who would award scholarships to the sons of servicemen, tenable at either Lincoln College or Canterbury University.

The trustees, some of whom (like Kippenberger, Hudson, and Cottrell) had been very close to Upham, were given a wide discretion in selecting candidates for the awards. But they considered that the fundamental purposes of the Fund would be honoured if they regarded qualities of manliness, self-reliance, and capacity for leadership as

S

primary qualifications, with scholastic promise and financial need as other criteria of only slightly less importance. The trustees have consistently over the years reaffirmed that qualities of leadership weigh more heavily with them than any other single factor.

Not only have they awarded scholarships, but frequently they have used the Fund to grant financial assistance to candidates who, while not obtaining a scholarship, have nevertheless shown themselves worthy of help.

Noble and generous in its conception, the Charles Upham Scholarship Fund remains to this day a living memorial to the stature of one man whose greatness has been that of character as well as action.

20

The New Life

DEEP in every man's heart is the picture of the home, or the farm, that he would like. So it was with Charles. Before the war he spent some time working for Douglas Macfarlane, a sheep farmer in North Canterbury, who owned an isolated station known as Rafa Downs. Tucked between the coastal ranges and the sea, Rafa had a glorious outlook, it was a hundred miles from Christchurch and the other distractions of town life, and the great bulk of the Kaikoura Mountains on the near horizon gave it a closeness to nature, and a grandeur, that had always remained in Charles's heart. When he dreamed of a farm, he dreamed of a place like Rafa.

It was before his return from England that Douglas Macfarlane rang Charles's parents and said: 'I'm thinking of cutting up Rafa Downs into three farms and selling off two of them. I know Charles always liked Rafa, so I'd like to keep one of the two for him if he wants it.'

Finding two ex-servicemen to settle on Rafa Downs became the task of the Land Settlement Board. One man was immediately available, but the other was not so easy to find. Phil Bennett, himself an ex-serviceman of the 1914–18 war, was the Board member given the task of locating a suitable second buyer.

Charles returned to New Zealand and Bennett very soon told him that portion of Rafa Downs might be available to him. He found Upham very interested, but chary of any suggestion that he might receive special treatment.

'There'll be no special treatment,' Bennett told him clearly. 'If you take this farm you'll pay for it just like any other returned man. You'd better come to Wellington and talk it over.'

Upham hedged. He muttered about publicity, his dislike of being recognized and stared at. Bennett understood, and promised that the visit would be arranged secretly.

Indeed it was. An Air Force plane with a spare seat for Charles was

275

laid on, and a few days later he was met at Wellington airport and brought to the Waterloo Hotel. Bennett was there waiting.

They met face to face—one the harried, over-wrought veteran of the war just ending; the other the veteran of an older war, but mature in judgment of exactly what treatment the returned men needed.

Bennett said: 'First of all—is there anything you'd like to do—anything you want?'

'There's only one thing I want,' Upham said shortly.

'And what's that?'

'I don't want to be treated differently from any other bastard.'

Bennett recoiled. He had expected the man to be highly strung and defensive—many ex-P.O.W.s were—but none had expressed themselves quite so violently.

He paused, looked Upham over steadily, then said: 'And why the bloody hell should you be?'

Upham stared at him for a few moments; then almost together the two men smiled at each other. They got on famously after that.

Charles's purchase of his portion of Rafa was put through the normal channels—the same mortgage obligations, the same interest, the same terms of repayment, as applied to thousands of other returned men going on the land.

Meantime, he remained at his parents' home in Christchurch, waiting for Molly's return from England.

He lived, and behaved, as he chose. He bought a new hat, along with other civilian clothing. The hat looked far too new. He didn't like new things. They made one conspicuous. He pulled it around, kneaded it between his hands, then finally held it under a tap and rolled it dry in front of a fire. He wanted it to look old.

'I love horses,' he blandly explained to his parents when one day they found a horse grazing on the lawn at the back of the house. 'A man on a farm needs a horse and gig,' he added.

'A *gig*?' they asked, prepared to be understanding, but a little stupefied at this one.

'Yes, a horse *and gig*. Mother—you'll have the first ride. I'm getting a gig tomorrow.'

Sure enough, he arrived home next day with the horse harnessed to a genuine gig, fresh from the pages of the *Tatler* of 1905.

'Come on, Mother. She's an old race-horse, but I can hold her all right. One of you others hold her head, will you? Yes, I know the step's a bit high.'

Mrs. Upham drew a very deep breath. It was trial enough to have a famous son. But now to have a horse and gig stabled on the back lawn, and to be asked to make a spectacle of herself like this on the sober streets of Christchurch—surely this was carrying independence too far.

Charles saw her hesitate. As if to reassure her he said: 'You hop up first. Actually the moment she feels anyone on the step she tries to take off. So I'll follow up behind you quickly to make sure you get aboard all right.'

Mrs. Upham had secret thoughts that it might work out quite differently—possibly that she might turn the corner into Rolleston Avenue at full gallop, clinging to the step with one foot, with Charles running vainly a hundred yards behind.

But, as she said later, she was determined she was not going to show that she was afraid or that she regarded this enterprise as at all odd. If Charles wanted to ride around in a gig, well, she'd humour him. The returned boys had had enough to put up with. Let them have their way when they came back home.

Manfully she approached the gig, placed her foot on the step, and, with an agility that surprised even herself, leapt up to the seat. Charles followed, and in a trice they were swinging away down Gloucester Street.

Charles smiled at her indulgently, as if to confirm that her unspoken fears had been groundless.

Past staring pedestrians they swung into Rolleston Avenue. Here now were the gates of Christ's College. Past them they swept and along the drive of stately homes that face on to Hagley Park. Turn right again, up through the suburban streets, into the city itself.

That this was an odd thing to do never occurred to him. He did it simply because he loved being close to a horse again; and he would never refrain from doing anything he wanted to simply because it was not 'conventional'. His mind possessed no sham, no shop-front concealing the wares behind. . . .

But December was not long in coming. As the happy day came near, Charles took the overnight sea ferry to Wellington, where, at long last, Molly waved to him from the deck of the *Mooltan* as the ship came alongside.

*   *   *   *

As 1946 dawned, it was all activity as they moved to Rafa. Their new home was still in the architect's hands, the road to it was just being formed, but the farm was theirs to look at and to plan for.

Given the temporary use of a farmhouse nearby, while their own home was abuilding, Charles and Molly set about the making of their

new world. For the site of their homestead they chose a high plateau
that gave a vista of twenty miles of coastline. Shrubs for the garden,
plantation belts to break the wind, implement sheds, plans for a wool-
shed, furniture to choose, colour schemes to devise, stock and farm
hardware to buy—there is no end to it at times like that.

Then they tempted him with politics. 'It does not matter what party
you would attach yourself to,' one prominent Parliamentarian wrote
naively, 'but the country needs the services of men like you. . . .' Charles
was indeed tempted a little. He had a strong sense of mission, a con-
tinuing hatred of injustice, but his singleness of purpose and absolute
mental honesty would have had to make compromises to fit in with the
devious demands of political life. He wisely kept away.

*   *   *   *

There came the announcement of the Victory Parade to be held in
London, and that a New Zealand contingent would travel there for the
occasion. As New Zealand's most illustrious son, Upham's name was
freely mentioned as one of the certainties for the trip.

Only a few days passed before the phone at home rang. It was the
Minister of Defence himself, the Honourable Fred Jones.

'We would like you to go to London for the Victory Parade, Captain
Upham,' came the request.

Charles called up all his reserves of tact and found several convincing excuses for refusing.

Then there was another phone call from a high military figure.
Again he refused.

A day or two passed, with Charles still determined, knowing that the
draft of men to travel to London by sea was already assembling. Den
Fountaine, one of his oldest friends of the 20th, would be one of the
senior officers commanding the contingent—so there would be old
times to talk about. But he looked out over his broken farm and counted
the months before he could make it even modestly self-supporting.

The phone rang again.

'Captain Upham? Hold the line, please. The Prime Minister wishes
to speak to you.' And the voice of the Premier, Peter Fraser, came
through the under-sea phone cable.

It was a long talk, and only the first of several, but Fraser won in
the end. He put it on the basis of duty, and a call to duty was Upham's
weak spot. That was one call for which there never was an answer, in his
mind, except obedience.

So they flew him to London, while the others went by sea.

'SHY DOUBLE V.C. UPHAM SLIPPED INTO LONDON—
DECLINED RECEPTION'

So said the *Daily Sketch* of 1st June 1946. The unsuccessful attempt
to provide a reception for him was equalled by the failure of newspaper
reporters to extract anything from Charles that touched on his war-time
deeds. When they quizzed him he talked back to them about the weather.
When they asked him about the £10,000 gift he said: 'No, I didn't want
it, but if you've got any cash to spare I'll take it back with me.'

Reporting to New Zealand Headquarters in London, he was told a
room had been set aside for him at the Fernleaf Club, where he could
stay in reasonable comfort.

'Where are the others staying—the rest of the New Zealanders?' he
asked.

'Oh, they're under canvas in Kensington Gardens,' came the reply.

'That's where I'll be,' Upham said shortly.

The march past at the Parade was a spectacular occasion, with the
forces of the Commonwealth presenting a very pageant of the earth's
people. The V.C.s were in the rear rank and on the flank nearest to the
saluting base. Charles himself was on the nearest end of the line. But he
had never been a good parade-ground soldier, and it was only because
the others liked him so much that they didn't berate him for the New
Zealanders' scraggy display as the last rank marched past the King.
For Charles unconsciously began stepping short, and at the vital
moment the New Zealand line became a dog's leg.

Whether or not the King noticed it, it did not dim his warmth when
a few minutes later he sighted Upham amongst the troops lining the
walks in Kensington Gardens, down which His Majesty slowly moved.
Signalling the Queen to join him, he moved to Charles, and the three
talked animatedly for several minutes.

In London Charles found himself noticed more and more, and he
never overcame his shyness at being saluted by generals, admirals, and
others, who were quick to spot the crimson on his uniform and whose
eyes popped at the sight of the *two* miniature Crosses superimposed on
the folded ribbon.

*   *   *   *

The phone began ringing again in 1950. This time it concerned the
opening of a memorial in Greece, erected by that nation to the memory
of the British, Australian, and New Zealand forces who had come to
Greece's aid in 1941.

Would Charles consent to go as part of a very small New Zealand delegation?

Once more the Minister of Defence rang. Once more the call came from the Prime Minister.

But Charles seemed adamant this time.

Then Kip rang; Major-General Kippenberger—then editor-in-chief of the official New Zealand War Histories, with his two painful artificial feet—Kip whom Charles always revered, and for whom he would always do anything.

'Charlie—I'd like you to go to Greece,' Kip said.

'I can't—I've got my shearing to do.'

'I knew you'd say that, so I've already arranged with one of your neighbours to do it for you. So you'd better come. In fact you're booked on the plane two days from now.'

'Will you be going?' Charles asked.

'Yes—just the two of us,' Kip said.

*   *   *   *

It was a rush to get ready for the official luncheon at the Palace. Kip was still doing up his uniform jacket as they boarded the taxi. It would be inconceivable for them to be late—at the very function where they were to be officially received and honoured by King Paul and Queen Fredericka, with other members of royalty present, to say nothing of Papagos and a variety of political and military big-wigs from the Balkans, as well as the Diplomatic Corps.

'Oh, my God!' Kip said suddenly. 'Look at my medals. These Greek ones—they're upside down. Help, what'll we do?'

Charles said: 'Well, it's too late to turn back. We'll change them over as we go.'

So as the taxi sped across Athens they wrestled with Kippenberger's coat, got it off over his shoulders and then, while he sat in his braces, they feverishly undid the offending medals, turned them round, and pinned them on again.

Kip was in a bath of perspiration, and only just struggling into the jacket again, as the taxi door was swung open by the officer of the reception guard.

The presentations were almost immediate. His Majesty . . . Her Majesty . . . Her Royal Highness . . . His Excellency . . . the Prince . . . General . . .

The two New Zealanders passed slowly down the receiving line. Then Kip came to the Crown Prince of ——. They shook hands, exchanged a word, and then Kip's eyes became suddenly riveted on the row of medals adorning the Crown Prince's chest.

For a second he was speechless and his jaw seemed to drop.

Because the Crown Prince wore the same Greek decorations as Kippenberger did himself. But—one of them was *upside down*, just like Kippenberger's had been; not only that, another was on *sideways*.

Kip's eyes fell to the ground, and he suffered yet a further blow—for below his brilliant uniform the Crown Prince was wearing *suède shoes*.

'We needn't have bothered, Charlie,' Kip whispered as they passed on down the line.

For Charles the function became a great success. After lunch King Paul drew him into a corner, and for about an hour monarch and man had their heads together, swopping reminiscences, laughing hugely at each other's jokes.

Then it seemed quite within recognized limits when Charles cheerfully asked Queen Fredericka what it was really like to be a Queen. Just as cheerfully she replied: 'One thing I like about it is that I always get the best seat on the train.'

All in all, it seems to have been a very successful party.

After the official functions in Greece there were a few days in England, in the course of which Charles and Kip dined with Eden in Downing Street; and then, soon after, the flight home, and the return to the rolling slopes of Lansdowne—the name Charles and Molly had given their farm, in memory of the home of an ancestor.

21

Passing Days

MANY years have now passed over Charles's and Molly's home on Rafa Downs. There they built a house to their taste, the rooms opening off a large central living-room with great windows and a terrace overlooking the sweep of the coast and the upsurge of the snow-capped Kaikouras.

It is seven miles to the diminutive settlement at Hundalee, which is hardly more than a general store. From Hundalee the road follows down the bank of the rushing Conway River, crosses over, then emerges into the coastal slopes. From the rocky shore of the South Pacific the land sweeps first gradually, then steeply, up into the hills. Here on the seaward slopes, in secluded freedom, locked by mountain and sea, Charles found his peace. The sea breaks on his land a mile to the east. Behind him the hills rear up. Around his home the sheep multiplied each year, his cattle grew fat, more of his 1200 acres become fit for grazing, and the brutal labour of the first hard years began to ease.

They have three children—all girls. Twins first—Amanda and Virginia (whereupon an old 20th friend infuriatingly said: 'Charles, you can't help doing everything *double*, can you?'). Then came Caroline, the youngest. Towards them Charles let the soft side of his nature run unchecked. He really gave them too much, Molly considers.

They have had their years of difficulty, like many others. But Charles had his farm in good shape by the time a world rise in wool prices suddenly made the burden easier. It was hard labour at first. But that was what he relished. He scorned the winds and the rains, or the difficulties of a steep climb, or the weight of the load. Just as in wartime, his ability to concentrate on one objective and put aside all distractions saw him tackle all his tasks with an indifference to personal comfort that startled even Molly, who knew him otherwise so well. She began to see the unbending, sometimes illogical, strength of his will. It worried her, too, for Charles's arm has never been right, and he squirmed in frustrated pain as it often failed to do the tasks he imposed upon it.

Hardship struck them early. In December 1946, before the house was even finished, they were living with friends on another part of Rafa. While pouring petrol into his car by the light of a hurricane lantern, Charles spilt some on the grass. There was a flash and a flame, and in a moment his trouser leg was alight.

'Your husband's swearing terribly,' a friend told Molly. 'He says it's nothing, but I think he's been burnt. He's beating himself with a sack.'

Next morning Charles again said that there was nothing wrong, and that he was fit to drive the hundred miles to Christchurch for a conference with the builder. He drove the car silently, deliberately proceeded with the conference, then made one or two calls he had planned. It was so like him—the planned objective would brook no diversion.

Only then did he consent to go to hospital for examination. One look at him and within an hour he was in the operating theatre.

Charles was in hospital and convalescent home for over four months.

There have been later attempts to persuade him into politics, but he has not succumbed. Locally, however, he has taken his share on Boards and in small public administration, and some of the girls' early prizes bear their father's signature as Chairman of the School Committee. He was appointed to the Board of Governors of his old' school, Christ's College.

He gradually, but reluctantly, became accustomed to his role as an heroic public figure. In the early post-war years his rejection of this role was uncompromising, and he defiantly shut himself away on his isolated farm. That was at a time when he was less tolerant, and more dogmatic, about many things on which he later mellowed.

But while resisting the status that his decorations imposed on him he has never shirked that status if he thought it a point of duty. At Returned Services' Association functions he has readily accepted the role of speaker, he has acknowledged the curtsies of débutantes, he has opened bridges, given away school prizes. When New Zealand undertook to send troops to the fighting in Korea, Upham lent his name and his voice in a national radio appeal for volunteers. And, in a smooth reversal of his former role as the recipient of awards, Charles has himself reviewed troops and has pinned pilots' wings on Air Force cadets at their passing-out parade.

Especially amongst his old battalion comrades there has never been anything held back. Charles never passes an old 20th man in the street. There is a barman here, a tobacconist there, a man driving a taxi, working in a shop, office or factory, a farmer from the Canterbury Plains. Each is met with a warmth and affection that shows no reserve. Eric Le Gros, too, see Charles from time to time, and they chuckle together over some of their unmilitary adventures.

The 20th had its birth in Christchurch, and every few years its reunion draws hundreds of former members. Upham never misses, and there are the shouted greetings, the back-slapping, the drinking of good beer, the silence for the fallen, and the pride which all of them feel, not just for Charles and their other decorated men, but for one another.

It was not till 1952 that 'Hoppy' Hopgood managed to attend his first 20th reunion. It was a far cry back to the days in the desert when he had been Charles's driver.

What a queue of V.I.P.s, Hoppy thought—Freyberg himself, Kippenberger, Jim Burrows, General Inglis, Charlie—all standing in a row shaking hands.

'Here—sign this, boss, will you?' Hoppy asked, pushing a menu card towards Charles.

Upham looked up. His face broke into a smile. 'Hoppy! Hoppy! It's you!' Then he suddenly bent closer, shielded his mouth with his hand and whispered furtively: 'I say, Hoppy. . . like to take the truck tonight, no questions asked?'

And as they roared their happiness together Hopgood knew that, two V.C.s and all, 'old Charlie' was just the same as ever.

*　　　*　　　*　　　*

The Queen and the Duke of Edinburgh, the Queen Mother, Anthony Eden, Montgomery. . . as royalty and other notables travel through New Zealand it is always Charles Upham requested by the, Government to be amongst the special guests. It is Upham who often appears alongside them in the Press photographs.

'What did she say, Charlie?'

'What were you and the Queen nattering about all that time, Charlie?'

'Come on, Charlie, give a little. The Queen was talking to you so long it made the party look like a duet. What does she know?'

Charles shrugged his shoulders, looked rather wonderingly over to where the Queen was now busy talking with another group. Then he turned back and said: 'What does she know? I'll tell you *one* thing. She

knows a bloody lot more about horses than anyone else I've ever met.
And that's what we were talking about.'

*   *   *   *

In 1956 came another journey overseas when the Victoria Cross
Centenary Celebrations were held in London.

There have since been a number of such trips. Usually to the V.C.
reunions, where Charlie is, of course, the star amongst stars.

Those who have not seen much of Charles since war days would like
to ask— how has he been? What is he like now?

Just the same, his friends will tell you. Meet him in a Christchurch
street, or on a horse near his front gate, and his first questions will be
of your family, your job, and your well-being. And in a few minutes he
is as like as not to say: 'I'll never forget that day you were stranded out
there with only a Bren gun and one mag. That was a wonderful job you
did! I don't know how you stuck it out. . . .' and he will look at you
admiringly as if it were only yesterday.

He has remained a complex personality. Now and then he will show
a spark of that old irrational obstinacy, and some of his opinions may
appear too rigid in these modern days when 'flexibility' is a convenient
word for vacillation. But the tales told about him, his own humility,
and his utter indifference to personal appearance (despite Molly's
efforts) have long conspired to present a false picture of his
personality; that is, to those who do not really know him.

The true picture, however, is of a man deeply thoughtful and
intelligent, one whose opinions are sought and respected. He became
the confidant of many of New Zealand's leading figures. They like to
hear him talk, for they find his views always fresh and refreshing. They
often envy his complete sincerity—his air of 'burning integrity' (as one
Governor-General of New Zealand described it).

The keen brain, capable of dedication to a single, unwavering
object, cloaked in modesty, and, sometimes, roughness—that is the
picture.

With a profound knowledge of international affairs, Charles has
clear views on present-day problems. But, as in all things, he is the last
to speak, and urges his friends to state their opinions first. He listens
to them intently, not out of flattery, but because he regards all life as
learning. Throughout his career, behind a façade that was sometimes
brash and sometimes humble, he has driven himself to understand and
evaluate the wisdom and experience of others.

He doesn't swear as much as in the old days. To his family and

friends his voice is quiet, his manner calm. But once in a while, if a
sharp word is called for, there is a lift, a ring, to his voice that has
almost an electrical effect. The voice rising above the din of the
battlefield seems suddenly real and understandable.

And what of his attitude now to his awards—still the only combatant
ever to have won two V.C.s?

The same as ever; just like the reception in London when
Mountbatten approached Charles and noticed he was not wearing his
medals—as prescribed by the order of dress for the occasion. When he
asked him why, Charles rather sheepishly produced them from
amongst the loose change in his trouser pocket, saying: 'My wife made
me bring them.'

Is he not, then, proud of the glory that he brought New Zealand,
and the honour that he so reluctantly carries? Yes—but proud in a way
that his old friends understand, but others take longer to appreciate.
You will find his pride when he talks around the fireside of an evening
or yarns over a pipe during a battalion reunion. But it is a pride of
memory; and the memories he treasures are those of the deeds of his
own boys, of the exploits *they* performed. And any attempt at having
him reminisce about war-days—not a difficult task— soon finds him
warming to the subject of the courage and dash of his friends and
comrades. He is uncomprehending and vague at any suggestion that
his own deeds are worthy of special memory. He has never accepted
that. He has attached himself for ever to the belief that the awards that
came to him were received in a representative capacity. That is the
only way in which his honours bring him personal comfort.

On one trip to London an interviewer pressed him to describe the
circumstances of the occasions for which he received his two V.C.s.

Charles is older, wiser, than in his more brusque earlier days of
fame. So this was his answer: 'The circumstances? Well. . . it is a long
time ago now. *I have forgotten.*'

Forgotten?

Locked deep away in memory, perhaps, so deep that few people
have ever known the real thoughts, the real attitude of mind, that
accompanied the deeds of those long-gone, more dramatic days.

But forgotten? No.

And as the years relentlessly push further into history the events of
1939-45, may the rest of us never forget, or allow to be forgotten, how
the young men of those times struggled to preserve their world for the
younger ones who enjoy it today.

Surely they were the men with the Mark of the Lion upon them.

*   *   *   *

Soon after the war a book was published about the prisoners of Colditz.[1] There are portraits of many of the captives, with pen-pictures of their exploits and their personalities. It is a monument as well as a history.

Opposite a full-page portrait of Charles Upham are a few words, set in small type in the centre of an otherwise empty page, and looking insignificant, though in a way impressive, against the blank whiteness of the rest of the sheet. The words are:

CAPTAIN C. H. UPHAM, V.C. & BAR

New Zealand Military Forces

An officer and a gentleman—determination and
singleness of purpose personified—loyal,
constructive, quiet, unassuming, and friendly.

---

[1] *Detour*. Edited by Lieutenant J.E.R. Wood, M.C. (Falcon Press).